Women's Liberation

WOMEN'S LIBERATION

Gender Inequality from Suffrage to Austerity

Pat Thane

polity

Copyright © Pat Thane 2026

The right of Pat Thane to be identified as Author of this Work has been asserted in accordance with the UK Copyright, Designs and Patents Act 1988.

First published in 2026 by Polity Press Ltd.

Polity Press Ltd.
65 Bridge Street
Cambridge CB2 1UR, UK

Polity Press Ltd.
111 River Street
Hoboken, NJ 07030, USA

All rights reserved. Except for the quotation of short passages for the purpose of criticism and review, no part of this publication may be reproduced, stored in a retrieval system or transmitted, in any form or by any means, electronic, mechanical, photocopying, recording or otherwise, without the prior permission of the publisher.

ISBN-13: 978-1-5095-6658-7
ISBN-13: 978-1-5095-6659-4 (pb)

A catalogue record for this book is available from the British Library.

Library of Congress Control Number: 2025945100

Typeset in 11.5 on 14pt Adobe Garamond
by Cheshire Typesetting Ltd, Cuddington, Cheshire
Printed and bound in Great Britain by Ashford Colour Ltd

The publisher has used its best endeavours to ensure that the URLs for external websites referred to in this book are correct and active at the time of going to press. However, the publisher has no responsibility for the websites and can make no guarantee that a site will remain live or that the content is or will remain appropriate.

Every effort has been made to trace all copyright holders, but if any have been overlooked the publisher will be pleased to include any necessary credits in any subsequent reprint or edition.

For further information on Polity, visit our website:
politybooks.com

Contents

Abbreviations vi
Acknowledgements ix

Introduction 1
1 Women Fighting for a Political Voice, 1900–1918 5
2 What Difference Did the Vote Make? 1918–1939 25
3 Gender in Wartime, 1939–1945 46
4 Making the 'Welfare State', 1945–1951 64
5 'Never Had It So Good'? 1951–1964 77
6 A Permissive Society? 1964–1970 98
7 The Seventies, 1970–1979 118
8 The Lady's Not for Equality, 1979–1997 138
9 Things Can Only Get Better? New Labour, 1997–2010 164
10 Austerity, 2010–2024 189
Conclusion 225

Notes 230
Index 252

Abbreviations

ACAS	Advisory, Conciliation and Arbitration Service
ALRA	Abortion Law Reform Association
APPG	All-Party Parliamentary Group
ATS	Auxiliary Territorial Service
AWS	All-Women Shortlists
BAME	Black, Asian and Minority Ethnic
BFBPW	British Federation of Business and Professional Women
BFUW	British Federation of University Women
BIPO	British Institute of Public Opinion
BMA	British Medical Association
CBI	Confederation of British Industries
CHE	Campaign for Homosexual Equality
CND	Campaign for Nuclear Disarmament
CPAG	Child Poverty Action Group
CRE	Commission for Racial Equality
CSA	Child Support Agency
CTC	Child Tax Credit
DHSS	Department of Health and Social Security
DLRU	Divorce Law Reform Union
DSS	Department of Social Security
DWP	Department of Work and Pensions
EC	European Community
ECEC	Early Childhood Education and Care
ECHR	European Convention on Human Rights
ECtHR	European Court of Human Rights
EMA	Educational Maintenance Allowance
EMS	Emergency Medical Service
EOC	Equal Opportunities Commission
EPCC	Equal Pay Campaign Committee
FANY	First Aid Nursing Yeomanry

ABBREVIATIONS

FPA	Family Planning Association
FJAC	Finer Joint Action Committee
GLA	Greater London Authority
GLC	Greater London Council
GLF	Gay Liberation Front
GMA	Guaranteed Maintenance Allowance
GRC	Gender Recognition Certificate
HLRS	Homosexual Law Reform Society
HRT	Hormone Replacement Therapy
ICW	International Council of Women
IFS	Institute for Fiscal Studies
ILP	Independent Labour Party
IS	Income Support
JRF	Joseph Rowntree Foundation
LCC	London County Council
MOH	Medical Officer of Health
MWA	Married Women's Association
NAB	National Assistance Board
NAWCS	National Association of Women Civil Servants
NAO	National Audit Office
NCUMC	National Council for the Unmarried Mother and her Child
NCW	National Council of Women
NHI	National Health Insurance
NOP	National Opinion Polls
NOW	New Opportunities for Women
NSPA	National Spinsters' Pensions Association
NUSEC	National Union of Societies for Equal Citizenship
NUWSS	National Union of Women's Suffrage Societies
NUWT	National Union of Women Teachers
NUWW	National Union of Women Workers
ONS	Office for National Statistics
OWAAD	Organisation of Women of Asian and African Descent
PC	Pension Credit
PEP	Political and Economic Planning
RAF	Royal Air Force
SBC	Supplementary Benefits Commission
SEND	Special Educational Needs and Disabilities

ABBREVIATIONS

SHRG	Scottish Homosexual Reform Group
SNP	Scottish National Party
SPUC	Society for the Protection of Unborn Children
STEM	Science, Technology, Engineering and Mathematics
TGWU	Transport and General Workers' Union
TUC	Trades Union Congress
UC	Universal Credit
VAD	Voluntary Aid Detachment
VD	Venereal Disease
WAF	Women's Aid Foundation
WAAC	Women's Army Auxiliary Corps
WAAF	Women's Auxiliary Air Force
WASPI	Women Against State Pension Inequality
WCA	Women's Citizens Association
WCG	Women's Co-operative Guild
WFL	Women's Freedom League
WFTC	Working Families Tax Credit
WHO	World Health Organization
WI	Women's Institute
WLGS	Women's Local Government Society
WLL	Women's Labour League
WLM	Women's Liberation Movement
WOTAG	Women's Taxation Action Group
WOW	Wider Opportunities for Women
WRAC	Women's Royal Army Corps
WRAF	Women's Royal Air Force
WRNS	Women's Royal Naval Service
WSPU	Women's Social and Political Union
WTC	Working Tax Credit
WVS	Women's Voluntary Service

Acknowledgements

I am very grateful to Louise Knight of Polity for suggesting that I write this book. I would not otherwise have thought of it. Also to her and her colleagues for their friendly and efficient work on producing the book.

Introduction

'Gender inequality' describes inequality related to the personally acknowledged or perceived gender of each individual and its associated characteristics. 'Gender' came into use in this context relatively recently, replacing 'sex' when the culturally entrenched belief that there were fixed and natural differences from birth between females and males was challenged, replaced by the notion that perceived or assumed differences between the sexes were culturally not biologically constructed and were not fixed. They might change over time, vary among individuals and groups, even overlap between males and females. It was not denied that there were differences between men and women, but their fixed, universal characteristics and their origins were challenged along with the assumption that both were homogeneous groups, and it was argued that there is no impenetrable barrier between them. Historian Joan Scott described this process of change and argued, when use of the term gender was relatively new, that it came into use due to growing awareness of 'the instability and malleability of the categories "women" and "men"'.[1] She wrote: 'We need a refusal of the fixed and permanent quality of the binary opposition' and to find ways to analyse how it comes about and changes,[2] for the characteristics and meanings of gender differences 'vary across cultures, social groups and time'.[3]

This book seeks to explore this variance through British history from c.1900 to the present, and its effects, especially the wide range and persistence of inequalities between people defined as 'men' or 'women', mostly disadvantaging women. It aims to understand how and why profound present-day gender inequalities, including in employment, political representation, experience of sexual violence, have survived despite over a century of protest against them, mainly by women, and some resulting improvements. Exploring how present inequalities came about historically should help to increase our understanding of them and suggest means to resolve them. The book seeks to discuss as comprehensively as possible the range of gender inequalities over time, their causes, how they have or have not changed and influences upon their persistence or change – cultural, social, economic, legal or political – sometimes resulting from pressure by women, more occasionally from men, sometimes together with other influences.

It starts at a time when significant numbers of women assertively challenged culturally accepted gender differences as inequalities especially disadvantaging women, and continues to the present when women still campaign against pervasive disadvantages in their lives compared with men's. Yet disadvantage due to gender inequality is not confined to females, though more women than men experience it in more areas of their lives. Some men have always resented inequalities due to gender identity, mainly homosexuals and transgender men. They long felt forced by cultural antagonism to be silent about their perceptions of their gender, but, as we will see, this changed in the later twentieth century when they found a voice, demanded recognition of their needs and achieved some support and improvement. But, overall, we do not know enough about male perceptions and experiences of gender inequality. As we will see, men have been persistently accused of creating women's disadvantages through their prejudice and discrimination rooted in centuries of 'patriarchal', as it is known, domination of males over females. It remains hard to understand how such attitudes came about and why they have continued, even perhaps intensified, over time but the coming chapters will attempt to do so.

We know more about perceptions and experiences of inequality among women because their protests, like their experiences, have been so extensive, long-lived and well documented. This documentation in a wide variety of sources provides much of the content of this book. In the 1900s, protest focused on the national vote, which was denied to all women and to working-class men. Women, and men, demanded it partly to remove a major signal of inequality, also to gain the political power to overturn other inequalities established and sustained by a political system dominated by better-off men. As we will see there were always some female opponents of change, including to the equal franchise itself, due to cultural, political or religious convictions. Adult women partially gained the vote along with all adult men in 1918 and were enfranchised equally with men in 1928. Gradually some of them used this power to achieve equal rights in marriage, including custody of their children, in divorce and control of their own property, among other advances. But their power was limited by their under-representation in parliament despite women being a majority of voters from 1928 and a majority of the adult population from long before 1900 to the present. Their representation grew very gradually, as we will see, reaching 40% of the House of Commons in the 2024 general election, improvement but still a minority.

Some severe disadvantages have never gone away. Since the late nineteenth century, women have demanded equal employment opportunities and equal pay with men and still need to do so in 2025. As we will see, there is ample information about gender inequalities in the labour market in the records of campaigning organizations, the personal records of campaigners and, increasingly over time, in the press and other media. From the 1950s, the growth of the social sciences produced valuable surveys of inequalities in work and pay on which later chapters will draw. Thorough, often well-publicized, documentation of gender inequalities has often led to their reduction but not to their eradication.

Women have also long been victims of male physical and sexual violence at home, in the streets, at work and elsewhere, but this is much harder to trace over time. Around 1900, as for long before and decades after, another symptom of gender inequality was that it was unacceptable for women to speak publicly about matters like domestic violence, rape and sexual harassment, which they suffered far more than the relatively few male victims, but the culture regarded these incidents as too shameful for public discussion. Public awareness of this gendered violence has grown over time and, following pressure from women, the justice system has gradually increased its attempts at punishment and control, but its full extent remains uncertain because women remain often unwilling to report it for reasons of shame, fear of retribution by the perpetrator, or that police and the courts will not take them seriously, as is still too often the case, another symptom of gender inequality. Male physical, mental and sexual violence against women, and gay men, remains widespread and shows little sign of decline; indeed, as we will see, it may even be growing as misogyny and homophobia spread in the early twenty-first century through the growing power of social media.

And still in 2025 many women experience poorer treatment from health services and more women than men suffer poverty, increasingly so as in recent decades poverty and inequalities between rich and poor have returned to levels comparable with 1900.[4] Also, over the time period under consideration Britain has become more ethnically diverse, so we must also explore the experiences of women and men in different ethnic groups. As we will see, women and men experience inequalities, especially of race and class within their gender groups. Also, inequalities vary over the life course – for example in opportunities for retirement as we will see – to a greater extent than is always recognized.

There may still be gender inequalities remaining hidden and awaiting public notice. Over time, changing awareness of gender inequalities and attempts to resolve and to sustain them have had diverse origins, including political movements and government action. As we will see, political parties have taken different attitudes to gender inequality at different times, both promoting and reducing it. Above all, this book seeks to ask why, after over a century of women's protests, is there still profound gender inequality in 2025? How can it be eliminated?

ONE

Women Fighting for a Political Voice, 1900–1918

In 1900, women experienced gender inequality in every area of their lives. From the mid-nineteenth century they increasingly protested against it as the numbers of educated, independent-minded women grew. The law essentially subordinated women, especially married women, to men. Women campaigned for equal education and career opportunities, against male violence and much more.[1] Among many other injustices, a woman lost on marriage all financial and property rights. As suffragist Millicent Garrett Fawcett pointed out, if a married woman's handbag was stolen, in the eyes of the law it belonged to her husband. Fathers had sole custody rights over children from age seven even if a marriage broke up. In England and Wales husbands could divorce their wives for adultery, but wives wanting divorce had to prove an additional offence – cruelty, desertion, incest. Adultery was judged normal for men, outrageous for women. In Scotland, where the law and culture differed from England in many ways, men and women had equal divorce rights.[2]

Family life was strictly divided along gender lines. It was the cultural norm that wives cared for the home and the children – the only acceptable ambition for a woman – while the husband was the family 'breadwinner' and the patriarchal authority, controlling his wife's existence and a distant, authoritarian figure to his children. These were essential elements of the 'masculinity' to which men were expected to aspire. Not all men or families wholly conformed to this stereotype, but it was expected of all classes and men who publicly challenged it – e.g., by playing with their children in public – were derided and stigmatized.[3] Women who sought to resist the stereotype faced profound opposition to their career ambitions, whether as artists or doctors. And there have always been opportunity and lifestyle inequalities within as well as between gender groups, including in 1900 and long before between rich and poor women and men, including between the millions of live-in domestic servants and their mistresses, profound differences in their everyday lives, while experiencing many similar inequalities with men; and rich men lived very different lives from their butlers.

One inequality women of all classes experienced on marriage was that British nationality was for life for all British-born men – and all men born within the mighty British Empire – but not for women. From 1870, a British-born wife was required on marriage to take the nationality of her husband. If he was not British, she lost her British nationality and all rights associated with it. She could apply for re-naturalization as British five years after widowhood or divorce. In 1914, following protests, widows were allowed to revert to British nationality immediately on widowhood, but not divorced women, who were much stigmatized. The importance of national identity grew as UK civil rights increased, in particular when in 1918 British women partially gained the vote. The British-born wives of 'aliens' (people lacking British nationality) were excluded from the vote even when resident in Britain. After the First World War, women's nationality became an international campaigning issue, but the British law did not change to provide gender equality until 1948.[4]

Men promoted and gained from gender inequalities and were more rarely disadvantaged by them than women. The most severe gender-related inequality men experienced was criminalization of any form of behaviour represented as homosexual. This became punishable by death in the *Acte for the punishment of the vice of Buggerie* in 1533, though such extreme punishment was not implemented in the twentieth century and capital punishment was permanently abolished in 1969. By contrast, lesbianism was never taken seriously enough to be criminalized, as all female activities were belittled in British culture. This disparity did not begin to diminish until 1967 when homosexuality was partially decriminalized, as discussed in chapter 6. In 1900, public discussion of homosexuality was effectively censored along with other forms of sexuality. Homosexuals did not protest because they lived in constant fear of identification and imprisonment and, when identified, were severely treated in the justice system.[5]

Votes for Women

Early female campaigners achieved some limited gains, but the patience of many of them was running out by the 1900s. They believed that only when they had the national vote could they achieve the equalities and social improvements denied them by an exclusively male parliament. Campaigning had gained some of them the local government vote in 1869, but only for the minority of women who were independent property holders, mainly better-off widows and unmarried women. It passed easily through parliament two years after it rejected John Stuart Mill's attempt to extend the national vote to women in the 1867 Parliamentary Reform Act which enfranchised skilled working men. MPs shared a common belief that women could usefully contribute to local government because it dealt with social issues, including public health and poor relief, which was believed to lie within the 'female sphere' of interest and competence, but major matters of state did not. Some women shared this view. In 1889 the novelist and philanthropist Mrs Humphrey Ward organized 'An Appeal against Female Suffrage' eventually signed by over 2,000 women. Mrs Ward and many of the signatories shared the conventional view that, as local government voters, women had control of all policies that lay within their competence and they did not need the national vote. Many signatories of the Appeal, including Beatrice Webb, later changed their minds and regretted it.[6] Women have never been unanimous in their attitudes to gender inequalities.

Women made an impact in local government, then and for long after, especially by improving social services. They were allowed to stand for locally elected School Boards when they were established in 1870 to develop state schools and the transition to compulsory education. After a struggle, they gained election to Poor Law Boards from 1875, then to the small Rural and Urban District Councils established in 1894, to the more important County and Municipal Borough Councils not until 1907. In 1900 there were about one million female electors and 1,589 elected women, by 1914–15, 2,488. A Women's Local Government Society (WLGS) was established to encourage qualified women to vote and stand for election, as it did very actively for several decades.[7]

Before they gained the national vote, women made some impact on national politics through organizing and campaigning against gender inequalities, putting external pressure upon parliament. In 1878 they gained the right to legal separation, with maintenance, for wives for whom divorce was too difficult or too expensive, also minor improvements to married women's previously non-existent property rights, and the right to petition for, but not necessarily gain, custody of their children up to age 16[8] – limited gains which encouraged demands for the vote and further change.

Women were active in pressure groups of all kinds and became indispensable to the political parties that denied them the vote, though in subordinate roles, and they were denied full membership of the major political parties – Conservative, Liberal and, from 1900, Labour – until after the First World War. Meanwhile they worked as canvassers, fundraisers and organizers of local branches of all political parties, hoping to influence party policy. By 1906 even anti-suffrage male politicians found it helpful to have women speak on their electoral platforms, and all political parties established or acknowledged substantial women's support organizations.[9]

Many better-off married women sought activities outside the home as their children grew and servants cared for them and performed all the domestic work. They were prohibited from paid work, culturally and by occupational rules, and many of them occupied their time in the thriving world of charity, reinforcing the conviction that women had special talent for care of those in need.[10] Their limited opportunities for other activities outside the home freed many women to campaign for greater opportunities. The more active women were in politics at all levels, the more absurd their exclusion from the national vote appeared, the more so when it was granted to women on equal terms with men in New Zealand in 1893, in some Australian states in the 1890s and throughout the country in 1902, and in Finland in 1906. Even in the Isle of Man from 1881 female property-holders could vote for its parliament, the Tynwald. These victories for women stimulated the women's suffrage movement in Britain. The National Union of Women's Suffrage Societies (NUWSS) was formed in 1897, led by Millicent Garrett Fawcett. She was a Liberal, married to a radical Liberal politician. The NUWSS consisted mainly of women who supported the Liberal Party and were disappointed by the lack of support from the party leadership for women's suffrage. It was committed to peaceable lobbying and moderation, initially demanding the vote on the same terms as men, which would have limited it, like the local vote, to better-off single and widowed women. This was a tactical first step, but it was divisive and alienated more radical women.

The Women's Social and Political Union (WSPU) was founded in 1903 by Emmeline Pankhurst, an Independent Labour Party (ILP) stalwart from Manchester, soon joined by other women from Manchester and elsewhere and her daughters, Christabel, Sylvia and Adela.[11] It also supported the limited franchise as a first step, since only this seemed realistically attainable in the foreseeable future. The WSPU was committed to active public campaigning for the vote, impatient with the quiet, apparently unsuccessful, tactics of the NUWSS. Textile workers from Yorkshire and Lancashire, shop workers and members of the working-class Women's Co-operative Guild (WCG), the largest working-class women's organization, founded in 1883, campaigned alongside middle- and upper-class women in both organizations.[12] Some men supported women's suffrage, sometimes expressed in imagery of 'manly' chivalry, presenting men as champions and protectors of women's rights.[13] On the other hand, horror at the 'unfeminine' public campaigning of the WSPU led the right-wing *Daily Mail* to label them 'suffragettes', intending the term to be disparaging, with striking lack of success.[14]

Women's suffrage was not a prominent issue in the election campaign of 1906, which saw victory for the Liberals, with Labour support, after years of Conservative government. The WSPU, frustrated by the politicians' lack of response, interrupted Ministers' public speeches, shouting 'Votes for Women!' In 1908 they moved to public demonstrations, window smashing and other forms of criminal damage, later to arson attacks. They did not harm people but themselves experienced physical and sexual assault, including from police, and arrest, fines and imprisonment. They responded with hunger strikes in prison, then resistance to the forced feeding that followed. The behaviour of the women and of the police and prison authorities shocked opponents and supporters, provoking some members of the WSPU to defect to the growing NUWSS. But the WSPU placed Votes for Women firmly on the public agenda by 1910 due to quiet as well as noisy tactics. In 1911 an unknown number of suffrage campaigners boycotted the National Census arguing, 'If women don't count neither shall they be counted.' They evaded it by joining all-night hikes or parties on census night, some roller-skating on a rink in central London. Emily Wilding Davison hid overnight in a broom cupboard in parliament.[15]

All three male-only British political parties and the very active mixed-gender Irish nationalists included both suffrage supporters and 'antis', as did their female support organizations. Only Labour was formally committed to votes for all men and women at age 21. The NUWSS shifted towards the equal adult franchise and to Labour by 1912. Most male Liberals and Conservatives feared the political outcomes of enfranchising all adults, which would massively and unpredictably increase the electorate, but by 1912 the Liberal government was persuaded to propose universal adult suffrage. This caused a hopeful lull in campaigning, until the Speaker of the House of Commons ruled women's suffrage out of order and hope collapsed.

WSPU militancy then increased: public letter boxes were set on fire, Emily Wilding Davison died after throwing herself under the hooves of the King's horse in the 1913 Derby. The NUWSS supported Labour candidates against anti-suffragists in by-elections and by 1914 campaigned against all Liberals, winning support from more working-class women. In 1914 Prime Minister Asquith promised to include women's suffrage in the government's next attempt at electoral reform, but this and the whole suffrage movement were overtaken by the outbreak of war.[16]

Poverty, Ill-health and Gender Inequality

Women demanded the vote for its own sake, as a symbol of gender equality, also to give them power to end other social and legal inequalities. Women suffered greater poverty than men, with a wide range of ill effects, which better-off women observed through charitable work, leading to campaigns for reform. Childbirth was especially dangerous for poorer mothers because they could not afford qualified health care. The UK birth rate declined from the 1870s, for the first time in over a century, easing the lives of many women, but arousing concern among politicians who feared a declining workforce in an increasingly competitive world. Births were conventionally believed to be falling fastest among the middle classes, because they were careful people seeking to improve their families' living standards, while the feckless lower classes had too many children who were malnourished and feeble, creating over the generations what was described as national 'physical degeneration' and potential economic and military decline. Such fears were deepened by the difficulties experienced by the mighty British imperial army in defeating inexperienced farmers in the Anglo-Boer war of 1899–1902. This was attributed by military leaders to the inherited physical weakness of many volunteers, without clear evidence.[17]

Women activists took advantage of politicians' fears to demand action to tackle the high death rate of infants, especially in poorer families, and the high levels of death and ill-health among their mothers due to lack of affordable health care. They argued that an obvious way to compensate for the babies who were not being born was to save the lives of the many who were at risk of dying and to help them grow up fit and healthy. In England and Wales in 1898–1902, 154 infants per 1,000 live births died in their first year, in Scotland 128 and in Ireland 108.[18] In the poverty-stricken textile town of Batley, Yorkshire, 172 died – almost one in six live births. Women's groups, including the WCG, demanded free medical care for babies and their mothers before and after childbirth; also, advice and support for working-class mothers provided by free local welfare centres, since many mothers admitted they were ill-informed about how best to feed and nurture their babies or themselves.[19] The WCG and the Women's Labour League (WLL, a Labour Party support group founded in 1906[20]) among others, raised voluntary funds to establish such centres, helping mothers overcome some of their worst difficulties, including providing pure milk free of charge. Some radical local authorities followed their example.[21]

The infant death rate fell, probably in consequence: in England and Wales to 118 deaths per 1,000 live births in 1907, 105 in 1914, with similar declines in Scotland and Ireland. In 1911 the Liberal government, as part of the new National Health Insurance (NHI) system it was introducing, provided wives of insured men (only) with a payment of 30 shillings (£1.50) to fund childbirth, financed by workers' contributions. Initially it was to be paid to the man. Women protested that it might go to the pub not to the woman and gained payment directly to mothers. But the wider NHI scheme, providing free GP care and sickness benefit, was not available to the families of insured workers and largely excluded low-paid workers and women, those most in need of health care. Inequalities and campaigns for state-funded health care for all continued.

The birth rate continued to decline as more households recognized that, with fewer mouths to feed, their living standards rose. And, as more women sought freedom and equality, the less they could tolerate, for themselves or others, repeated pregnancy, childbirth, miscarriage, sometimes secret, illegal abortion, and the death of infants, all with serious long-term effects on women's physical and mental health. But falling pregnant was hard to control, especially for poorer women. Contraceptive condoms, caps and sponges were becoming available, but they were much disapproved of, difficult and, for poor people, expensive to obtain, along with access to knowledge about them. The most prevalent birth control methods were the oldest and most stressful, *coitus interruptus* and abstention from sex. Women's groups did their best to give poorer women advice on birth control and free appliances.[22]

Due to fears about the health and fitness of the population and under pressure from women, more local authorities appointed school medical officers to identify and treat ill-health among schoolchildren whose families could not afford medical care. Under Conservative governments the central state did little for the poorest, which contributed to the success of the Liberals in the 1906 election. They then worked to reduce social inequalities but showed less awareness of gender inequalities, though there was some progress due to women's pressure. In 1906 a Labour MP initiated legislation providing free meals for needy schoolchildren, to improve their health, fitness and capacity to benefit from education. Further reforms followed. Women were excluded from the innovative Unemployment Insurance scheme as they were from NHI, which was introduced alongside it. Both were intended to improve the security of skilled male workers in order to promote economic growth in an increasingly competitive world economy.[23] More women gained from the introduction of old age pensions in 1908: two-thirds of the 490,000 recipients of the first pensions were female; because they had longer life expectancy than men, more lived to old age and more were poor. The pension was not paid until age 70, strictly means-tested and confined to the very poor, and it was and long-remained too low to live on without a supplement.[24]

Women were the main beneficiaries of the Trade Boards Act, 1909, which established a system for negotiating improved pay and conditions in the notoriously low-paid, exploitative 'sweated' trades, as they were known, including tailoring, cardboard-box making and chain making, which overwhelmingly employed women in small workshops or their own homes. It followed a campaign by the Fabian Women's Group, the WCG and others. In 1905 they organized with other women's associations a London exhibition displaying women's poor working conditions. The publicity, plus pressure from the Labour Party and trade unions, persuaded the government to introduce the legislation. But the resulting pay was low, the law was not strongly enforced and it had limited impact.

The Fabian Women's Group was part of a moderate socialist reform organization, the Fabian Society, affiliated to the Labour Party. The Women's Group was formed in 1908 to demand the vote and improved social and working conditions, particularly for women, and was led by Maud Pember Reeves, wife of the New Zealand High Commissioner, a successful campaigner for the vote in her home country. It worked to increase public awareness of gender inequalities, including through a survey of the budgets and daily lives of families in Lambeth, south London, asking, 'How does a working man's wife bring up a family on 20s a week?' The report, *Round about a Pound a Week*, published in 1913,[25] included details of incomes and budgets and described housing, diet, health and family life, stressing how carefully most poor women managed inadequate, insecure incomes, contrary to the 'improvidence' perceived by critics ignorant of their lives. Most Lambeth wives were not in paid work; they had work enough at home, sometimes supplemented by part-time employment as cleaners or letting rooms to lodgers. To improve family living standards, the Fabians advocated a state-guaranteed national minimum income, sufficient to keep a family, which New Zealand had been the first to introduce in 1894, followed by Australia in 1896.

The National Union of Women Workers (NUWW), founded in 1895 (from 1918 the National Council of Women, NCW, signalling its membership of the International Council of Women, ICW), supported these campaigns for improved working conditions for women. It was not, as the name suggests, an organization of working-class women, but of middle- and upper-class women not in paid employment but dedicated to work in voluntary philanthropy to help the poor, especially poor women, so they were well aware of their disadvantages. They were profoundly committed to protecting young women against sexual exploitation, including the all-too-prevalent 'white slavery', as it was known, forcing impoverished women and girls into prostitution and suffering and transmitting venereal disease (VD). They sought to support and rehabilitate victims and advocated appointment of the first policewomen to protect women. They aimed to ensure that women arrested for prostitution no longer suffered sexual harassment from policemen and that any women could safely report rape or other forms of sexual violence to a police representative without fear that they would be ignored or suffer further assault. This campaign was unsuccessful before the First World War.[26]

VD (syphilis or gonorrhoea) was a widespread problem not only for prostitutes but for wives contracting it from unfaithful husbands. It could cause miscarriages, stillbirths, the death of infants, underweight births and longer-term effects on mother and child. Women's organizations promoted the growing range of effective treatments for VD and sought to persuade men to reject cultural norms and to practise chastity outside marriage.[27] Christabel Pankhurst demanded 'Votes for Women, Chastity for Men', arguing that women needed the vote to gain protection against male sexual aggression and the danger of VD.[28]

With other women's organizations (the Women's Freedom League, WFL, was very active in this area), the NUWW was concerned about women's difficulties in obtaining justice as victims of sexual offences, the dismissive treatment by the criminal justice system, including the police, of female victims of any crime, while women accused of any offence were harshly treated by all-male courts. Concerns were intensified by the treatment of militant suffragettes and by the practice of clearing all female spectators from courts dealing with 'sensitive', i.e. sexual, issues, leaving female victims of sexual crime unsupported. The NUWW, with others, campaigned for the appointment of women lawyers, magistrates and jurors to support women in court. They recruited female volunteers to attend court hearings as 'friends' supporting women in all types of case, when they were allowed.[29]

Inequalities in Marriage

Inequalities in marriage were another cause of protest. Not all women married, despite cultural expectations, mainly because they outnumbered men in the population. This owed much to the longer life expectancy of females from birth. Male babies had higher death rates than females at this time of high infant mortality, and young adult men, especially working-class men, had higher death rates due to accidents at work or to military service, and more men than women emigrated alone for work in the United States or the British colonies. In England and Wales there were 15.5 million adult males to 16.6 million females in 1901; in 1914, 17.8 million and 19 million, with similar proportions in Scotland and Ireland. Not all men married. Around 14% of women and 9% of men never married in England and Wales, continuing to the Second World War. These were long-established patterns. Male non-marriage may have been due to men believing their incomes were too low to support a family, or to secret homosexuality. Marriage ages had long averaged about 27 for men and 25 for women.

Marriages did not always last. Their greatest destroyer was death. Of marriages in England and Wales in the 1880s, 13% were ended by death, most often of the husband, within 10 years, 37% within 25 years.[30] Widowers were more likely than widows to remarry, seeking care for their children and themselves. Women often preferred the independence of widowhood, including gaining control of their own property and custody of their children, compared with the legally enforced dependence of wifehood, while men could be reluctant to support another man's children. But low pay and limited work opportunities made poverty almost unavoidable for lone mothers without independent wealth. Impoverished single mothers were as numerous in the early as in the late twentieth century; in 1900 the main cause was widowhood, in 2000 divorce, separation or choice, as we will see in later chapters

Marriages broke down for other reasons. Divorce was possible in England and Wales from 1857, but, as we have seen, it remained easier for a man than a woman, and for most working-class people it was prohibitively expensive.[31] In Scotland divorce was available to men and women equally for desertion as well as adultery, though it was not always cheaper. Many churches forbade remarriage and there was no civil marriage, as there was in England and Wales from 1836. But 'irregular' unmarried partnerships could be officially registered, as they could not in England and Wales, forming 12% of all registered partnerships, including marriages, between 1855 and 1939.[32] This was similar to the number of unmarried partnerships throughout Great Britain in the late 1990s.[33]

In England and Wales from 1878, a wife could claim in court a separation order and an allowance of up to £2 per week from her husband if she left him due to violence or he deserted her. This followed a feminist campaign against 'wife torture', as they described domestic violence, but extracting payment could be difficult and he could claim custody of their children. In 1900, the Divorce Court granted 494 divorces in England and Wales, while magistrates made more than 5,000 separation orders, which did not allow remarriage. Some couples cohabited, presenting themselves as married, because they could not divorce and remarry, often having children; how extensive this was is unknown. The situation continued despite protest by men and women and proposals for divorce reform by official commissions, which listened to women's views despite King George V's assertion that divorce was 'not a subject on which women's opinions could be conveniently expressed'.[34]

Public discussion of sex and sexual relationships, in and out of marriage, was unacceptable and they were little understood. It was generally believed that the biological differences between men and women created differences in their capacities and purpose in life. Women's central purpose was represented as reproduction followed by care for the family, leaving little energy for intellectual growth; men's was assisting population growth, and improving national health and economic growth through their hard work as family providers. Biological differences were assumed to justify the subordination of women to men.

The 'Great War'

The war that came in August 1914 reinforced perceived inequalities between heroic men who fought to save their country and women whose role was to look after the domestic front, but it also gave women some new opportunities, including helping to persuade the government to concede the vote to some women in 1918.

The WSPU immediately suspended public protest. Emmeline and Christabel Pankhurst believed the vote would be the reward for patriotism and that, as Christabel put it, 'To win votes for women, national victory was needed for, as Mother said, "what would be the good of a vote without a country to vote in!"'[35] Some WSPU members supported the war by forming the first, initially unofficial, uniformed Women's Police Service, to maintain public social, especially sexual, propriety in wartime, including protecting women from assault. They gained Home Office support but not powers of arrest, though they were a visible, watchful presence, totalling 4,000 patrols nationwide. A similar body formed by the NUWW established about 5,000 patrols. The NUWW continued its pre-war campaign for the permanent appointment of policewomen and established courses which had trained over 1,000 by 1920. The first woman was appointed to an official police force in Grantham, Lincolnshire, in 1915. After the war more women became official policewomen.[36]

Emmeline Pankhurst became increasingly Conservative, while her daughter, Sylvia, moved left, opposing the war and joining the newly formed Communist Party in 1920. There were more opponents of the war in the NUWSS, and they gained some dissident refugees from the WSPU, which was divided about the war. Millicent Garrett Fawcett judged it wise not to support or oppose the war in public and urged her supporters to take up relief work 'to give aid and succour to women and children brought face to face with destitution in consequence of the war'. Many firm pacifists left the organization. Fawcett suspended political activity since it was unlikely to be effective in wartime and chose to prove the skills of women in the NUWSS by developing relief services. Their valuable work included equipping and staffing hospital units for soldiers at the front, working with Belgian and Russian refugees, providing 'comforts', such as warm clothing, for the troops, and much more.[37]

Families at War

At first the war caused unemployment for women and men. Many female domestic servants found themselves jobless as employers used the war as a reason to dismiss them. Then, as the war economy opened new opportunities, others left for better pay and conditions in work that allowed them more independence. Domestic servants declined by 400,000 over the war period. As the war economy expanded, the labour shortage due to the absence of men in the services created full employment for civilian men, unknown in peacetime, and new work opportunities for women, which together improved the living standards of many working-class families.[38]

But many servicemen's families faced poverty when the men went to war: families lost their wages and the government was slow to give them support. Sylvia Pankhurst devoted herself to assisting such families in east London, horrified by the conditions she found, as she later described:

> Women gathered at our door asking for 'Sylvia' . . . they turned to her now in these hours of desperate hardship; poor wan, white-faced mothers, clasping their wasted babies, whose pain-filled eyes seem older than their own. Their breasts gone dry, they had no milk to give their infants, no food for the elder children, no money for the landlord.[39]

She did her best to help.

From October 1914, the government paid allowances to servicemen's families, after a while even to cohabiting 'unmarried wives', when these emerged in unexpected numbers. They were payable only where the relationship had preceded the serviceman's enlistment by at least six months, there was at least one child, 'evidence that a real home had been maintained', and the woman had to prove that the serviceman was her sole support and she 'would otherwise be destitute'. The allowance was paid even if the serviceman had a legal wife.[40] From November 1915 families of the war dead, including 'unmarried wives', also received pensions. Most allowances and pensions were small, often paid only after long delay for assessment, and could expose wives (married and unmarried) to moral policing, since payments could be withdrawn as punishment for 'immoral behaviour'.[41] The government intended them to be at least minimally adequate for subsistence and, low as they were, their regularity (unlike the pay at work of many poorer men) improved the well-being of poor families so visibly that after the war feminist Eleanor Rathbone started a long campaign for their continuation as peacetime 'family allowances' to reduce family poverty.[42]

Another source of wartime hardship for many families was rising rents in centres of war production, such as Glasgow and London, due to pressure of demand on a limited housing supply from the influx of workers and the greed of some landlords. Even before the war, there was a serious housing shortage in the cities and the war made things even worse. The first of a series of rent strikes began in Glasgow in May 1915, led by women, followed in London, Coventry and elsewhere. In Glasgow:

> Mrs Barbour, a typical working-class housewife became the leader of a movement such as had never been seen before . . . street meetings, backcourt meetings, drums, bells, trumpets – every method was used to bring the women out and organize them for the struggle. Notices were printed by

the thousand and put up in the windows: wherever you went you would see them. In street after street, scarcely a window without one: WE ARE NOT PAYING INCREASED RENT.[43]

The Chancellor of the Exchequer, David Lloyd George, immediately established rent controls which remained in force, with amendments, until Margaret Thacher abolished them in the 1980s.[44] A success for women campaigners, though wartime housing conditions remained poor.

Work for Women

As more men were killed, for the first time women were recruited to the services. The Women's Army Auxiliary Corps (WAAC) was formed in 1917 to undertake non-combatant tasks behind the lines and release men for the front. It had four sections: Cookery, Mechanical, Clerical and Miscellaneous. Its formation was strongly resisted by senior members of the armed forces who accepted it only due to the shortage of men. About 80,000 women enrolled by the end of the war. At the end of 1917, the Women's Royal Naval Service (WRNS) was formed for the same purpose. In April 1918, the Royal Air Force (RAF) was founded, with a woman's branch from the start, the Women's Royal Air Force (WRAF). In none of the services were women allowed to bear arms or take part in combat. In war as in peace, women were expected to serve men. A Women's Land Army worked on farms to help meet the growing wartime food shortages, replacing men serving in the war. Female voluntary aid detachments (VADs), mainly engaged in nursing behind the lines often in horrifying conditions, were formed pre-war and included 40,000 women in 1914, 80,000 in 1918. They worked alongside the Women's Sick and Wounded Convoy Corps and the First Aid Nursing Yeomanry (FANY), both founded in 1907.[45] Dr Flora Murray and Dr Louisa Garrett Anderson formed the Women's Hospital Corps in 1915, providing female doctors to supplement the men at the front.

Medical training expanded – temporarily – for women as male doctors were needed at the front, creating an acute shortage at home. In London none of the eleven male medical schools admitted women in 1914, only the London (Royal Free) School of Medicine for Women, established in 1877. Elsewhere most university medical schools admitted just small numbers of women. By 1915, women were urged to rise to the nation's need and train as doctors, but the opportunities remained limited, while medical schools emptied as men went to war. Then they gradually admitted women, and by 1918 seven of the all-male London schools and other universities increased their intake, generally making clear that this was just for the duration of the wartime emergency. After the war some reverted to male-only status and everywhere places for women were severely cut, with little change until the 1970s.[46]

By the end of the war, about 1.6 million women had entered new wartime employment, about half in manufacturing, almost a million in the metal and chemical trades compared with 200,000 before the war, a quarter directly employed to produce munitions. Wartime work often brought more freedom, independence and higher pay for women but, all too often, also illness and stress from working long hours in sometimes poor conditions. About 300 'munitionettes' died, and others were physically and/or mentally impaired due to chemical poisoning or explosions.[47] About 100,000 women were employed in transport, taking over traditionally male jobs as the war progressed, most visibly as ticket collectors and conductresses on buses and railways, some, shockingly, even driving trams, buses and ambulances.

In the UK about 7,311,00 women were employed at the end of the war compared with 5,966,000 in 1914, including in the women's branches of the armed services. Many were in wartime-only jobs, temporary because, like munitions, they were less needed in peacetime, or because, like bus conducting, they would be repossessed by returning men. The most significant, and lasting, growth of women's opportunities was in middle-class, 'white blouse' occupations as they were known, echoing the common designation of comparable male employment as 'white collar'. The women worked mainly as low-status clerks, secretaries, telephonists, speeding up a pre-war trend as the scale of government and business grew permanently during the war. About 400,000 more women were employed in banking, finance, commerce and public administration in 1914–18, but most at low levels in gender-specific work. More women were employed in the growing trade of retailing.[48]

In no occupation were women paid equally with men in wartime as in peace, though many earned more than before the war, especially in munitions. On average, women's rates of pay rose from half to two-thirds of those of men. Where they took over men's industrial jobs, unions and employers widely agreed to 'dilute' the work, redesigning skilled work into a series of semi- and unskilled tasks judged to be within the capacity of unskilled women, at lower pay. This aroused realistic fears among male trade unionists that employers would find it profitable to continue such arrangements after the war, depriving men of work, and strikes forced employers and the government into commitments to restore pre-war practices after the war.[49] Some trade unions were persuaded to demand equal pay where men and women were doing the same work, not necessarily out of commitment to gender equality but to protect male pay rates.[50]

Such debates made equal pay a more prominent issue during the war. It was considered by the War Cabinet Committee on Women in Industry, established in 1918 to exonerate government from claims by striking female transport and munitions workers that they had not honoured their promises to award equal pay to women doing men's work.[51] Its Majority Report, in 1919, recommended that women doing the same, or similar, work to men should receive equal pay in proportion to output. They accepted male arguments with no evident basis that women were only two-thirds as productive as men and should not receive equal pay rates. The idea of comparing pay for exclusively female work with rates in exclusively male work was rejected as impossible.

Infant and Maternal Care

The birth rate fell faster than before the war, while pre-war concern about infant and maternal welfare and high infant death rates continued to drive campaigns for health services, mainly by women but now with greater male support due to the need to replace adult males killed at war. As the Bishop of Fulham told an audience: 'While nine soldiers died every hour in 1915, twelve babies died every hour, so that it was more dangerous to be a baby than a soldier.'[52] Concern was further aroused by the large numbers of male volunteers judged physically unfit for the armed services.[53] Just before the war the government offered to fund 50% of the cost of clinics, health visitors for expectant and new mothers, additional hospital beds and skilled midwives, all provided by local authorities as women campaigners proposed. In 1915 it added funding for local authorities to establish milk depots selling milk for infants at cost price and for childcare classes for mothers. By 1916 concern about war deaths grew and it offered to pay the full salaries and expenses of nurses, health visitors and inspectors of midwives, of doctors and midwives for poorer mothers, especially in more deprived regions, to keep more babies alive and healthy. The number of full-time health visitors in England and Wales rose from 600 in 1914 to 1,355 in 1918. Poorer mothers gained improved health care to ensure adequate supplies of male workers and fighting men for future wars.

The improved services owed much to their being run by women who saw this as their war service, paid or voluntary, and they raised substantial voluntary funds to further improve health and welfare. Deaths in the first year of life fell after the first year of war.[54] In relatively deprived Wigan (Lancashire), the death rate was 139 per 1,000 on the eve of war, 119 by November 1918.[55] This probably also owed much to improved family living standards. Maternal mortality did not decline but nor did it arouse as much official concern as infant and male deaths, despite pressure from women's organizations who lobbied for free health services and benefits for low-income mothers.

Through the war the proportion of 'illegitimate' births rose to around 9% of all births, compared with around 4% before the war. This unleashed a moral panic about the deterioration of morals among young people, especially women, in wartime. More probably, as was shown in the Second World War and discussed in chapter 3, it was due to the absence of young men at war delaying marriage following discovery of the pregnancy. Premarital sex was more common in the early twentieth century than conventionally believed, and society, including women, less sexually inhibited, as the numbers of unmarried cohabitees also suggested. On another health issue, VD increased during the war. In 1917 about 55,000 British soldiers were hospitalized with it, increasing women's pressure for their protection.[56] From 1916 a system of free treatment was established nationally.[57]

The Vote

The inequalities experienced by women during the war strengthened the demand for women's suffrage, while conscription, introduced for the first time in Britain in 1915, made it difficult for the government to refuse extending the vote to men who risked their lives and sometimes suffered serious injury for their country. The war gave some a further reason to oppose votes for women on the grounds that they did not fight, though others argued that they deserved the vote for their wartime work and service. In 1916 the government set up a cross-party Speaker's Conference to consider voting reform.[58] This encouraged the NUWSS to resume lobbying, together with smaller suffrage organizations, the Women's Freedom League and the United Suffragists. They recognized that because women were a majority of the adult population there would be opposition to an equal adult franchise leading to a female-majority electorate. They proposed instead a higher age limit for women voters, as a first step to full adult suffrage, strongly supported in the Commons by a minority of male MPs.[59] The WSPU refused to renew campaigning, while Sylvia Pankhurst's left-wing Workers' Suffrage Association demanded full adult suffrage at age 21 and rejected any compromise.

In March 1917 the Speaker's Conference recommended granting the vote unconditionally to men aged 21, or younger if they fought in the war, and not at all to conscientious objectors who refused to serve. A majority supported women's suffrage limited to women from age 30 or 35 who were independent householders entitled to the local government franchise or wives of householders, thus retaining the property qualification to be abolished for male voters. Some suffragists objected that the age limit would exclude young women munitions workers and others who had made a significant contribution to the war effort, if they or their husbands owned or rented insufficient property to qualify. Millicent Fawcett agreed but opted to accept a compromise, then to campaign for a full democratic franchise, as the suffragists subsequently did.[60]

The Representation of the People Act, 1918, embodied these proposals, setting women's voting age at 30. It passed through parliament quite easily in February 1918. The higher qualifying age for women especially appealed to many Conservative and Liberal men because they believed older women would be more conservative than irresponsible young women and would help counter the danger that newly enfranchised working men would support Labour or, worse, Communism following the 1917 revolution in Russia. Later in 1918, more easily still, parliament granted women the right to stand for parliament before they could vote, at age 21 and regardless of their property status. This apparent anomaly was, as MPs pointed out, logical since adult men disfranchised by the property qualification (e.g., if they lived in their parents' property as wealthy men often did before marriage) had long been able to stand, including some leading current MPs.[61]

Over half a million men were missing after the war, widening the female majority in the population though less dramatically than is sometimes thought: from 107 adult women to every 100 men in 1911 to 110 in 1921 in England and Wales; 106 to 108 in Scotland. The gap was widest among those in their twenties: in 1921 there were 19% more women than men in this age group in Great Britain, compared with 11% in 1911. Contrary to persistent myths of a generation of embittered spinsters left by a 'lost generation' of men killed in the war, the proportion of women in this age group who married changed little, since a high percentage had never married previously.

Conclusion

In the early years of the twentieth century women exposed and challenged more gender and social inequalities than before, in particular unequal voting rights, rights within marriage and social, including health, disadvantages suffered, especially by poorer women. They had limited effects before war came in 1914. This brought more significant changes, especially in women's working opportunities, some of which outlasted the war, in social reform including rent controls, and health care, especially for poorer mothers and children. And they gained the vote, though on terms decided by men and not equal with theirs, but enough to stimulate further campaigns for equality.

TWO

What Difference Did the Vote Make? 1918–1939

Newly enfranchised working men did incline to vote Labour, but women voters were not as conservative as some politicians hoped. From 1918 there was more radical activism by women, some with voting rights, some not, challenging more gender inequalities than before the war, and there were more women's organizations, mostly speaking up for women's rights. Meanwhile women were allowed to become full members of the political parties for the first time and remained active, hoping to influence their actions in the still male-dominated political world. By 1928 the Conservative women's organization, which became part of the party in 1918, had about one million members, the Labour Party about 300,000, half the individual membership of the party, the Liberals over 100,000.[1] As voters they had greater influence upon politicians and bombarded them with letters and organized protests and delegations to Ministers demanding gender and social equality. They had some successes, but most inter-war governments were Conservative-controlled and not anxious to promote gender equality.

Six million women gained the national vote; five million joined the local government electorate, along with 1.25 million men. About two million women over 30 were disqualified from voting, nationally or locally, because they did not meet the required property qualification. A small number of women and many more men had two national votes if they were university graduates who were qualified to vote in one of the nine UK university seats. The right of male businessmen to vote twice if their residence and business premises were in different constituencies did not apply to businesswomen, including the many female owners of small shops. Equally irrationally, three single men 'jointly occupying' a rateable property each had the vote, whereas if three women did so, only two could vote. Such anomalies further stimulated the vigorous women's campaign for a universal equal franchise at age 21.[2]

How many women voted, and how, is and was unknown, though there is no reason to expect 'women' *en masse*, any more than 'men', to show predictable, uniform, voting preferences. Despite the belief of some historians and political scientists in a persistent preference of women to vote Conservative, there is no good evidence of female or male preferences in the absence of reliable opinion polls before the Second World War.[3] Journalists between the wars were as curious as politicians and crowded around polling stations at elections, questioning women, generally concluding that, like men, they varied in their voting preferences among themselves and from election to election, depending on their evaluation of the issues, influenced by class and other variables, as polls suggest they have done since 1945.[4] Class was probably a stronger influence on voting than gender.

There is every sign that women, after the generally low turnout in the 1918 election, used their votes. It was once argued that, after partially gaining the vote, the women's movement believed it had won, then splintered and collapsed and women made little use of their new rights, while those who did so inclined to Conservatism and did not campaign for further gender equalities.[5] But leading feminists, including Millicent Garrett Fawcett, Eleanor Rathbone and Sylvia Pankhurst, from their different perspectives, recognized that partially gaining the vote was not the end but the start of another battle, for women to *use* the vote to achieve full gender equality, including equal voting rights and improved social conditions. The NUWSS in 1918 became the National Union of Societies for Equal Citizenship (NUSEC) and campaigned with other organizations to encourage women to use their votes, to inform them about political issues and press parliament for essential reforms promoting gender equality.

Women's campaigns for equality multiplied. Organizations divided over which of the many inequalities they could most effectively target. In 1919 NUSEC resolved that certain causes were especially urgent: equal pay for equal work; reform of the laws on divorce and prostitution, to establish 'an equal moral standard' between women and men; pensions for civilian widows; equal parental rights to child custody; opening the legal profession to women. Through the 1920s there was progress on all of these except equal pay.

Political parties worked hard to attract women voters. Women continued to be active in all political parties and were a substantial part of their membership now that this was allowed by all parties. But they were still regarded by male party activists mainly as useful canvassers and fundraisers and had little influence upon policy.[6]

Women in Parliament

Seventeen women stood in the 1918 election, but only Countess Constance Markiewicz was elected, for the Irish Nationalists, who had substantial female support. She was in Holloway prison at the time for her part in the Nationalist Dublin Rising of 1916. She refused to take her seat because Nationalists, seeking Irish independence, opposed rule by Westminster. Nancy Astor, Conservative, American by birth, was the first woman to take her seat in parliament, in 1919, for Plymouth, replacing her husband when he inherited his father's title and seat in the House of Lords. She was acceptable to local selectors who assumed she would be guided by her husband. She retained the seat until she was defeated in the Labour landslide of 1945. She found the Commons a lonely and often hostile place, a situation that improved when Liberal Margaret Wintringham also took her husband's former seat in a by-election in 1920, following his death. Unlike Astor, she was a former suffragist, active in women's organizations as well as in the Liberal Party, but they co-operated and Astor supported causes promoted by women's organizations. Male antagonism in parliament made her more feminist.

In the 1922 election they both won again, the only female victories, while 31 other women stood unsuccessfully across all parties. In 1923 three Labour women were elected. In 1924, following Labour's first, brief, minority government, Ellen Wilkinson was the only woman who stood successfully for Labour. She was over 30 but because she was unmarried and from a low-income working-class background with little property, she did not qualify for the vote. The largest number of women elected to parliament between the wars, among 615 MPs, was 15 in 1931, including 13 Conservatives following the collapse of another minority Labour government. The small number of women MPs was not because they did not seek election, but they found it hard to gain selection for winnable seats; prejudice against women in politics ran deep and has never gone away.

Throughout the UK women continued to have more success in elections for local government.[7] Local authorities still carried most responsibility for social services, with considerable independence from central government. Women were still conventionally believed to have special skills concerning social issues and they had more time and enthusiasm for this unpaid work than many men. Women of all classes continued to work to improve social services, including housing and the still inadequate health care of poorer women, with greatest success in the growing number of Labour-controlled authorities. The number of female local councillors increased from 259 to 754 between 1914 and 1923; the number of female Poor Law Guardians rose from 1,536 to 2,323.[8] Locally elected women, and men, were not necessarily affiliated to parties since Independents were active and successful in local government, though not in parliamentary elections.

Party members or not, elected or not, women could wield influence at the local level. Preston, Lancashire, was transformed from a Conservative to a Labour stronghold in the 1920s when working-class women formed a strong local Labour Party Women's Section and persuaded an initially unsympathetic local party to adopt and, following success in local elections, implement a programme of improvements in education, maternity and child welfare, health care, housing and provision of public amenities important for poorer women, including baths and wash houses.[9] Women were similarly active elsewhere, making real differences to the quality of life.[10]

Party membership and election to parliament were not the only ways that women influenced national politics. Activists realized that politicians wanted their votes, and they could be effective through collective organization in pressure groups focused upon specific aims. They also recognized that comprehensive gender equality could only be achieved through a wide spread of activism. Eleanor Rathbone formed the Women's Citizens Association (WCA) in Liverpool in 1913 with this objective. She also chaired NUSEC from 1919 and the organizations worked closely together.[11] Both were determinedly independent of party politics in order to include women of diverse political views, though their members might join parties and support party candidates, male and female, who supported their causes in local and central government elections.[12] Other organizations committed to similar aims and methods included Women's Institutes (WIs), founded from 1915 by suffrage campaigners, including former militants, on a model initiated in Canada, to give countrywomen opportunities for personal and political development in spaces free from the traditional rural social hierarchy, dominated in Britain by the wives of squires and clergy. WIs, like Labour Party women and others, including Eleanor Rathbone, encouraged women who worked in the home to value their domestic work and skills and their important contributions to society and the economy in raising children and supporting working men. They campaigned for recognition of this indispensable, unpaid, hard work as *work*, as valuable as paid work, and they fought for improved conditions for women in paid work. WIs and other organizations also co-operated in increasingly successful campaigns to improve often appalling rural housing and access to water and electricity supplies, still lacking in much of the countryside in the 1930s.[13]

Women's political awareness and their capacity for campaigning was promoted, alongside other goals, by the growing number of women's trade unions and professional, faith-based and single-issue groups, including the National Union of Women Teachers, the Council of Women Civil Servants, the (Roman Catholic) St Joan's Social and Political Union, the Union of Jewish Women and the Anglican Mothers Union, alongside established organizations, including the WCG and the NCW.[14] They had active members in all political parties but none who campaigned on a range of issues. Among others, the League of the Church Militant (founded 1909 as the Church League for Women's Suffrage) campaigned for greater representation of women in the male-dominated Church of England and, particularly, for the ordination of women (achieved in 1994). Women were admitted more readily to the ministry of nonconformist churches: by the Congregationalists in 1917 and Baptists in 1926.[15] At least 130 women's organizations were active in the 1920s, almost certainly drawing into public life a larger number and wider social range of women than ever before, increasing gender equality in public life.[16]

An early parliamentary response to women's campaigns was the Sex Disqualification (Removal) Act, 1919, which, in principle, abolished disqualification by sex or marriage for employment in the professions or the exercise of any public function. Parliament would only accept a compromise with Bills promoted by Labour and women's organizations which included the equal franchise, and the Act did not go as far as many campaigners wanted.[17] Women still experienced prejudice and restricted entry to occupations and public roles, including limited promotion prospects and lower pay than men for the same work. The marriage bar, prohibiting recruitment of married women and requiring them to resign on marriage, remained throughout the public and much of the private sector, including for teachers and civil servants, despite campaigns against this and other inequalities throughout the inter-war years.[18] Men introduced it in the late nineteenth century when women started to enter the civil service and other professions, and they maintained it to protect themselves from competition for promotion.

The 1919 Act enabled women to become lawyers and magistrates and to sit on juries for the first time in their long history. In the early 1920s, the first women were called to the bar, though they faced prejudice and discrimination.[19] In 1920, 200 women were appointed magistrates, presiding over the ancient, lowest, unpaid, but indispensable level of the judicial system. No longer did women involved in legal processes, including marital or family cases or concerning physical or sexual assault, always alone face courts wholly composed of men, though they continued to experience problems, as we will see. There were 1,600 female magistrates in England and Wales by 1927, out of a total of 25,000.[20]

Like all reforms of the period, these were imperfect and women's and penal reform organizations worked together to further improve the treatment of women and young people in the justice system. Their campaigns and lobbying achieved greater support and rehabilitation of young offenders in place of imprisonment, improved the treatment of women in police cells, and ended the initial exclusion of women magistrates from juvenile courts. The NCW campaigned to increase the numbers of women jurors, including by abolishing the property qualification which existed for female but not male jurors and excluded most married women, but women did not gain equal access to jury service until 1972.[21] The law allowed defendants to demand an all-male jury and judges to exclude women from juries due to 'the nature of the evidence', often sexual. Through the 1920s, in some places for longer, women were still cleared from courts hearing sexual cases. Women's organizations campaigned against these restrictions and, with penal reform organizations, pressed for the appointment of more women to administer women's prisons, which were run overwhelmingly by men. A very few, mostly junior, female appointments were made. In 1945 the first woman was appointed governor of Holloway in London, England's main jail for female convicts.[22]

Inequalities at Work

Women gained and lost in the post-war labour market. Better-off, better-educated women made the most lasting gains, poorer women the least. Women had to leave work that was primarily war-related, such as munitions, or to which men expected to return. The labour market again became strictly gender-divided. Many working-class women returned reluctantly to domestic service, where the numbers gradually climbed close to pre-war levels: in 1911 there were 1,662,511 living-in servants, in 1931, 1,600,017, and it was the largest occupation in the UK for women or men. Respectable 'white blouse' work offered more opportunities, mainly for younger, unmarried, educated, better-off women. These included employment in the civil service, local government, teaching and nursing, all of which increased as the public sector expanded. Private businesses, including banks, grew in number and size during and after the war, creating well-paid jobs for many well-qualified men but mainly low-level secretarial and clerical posts for women. In none of these occupations did women have anything approaching equal opportunities for promotion and pay with men. Often, as in teaching, women did identical work with men, but earned less, had more limited promotion prospects and were required to leave on marriage, which was still represented as women's only acceptable career.[23]

The BBC, founded in 1922, and the John Lewis (department store) Partnership, founded in 1918, were unusual in having no marriage bar and providing equal pay and opportunities for women, at least in principle. The BBC in its early days found it difficult to attract talented men to an innovative institution with an uncertain future and had little choice but to recruit talented women, some married, who gained exceptional opportunities in developing the service. But when its success and significance were clearly established by the 1930s, men came forward and the BBC preferred to appoint them. It instituted the marriage bar, increasingly marginalizing women from top positions, though the bar was less strictly enforced than elsewhere and well-regarded married women remained and progressed. Women still had a better deal at the BBC than in most institutions, though they were not thought authoritative enough to be radio announcers or newsreaders until the Second World War brought another shortage of men. When it was suggested, the *London Evening*

News expressed horror at 'a Hobb's century [at cricket] being announced in a pleasant soprano, or the details of a heavyweight fight related by a girlish voice'.[24]

Other new occupations emerged. The campaign for the appointment of official policewomen continued. As the war ended, some police forces appointed women. The London Metropolitan force appointed 100 women as full constables, mostly NCW members since the Commissioner rejected former suffragettes due to their past militancy.[25] An official report in 1920 was very positive about appointing policewomen, but as economic depression descended from 1921, another government committee in 1922 recommended severe cuts to public spending and services, including axing women police. 'Fierce intervention' by the NCW and other organizations, supported in parliament by Nancy Astor and Margaret Wintringham, resisted this. A deputation to the Home Secretary in 1922 was supported by 59 women's organizations, but the Minister declared that the work of policewomen was welfare work not police work, so public money intended for the police could not be spent upon them.[26] Female police numbers remained low throughout the inter-war years. London continued to employ policewomen – though only 20 following cuts – but many authorities resisted, despite continuing pressure from women.

Before marriage, most working-class women had no choice but to enter the labour market, most from age 14, the official school-leaving age, some at 12 or 13. Females aged 15 to 24 in employment increased from 47% to 63% between 1911 and 1921, mainly due to the middle-class influx.[27] In 1921 the largest female occupation (23%) was, again, domestic service, while 13% worked in the textile industries, 12% were clerks and typists and 9% shop assistants, another occupation which expanded during and after the war as consumption grew among the better-off. Women, like men, gained higher wages during and after the war, though unequal with men's, until 1920 when their value declined as prices rose.

New industries began to expand from the late 1920s: motor vehicles in the Midlands, new electrical and other consumer goods, especially employing women, at low levels and low pay, in parts of London and the South-East. But there was severe, continuous unemployment in the old industrial and mining areas of northern England, southern Scotland and south Wales affecting men and women. Everywhere, young working-class women under 18 were the lowest-paid sector of the workforce, regarded as cheap, disposable labour, though their incomes could be vital to their families as unemployment grew, or if their mother was widowed or separated with younger children. The standard argument for unequal pay by employers and unions, that men supported families whereas women did not, overlooked such realities and the fact that unmarried men benefitted from higher pay.

Unequal pay was a major source of female discontent at all levels, a major issue throughout the inter-war years and the object of growing campaigns, very actively in the civil service. In 1935/6 equal pay for civil servants was debated in parliament but rejected by a Treasury Minister on the grounds that women did not do work of equal value with men: they were less efficient, took more sick leave and left the service on marriage (as they were compelled to do). An NCW memorandum to the Minister 'recorded their pride in the work of women civil servants, challenged the truth of [his] statements . . . and called on the government to give equal pay to men and women in the common grades [of the civil service]'. The House of Commons voted in favour of the proposal. Then the Conservative Prime Minister, Stanley Baldwin, declared that equal pay was a matter of confidence in the government and the vote must be withdrawn. The House obeyed.[28]

Women campaigned persistently on behalf of women working both within and outside the home. Like WIs and many others, Labour Party Women insisted that unpaid work in the home should be respected as indispensable, that domestic work conditions should be improved by well-designed housing, and hard-working 'housewives', like male employees, deserved an eight-hour day – 'eight hours work, eight hours sleep, eight hours leisure' – not their normal relentless labour. Also that women workers in or out of the home deserved the support of social services, including day-care for children, enabling them genuinely to choose whether or not to take paid employment.[29] They believed that the choice would be more realistic if work at home was paid – 'wages for housework' as it was known much later, as discussed in chapter 7. This was the aim of the campaign for family allowances, promoted by Eleanor Rathbone. Rathbone did not share the conventional belief that married women *should* stay at home but argued that those who did so deserved payment by the state for their essential work in raising children and helping male workers keep fit and active, just as service families had received wartime allowances, whose success inspired her campaign.[30]

In 1935 unmarried working women, led by Florence White, owner of a small confectionery business in Bradford, formed the National Spinsters' Pensions Association (NPSA), revealing another dimension of gender inequality at work. They demanded state pensions at age 55 on the grounds that unmarried women were often forced by employers to retire at earlier ages than men, most of whom received state pensions from age 65 following extension of the pension system to all workers insured under NHI in 1925. In people-facing jobs, like shop assistants, where appearance was believed to matter, women were forced to retire sometimes in their thirties or forties without pensions, and unemployed older women found it even harder than older men to find work.[31] Also, many middle-aged women gave up work to care for ageing parents, then were left destitute as they grew older. Following an official investigation, all women gained a reduction in the female pension age to 60 in 1940, on the grounds, not of discrimination, but because it was reckoned that, on average, husbands were five years older than wives and the reduction would enable husbands and wives to retire together on pensions.[32]

Gender, Sexuality, Marriage and the Family

Despite persistent gender inequalities at all levels of employment, young, unmarried, middle-class women gained new freedoms between the wars, when they could earn a living and live independently, enjoying new leisure activities, easier social relationships with men and more relaxed dress codes, arousing the disapproval of conventional moralists. More felt able to choose their own marriage partners, who previously had been subject to the approval, or choice, of parents. Marriage rates increased. Fewer men emigrated alone, and more men married, at younger ages than before. There was growing encouragement of the idea of marriage as an equal, enjoyable 'companionate' relationship of sexual fulfilment, clearly expressed in Marie Stopes's best-selling book *Married Love* (1918). Stopes received many letters from women and men, women often expressing their gratitude that she had diminished their ignorance and fear of sex and birth control.[33] This was an indication of a gradually increasing, though still limited, willingness to openly discuss sex and associated aspects of the lives of men and women. A British Society for the Study of Sex Psychology had been formed in 1914, led by homosexual Edward Carpenter, aiming to increase public discussion of sexuality. It arranged talks and issued publications, including about homosexuality, with limited public impact except among radical intellectuals. The Soviet Union in its early post-revolution days also appealed to radical intellectuals in Britain when it supported gender equalities, legalized divorce and abortion, encouraged birth control and decriminalized homosexuality, though it retreated from cultural liberalism in the 1930s.[34]

Lesbianism became somewhat more visible, featuring in novels, though Radclyffe Hall's *Well of Loneliness* (1928) was judged by the Home Office to go too far and was banned. Like other 'obscene' publications, it was then distributed from abroad until it was prosecuted under the Obscene Publications Act, when it received 5,000 letters of support. Publication was permitted in 1949. Also in 1928, Virginia Woolf celebrated her liaison with Vita Sackville-West in her novel *Orlando*. It was less explicit, aroused less condemnation and was very popular.[35] Sympathy for male homosexuality gradually increased, though it was still not openly discussed, and manifestations of its practice were fiercely policed, with growing numbers of prosecutions through the 1930s.[36]

But sex was still widely regarded with fear and ignorance. Sex outside marriage was condemned and stigmatized and assumed to be rare, especially among women, though the popular press took pleasure in reporting detailed accounts of adulterous behaviour revealed in court cases for divorce and related misdemeanours.[37] Many people, especially women but also many men, were ignorant about sex when they married, another reason for the popularity of Stopes's *Married Love*, which provided guidance. The extent of ignorance aroused demands for sex education in schools. In 1927 the Board of Education recommended it, but it was discretionary and by 1944 only about one-third of secondary schools provided it in any form, generally lectures on the ethics of married life.[38] In 1938–9, for the first time, parents were required to record their date of marriage when registering the birth of their first child. The Registrar General delivered the shocking report that in the first year, 30% of first births were recorded as occurring within nine months of the parents' marriage, suggesting substantial pre-marital sex. There was no reason to believe that this was something new.

Women's extra-parliamentary campaigns achieved some legal reforms concerning sex and marriage. They demanded protection of women and children from sexual and physical harassment and abuse, within and outside the family, through tighter laws and the appointment of more policewomen to support victims.[39] The Criminal Law Amendment Act, 1922, raised the age of (heterosexual) consent from 13 to 16. Also in 1922, the maximum maintenance for women and their children under separation orders was increased, easing escape from intolerable marriages. In 1925 the grounds on which either partner could obtain separation were extended to include cruelty and drunkenness and women were no longer required to leave the marital home before applying for a separation order. The Matrimonial Causes Act, 1923, initially drafted by NUSEC, following a succession of unsuccessful Bills and much parliamentary wrangling, enabled wives as well as husbands in England and Wales to gain divorce for adultery alone, but it remained expensive and inaccessible to many.[40] Still no divorce was possible in Northern Ireland except by the expensive process of a private Act of Parliament; Protestant and Catholic churches were powerful there and both opposed it. In 1924 mothers acquired equal rights with fathers to claim custody of children over age 7 following marriage break-up. Lack of custody rights had also trapped women in unhappy marriages, though, again, the costs of legal proceedings were prohibitive for many mothers and the law courts still inclined to support fathers over mothers.

The Bastardy Act, 1923, legalized legitimation of children following the subsequent marriage of their parents, improved procedures whereby unmarried mothers claimed maintenance from the fathers of their children and doubled to £1 the maximum weekly maintenance. It was introduced in parliament by Neville Chamberlain, Vice-President and later President of the National Council for the Unmarried Mother and her Child (NCUMC), a Minister in the Conservative government and future Prime Minister. Since its foundation, mainly by women, in 1918 the NCUMC had supported often impoverished, stigmatized unmarried mothers and their children and promoted improvements to their public support. It was committed to helping mother and child stay together, resisting the adoption of 'illegitimate' children enforced in Ireland, Australia, Canada and parts of the United States. In Britain this was common in Christian-run maternity homes, causing intense pain to unmarried mothers. More fortunate women returned to their parents' home, where the children grew up, sometimes told that their grandparents were their parents, to hide the shame of illegitimacy. Other mothers were assisted by the NCUMC and others to live in hostels, to take live-in domestic work where their children could join them, or place their children in foster care while they worked.[41]

The NCUMC and other women's organizations recognized that adoption was sometimes unavoidable when mothers could not cope. They supported legislation to control a practice that was wholly unregulated and could lead to abuse of children, because adoption was easy and prospective parents were not vetted or supervised. Legal adoption was introduced in 1926, including enabling unmarried mothers to adopt their own children.[42] Previously, 'illegitimate' children were legally *filius nullius* (nobody's child) because they had no legal father and in this patriarchal culture they lacked all legal rights, even to inherit from their mother if she died intestate.[43] Many mothers subsequently adopted their own children, giving them legal status. But the law was imperfect, abuse of adopted children continued, along with campaigns for further reform.

Another significant parliamentary response to women's campaigns was the New English Law of Property, 1926. This enabled married women, like those who were single, to control their own property, real and personal, on an equal basis with men.[44] These legal changes signified gradual shifts towards gender equality, including concerning marriage, the family and parenthood. Established cultural norms persisted but more fathers challenged them, spent more time with their children and recognized that they could influence their lives for good without imposing patriarchal domination. This was partly because wider cultural attitudes to the family changed as family size fell, living standards and expectations rose, more women asserted their right to independence and equality within and outside the home, and psychology grew in cultural and political importance, deepening understanding of the influence of parents upon children's lives. And more, especially better-off, fathers worked fewer hours and had more leisure time, more leisure activities could be enjoyed as a family and more families had comfortable homes and gardens, encouraging conceptions of the family as a self-sufficient nuclear unit, as it was increasingly represented in films and the popular press.[45]

These changes became more prevalent in the 1930s but not universal. Many fathers still tried to hide their involvement in childcare for fear of stigma. Only gradually did they feel able to push prams or play with their children in public. They rarely changed nappies and were still represented as the disciplinary figure in the family. Gendered expectations of parents continued as a cultural norm upheld by politicians and journalists.[46] Poorer, including unemployed, families could generally enjoy fewer leisure pursuits, and had less income and space. When cash for food was short, fathers and sons still had preference at mealtimes, to keep them fit for work.

Another change promoted by NUSEC and other women's organizations, the introduction of pensions for civilian widows (10s. per week) and orphans (5s.) to match those for war widows and their children, was introduced also by Neville Chamberlain as Conservative Minister of Health in 1925. It was confined to the families of male contributors to the NHI scheme, mainly better-paid skilled manual workers. It gave (minimal) income security to the largest group of single mothers. Chamberlain was not alone among male politicians in supporting women's proposals. Most of the legal reforms of the 1920s, initiated and often drafted by women's groups, were guided through parliament by a dedicated group of male MPs, since women MPs were so few. The legal changes did not create gender equality, but it edged closer. Women became a stronger, more assertive political presence after 1918, while fighting on for the equal franchise.

Equal Suffrage

They never stopped campaigning for equal voting rights. Conservative leader Stanley Baldwin announced in the 1924 election campaign: 'The Unionist Party is in favour of equal political rights for men and women.'[47] The Prime Minister before the election, Ramsey MacDonald, leader of the first – short-lived, minority – Labour government, supported a Labour backbencher's Equal Franchise Bill, but lost office before it could proceed. The Liberals also officially supported equality. After the Conservatives won the election it was not mentioned. Baldwin was perhaps deterred by hostility on the Conservative backbenches to enfranchising 'irresponsible' young women, creating a majority-female electorate, and by the predictions of the incorrigible *Daily Mail* that:

> If the women come to use their power (and they may gradually come to do so) they can dominate the state and control all its departments. They will almost certainly claim in the immediate future a much larger proportion of appointments, so that men will be steadily dislodged.[48]

This was more than the most ardent feminists dared aspire to, at least in the immediate future, but it expressed the views of male opponents. The strident opposition of the *Mail* and its sister paper the *Daily Mirror* to the 'Flapper Vote' was not driven just by crude sexism – the two papers normally appeared quite supportive of aspiring young women, not least because they needed their readership – but by the extreme anti-socialism of their proprietor, Lord Rothermere. He was convinced that the new voters were likely to be employed and therefore susceptible to trade union and socialist influence and would keep Labour in power. When the equal franchise finally went through parliament, the *Mail* warned it 'may bring down the British Empire in ruins'.[49]

Women repeatedly reminded Baldwin of his pledge. Early in the new government, Labour MPs William Whiteley and Ellen Wilkinson introduced another Equal Franchise Bill, one of several since 1919. The government rejected it but felt obliged to promise an all-party conference on the issue, perhaps in 1926. NUSEC and other associations organized demonstrations, meetings and deputations to Ministers, hinting at a return to militancy if Baldwin broke his promise. Another Labour Bill was introduced in March 1926. The campaign, with press publicity, peaked at a demonstration in July when 3,500 women of all parties and backgrounds marched to Hyde Park. The demonstrators included Emmeline Pankhurst (now an unsuccessful Conservative parliamentary candidate), Millicent Fawcett and other veteran suffrage campaigners, wearing their prison badges. Activism continued into 1927, courting maximum publicity and support – without response from the government.

In March 1927 Baldwin met a deputation introduced by Nancy Astor, including Eleanor Rathbone and Lady Rhondda, editor and founder of the feminist journal *Time and Tide*, previously a suffragette imprisoned for her militancy.[50] He excused his inaction on the grounds that he had been preoccupied by the 1926 General Strike and miners' strike and war in China and promised a statement soon. Lobbying continued until, in April, Baldwin announced the introduction of a Bill in the next session of parliament extending the franchise to women at age 21, not 25 as some Conservatives demanded to keep women voters in a minority. After so many broken promises the campaign continued, more intensely when the next parliamentary session was delayed until February 1928. On the day of the State Opening of Parliament, suffragists delivered a petition to the Prime Minister's house and a letter to the King at Buckingham Palace, while cars driven by women, festooned with placards demanding equal votes, circled Parliament Square to the sound of whistles and car horns. The King's Speech at the Opening of Parliament did not mention the franchise, but, that evening, Baldwin informed parliament that an Equal Franchise Bill would be introduced, enabling newly enfranchised women to vote in the election due in 1929. Introduced in March, it passed easily through parliament, though 218 MPs stayed away from the second reading, when there were just ten votes against.[51] Women were at last allowed to vote at age 21 on the same terms as men, enfranchising 5,221,902 women. The electorate became 53% female.

Health, Birth and Death

The local vote was also now extended to all adult women. Local authorities were the main providers of health care for working-class women and their children. Maternity and child welfare and school medical services improved gradually and unevenly, best in the growing numbers of Labour-controlled authorities, under continuing pressure from women's groups. By 1934 Labour controlled all major cities, including London and Glasgow. By the later 1930s all local authorities in England and Wales supplied milk to expectant and nursing mothers, free or at cost price. Ninety-seven per cent of babies received at least one visit from a health visitor. About 50% of mothers received free ante-natal care; more than 50% of babies attended local health and welfare centres staffed by doctors and health visitors. They treated only minor ailments and were often overcrowded and under pressure, but they dispensed free or subsidized food and milk. Those who benefitted welcomed them in comparison with past conditions, while women's organizations campaigned for more.[52]

But working-class women continued to have less access to health care other than in childbirth and child-rearing than many working-class men received through NHI or subscriptions to voluntary Friendly Societies, established since the nineteenth century to provide benefits and services to working-class people, mainly men.[53] Few families could afford also to subscribe on behalf of women and few women could afford it for themselves. A survey of the health of 1,250 working-class women by the feminist Women's Health Enquiry Committee in 1933 found that 404 had received no professional advice on health care, 591 learned all they knew from district nurses and ante-natal clinics, 245 from a health visitor, only 67 from a GP. Their report, *Working Class Wives*, described how women put the needs of their families first and were more anxious to learn how to care for their children than for themselves.[54] It gave a devastating account of working-class women's ill-health and the inadequacy of services, though it was positive about the work of welfare centres and health visitors in all but their numbers. It showed how much of women's ill-health still resulted from repeated pregnancy, miscarriage and sometimes illegal abortions without qualified medical care, all worsened by poverty and bad housing. One example was the wife of an employed miner in Durham:

> She is only 32, has been married fifteen years and has seven children the eldest of whom is 14. She lives in a colliery house; it has an open ash-privy at the back; the back bedroom is damp and the rain comes in; the kitchen ceiling is unsafe; there is no sink under the tap; the coal-house and ash-pit are at the end of a long garden and coal and ashes have to be carried through the sitting room which is used as a bedroom ... She gets up at 4 am and goes to bed at any time between 10 pm and midnight ... She does her own baking and the diet given is miraculous. She drinks a lot of water and gets a lot of green vegetables from their own garden including lettuce daily in summer. ... these are her own ailments, (1) Neuritis: from which she has suffered for two years owing, in her opinion, to getting wet, the heavy work of mangling etc. She rubs her shoulder with oils and puts on hot flannels with the advice of the colliery doctor. (2) Pyorrhoea: on the advice of the colliery doctor she has had all her teeth extracted; (3) Kidney trouble due to Bright's disease at 5 years; she takes medicine for this; (4) headaches and biliousness: lifelong due to the kidney trouble; she takes medicine for this; (5) Cystitis during her last pregnancy due to getting wet and heavy work; for this she rested in bed and kept warm; (6) Pain in right side during menstrual periods, due to ovarian trouble; the colliery doctor gives medicine for this by which 'he hopes to avoid an operation'.[55]

She was fortunate to have access to the colliery doctor, like her husband, if in little else.

To limit the effects of repeated pregnancies, women's organizations still campaigned for, and when possible provided, birth control assistance.[56] Techniques of control improved between the wars. Provision for poorer women came overwhelmingly from the voluntary sector, whereas better-off women paid doctors. Marie Stopes became a leading birth control campaigner and converted two horse-drawn caravans into mobile clinics which travelled the country providing free assistance. In 1931 the second Labour government responded to pressure from Labour women and others to make birth control more easily and cheaply available. Aware of the hostility of their substantial Catholic vote to birth control and that, as a minority government, they could not be sure of majority support in parliament, Labour proceeded cautiously. They permitted local authority health and welfare clinics in England and Wales to give free birth control advice to married women (only) whose health was endangered by pregnancy. Four years later, 224 councils of 474 in England and Wales provided birth control clinics, sometimes interpreting their role more flexibly than the government intended. Universal free birth control did not become available in Britain until 1974, as discussed in chapter 6.

In 1938 several, mainly female, voluntary organizations merged to form the Family Planning Association (FPA, which still exists) which developed a national network of free clinics, available to all women.[57] Births continued to decline in all classes, apparently achieved mostly by the cheapest methods, abstention from sex or *coitus interruptus*, men 'being careful' or 'getting off the bus early', as it was commonly known, though nothing is certain about something few people discussed openly and about which there was still much ignorance.[58] The reasons for limiting families are equally uncertain, though the desire for higher living standards, with fewer mouths to feed, and the growing realization that social mobility to higher social status and opportunities was now possible for children whose parents could afford to keep them at school were important, together with the growing desire of women for control over their lives and bodies and greater independence.[59] But the decline gave rise to panic in Britain and elsewhere in Europe because average life expectancy was also rising, creating the spectre of an ageing population burdening a shrinking younger generation with the costs of their care and damaging the economy. This caused anguished debate, continuing to the 1950s, involving such figures as Beveridge and Keynes, but no solutions, since there was no known way to increase the number of births. Hitler and Mussolini's attempts in the 1930s to reward mothers of numerous children did not raise their national birth rates.[60]

With better services and improved living standards, infant mortality continued to decline in England and Wales from 64 to 55 per 1,000 live births from 1930–2 to 1940–2. It remained somewhat higher in Scotland and above average in areas of high unemployment. It compensated somewhat for the decline in births, though another reason to have fewer babies was that they were now more likely to survive. In contrast, maternal deaths in England and Wales rose from 3.09 to 5.94 per 1,000 births, between 1921–5 and 1934.[61] They affected all classes, especially at first births, due mainly to sepsis. The rise may have been partly due to fewer births and the corresponding high proportion of first births, though poor diet in pregnancy and poor care still left poorer women especially vulnerable. Most confinements, in all classes, still occurred at home, in highly variable circumstances. The numbers, qualifications and state regulation of midwives improved, though by 1939 many poorer women still gave birth with unqualified assistance, unable to afford a doctor or medication if things went wrong. Maternal deaths declined permanently from the later 1930s following the discovery of penicillin to counter infection.

It was suspected that abortion was a significant cause of maternal death and was increasing. In 1930, 10.5% of maternal deaths were attributed to abortion, by 1934 20%,[62] when the Ministry of Health estimated that about 68,000 illegal abortions occurred, though only 73 were reported to the authorities.[63] It was believed to be commonest among older, married, working-class women. Women's groups campaigned for legalization. In 1936 the Abortion Law Reform Association (ALRA) was established by feminists, calling for safe, legal abortion for all women. They succeeded at last in 1967, as described in chapter 6. In 1937 a Committee was appointed to investigate abortion, in response to these pressures and the Ministry's concerns. Women's organizations submitted evidence. In 1939 it recommended against legalization but affirmed that abortion was allowable if pregnancy threatened a woman's life. This followed the legal judgment in the Bourne case in 1938, involving a doctor accused of performing an abortion following the gang rape of an underage girl by members of the King's Guard in London. This set a precedent by ruling the abortion lawful because it was intended to save the mother's life by preserving her psychological health.[64] Rape and sexual harassment of women continued to be frequent – we have no idea how frequent – but still not publicly discussed, with no legal controls.

The Struggle Continues

Gaining the equal franchise did not guarantee gender equality in other respects, and women's organizations fought on to improve the rights and status of women, building on their achievements since 1918, not always agreeing about priorities but with common ambitions for equality. Women's trade unions expanded, including in teaching and the civil service, still demanding wider work opportunities, equal pay and abolition of the marriage bar.[65] The organizations still encouraged women to vote and participate in local and national politics, promoting democratic citizenship, aiming to get more women elected, and they arranged continued local campaigning for social and health services and affordable, good-quality housing, contributing to gradual, real improvements.[66]

Divorce reform was still a major, divisive, issue, opposed by Anglican and Catholic women's organizations. Others supported the 1937 Matrimonial Causes Act, introduced by A.P. Herbert, the novelist and Independent MP. This extended the grounds for divorce in England and Wales, allowing husbands or wives to seek divorce after three years' desertion, or for adultery, cruelty or being of 'unsound mind and continuously under care and treatment' for at least five years; a wife could sue for rape or sodomy. According to its preamble, it amended the law 'for the true support of marriage, the protection of children, the removal of hardship, the reduction of illicit unions and unseemly litigation, the relief of conscience among the clergy and the restoration of due respect for the law'.[67] In England and Wales divorce petitions rose from 23,921 in 1931/5 to 37,674 in 1936/40,[68] though divorce remained expensive, impossible if one partner refused, and stigmatized, especially for women, and the campaign for further reform continued. In Scotland many of these provisions had long existed, the remainder were introduced in 1938. In Northern Ireland in 1939 divorce became possible for the first time other than by private Act of Parliament, but on more limited grounds than elsewhere in the UK since Catholic and Protestant churches still opposed it.

Conclusion

Through the inter-war years women were stimulated by possessing the vote – on equal terms with men from 1928 – to campaign even more vigorously than before to reduce the many remaining gender and social inequalities. They achieved change at national and local levels, with some support from male politicians, including further social reforms, to women's health care and pensions, for example. Especially middle-class, better-educated women gained access to a wider range of occupations, including previously closed professions, such as the law, and public offices, including as magistrates, though they still lacked equal opportunities in any occupation. They achieved greater, but still incomplete, equality before the law, including concerning marriage and parental rights. Gradual cultural change brought greater relaxation to family life and the leisure time especially of young middle-class women. There was much change towards greater gender equality between the wars, rarely initiated by governments, benefitting many women. But major inequalities, and strong opposition to equality, continued.

THREE

Gender in Wartime, 1939–1945

The Second World War, like the First, exposed and deepened gender inequalities, then ultimately slightly narrowed them. As in the previous war there was soon a labour shortage and, reluctantly when they could see no alternative, in December 1941, for the first time, the wartime coalition government conscripted women, at first unmarried women aged 18–30 for mandatory service in the armed services, the Land Army, teaching, nursing, the civil service or other essential services and occupations. The age limit was extended to 40 in 1942, and 50 in 1943, as the labour shortage continued. Married women without children under 14 or unavoidable household (mainly caring) duties were required to register for war work and prosecuted if they failed to take work to which they were directed. Some 2,067 were prosecuted during the war.[1] Ernest Bevin, the Labour Minister of Labour, and other members of the government were reluctant to enforce women's work because they feared damaging male morale if 'normal family life' was disrupted. As ever, they thought first of men's interests, but they went ahead as the labour shortage became severe.

Preparation for war began early and the government was better prepared than in 1914, drawing on that experience as war appeared increasingly likely despite the efforts of Neville Chamberlain, now Prime Minister, to avoid it with his policy of 'appeasement' of Hitler and Mussolini. His desire to avoid another war was widely shared among women and men until Hitler's vicious antisemitism and the territorial ambitions of both fascist leaders became inescapably obvious and very many men and women thought war against them essential.[2] The Auxiliary Territorial Service (ATS) was founded in 1938. It became the largest women's service, with 214,420 members by June 1943, working as cooks, waitresses, clerks, gaining skills including shorthand, switchboard operation or as motor mechanics to free and support men for combat, from which women were still banned. The Women's Auxiliary Air Force (WAAF) and the Women's Royal Naval Service (WRNS) continued as non-combatant support units. Women were forbidden to use weapons in any service, no matter how vulnerable their situation. They went on guard duty bearing sticks, while male colleagues carried firearms.[3] Recruitment posters appealed to women to join the WRNS to 'free a man for the fleet'; the WRAF 'to serve with the men who fly'.[4] Approximately 494,000 women were in the auxiliary services by 1944.[5] The Women's Land Army was re-launched in June 1939 to help maximize food production as in the last war. Again, some farmers were reluctant to employ women in normally male work as tractor drivers, field and plough workers, and shepherds, but they had little choice as men were conscripted from the start of the war. By 1943 there were 43,000 'Land Girls', plus 4,900 in the Timber Corps, cutting trees to provide fuel and managing forests.[6]

More men and women were recruited to the services than in the Great War and more survived. Around 360,000 British-born nationals, overwhelmingly male, died in war service. The services enabled some recruits to gain education and skills. Not altogether surprisingly, conscription revealed much poor literacy and an education service was established to meet these and other educational needs. But better-educated female graduates found their already limited career opportunities constrained further by conscription. If they dreamed of 'non-essential' careers, like architecture or film-making, it was forbidden until after the war, when they might be judged too old to train.[7]

Women in all classes again supported the war effort through voluntary action, this time directed and funded by the government. In 1938 the Home Secretary established the Women's Voluntary Service (WVS), initially to help with evacuation of children from areas at risk of bombing and with the effects of German bombing, which was expected as soon as war started, though the 'blitz' did not come until the autumn of 1940. The WVS fulfilled these and other functions throughout the war, invaluably supplementing stretched official services. It was a cross-class organization, with elite leadership, directed by Lady Stella Reading, widow of a former Viceroy of India, experienced in public and voluntary service.[8]

Evacuation

These activities, together with shared fear of bombing and invasion early in the war, then the experience of bombing, rationing and queuing, brought together women who might not otherwise meet. So did the rushed evacuation of children at a time when the potential psychological damage from suddenly taking children from their families into wholly strange environments was not understood. Many of them came from very deprived inner-city areas which were expected to be, and were, most vulnerable to bombing. The transition sometimes from very poor homes to those of better-off, or less deprived, families could exacerbate social divisions. Some hosts blamed mothers for the impoverished appearance, lice-ridden heads and poor table manners of underweight children from desperate homes, who wet their beds due to what was not recognized as trauma. Others felt compassion for depths of poverty they had never encountered and demanded reforms to end such conditions. Some evacuees were generously received and benefitted life-long from better education, food and environment than they might otherwise have experienced. Others suffered undetected abuse. Much was learned from the experience of evacuation, including about the psychological impact on children, though at some cost to the children and others.[9]

Evacuation could be stressful for women who were expected to look after sometimes more than one unknown, bewildered child. Billeting officers assessed who had bedroom space and evacuees were allocated according to standard overcrowding rules, though some richer families probably escaped. Women caring for evacuees were exempted from conscription. They received payments of 10s.6d. per week for the first child, 8s.6d. for others, more than the maximum service allowances of 5s. for the first child, but insufficient to cover the costs, especially when growing children needed shoes and clothing their families could not afford. Relatives caring for evacuees were unpaid. Reluctantly, against Treasury opposition, the Ministry of Health sanctioned small clothing grants. Following protests there were small increases for children over 14 in 1940.[10]

Social Conditions

Far more than in the previous war when a relatively small number were killed in Zeppelin and other raids, civilians at home in Britain suffered death and injury. Of 130,000 civilian adults killed or wounded by bombing, 63,000 were women. For the majority who survived, as in the last war, social conditions for most civilian manual workers and their families improved and there was some narrowing of socio-economic inequalities due to full employment from 1940 and government benefits. Allowances for service families, including again 'unmarried wives', as discussed in chapter 1, were provided from the start, more efficiently than before, though still not generous. The wife of a non-commissioned soldier with two children received 32s. weekly in 1939, 33s. in 1940, 38s. in 1941, 43s. in 1942. Average weekly male manual earnings in 1939 were 56s.9d. These payments were hard to live on. Public concern at poverty among servicemen's families led to an increase to 60s. by 1945. Officers' wives also received low payments by the standards of their class, and service personnel themselves were relatively low-paid.[11]

Food rationing was introduced sooner than in the previous war, in 1941. It prioritized healthy foods at controlled prices, improving the diets of many low-income families, and local authorities could, and most did, establish British Restaurants, as Prime Minister Churchill insisted they were called, providing low-cost, nutritious, off-ration meals. By September 1943, 2,160 British Restaurants served about 630,000 meals daily.[12] The government Food Policy Committee, chaired by Labour leader Clement Attlee, from 1940 approved grants of subsidized milk to mothers with children under five and daily milk and meals for schoolchildren. By February 1945 1,650,000 children received meals, 14% free, the remainder paying 4d.–6d. per meal; 73% of schoolchildren received free milk.[13] Free vaccination of children against diphtheria eliminated a major pre-war killer. Pre-war efforts to reduce the child death rate and improve health progressed, benefitting the poorest most. The government intervened to improve social conditions more vigorously than in the last war, following its greater activity between the wars. This was partly due to the influence of Labour in the coalition government, in which Attlee led on social policies. Rationing was also applied to clothing and essential household goods, including furniture, of basic, uniform design but good quality at low prices, further improving living standards for poorer households.

Rich people retreated to country homes from the dangers of the cities, including encountering other classes. They suffered some deprivations. The London social season was suspended, but they could still enjoy luxury foods in smart restaurants since all restaurants were 'off-ration'. If their children were evacuated, it was often to relatives in the Dominions, the long separation causing distress. As in the last war, one of the worst deprivations suffered by many better-off families was the flight of servants to more appealing work, this time permanently.

Reorganization of health services to meet wartime needs featured in the careful pre-war planning. An Emergency Medical Service (EMS) was established immediately, a centralized state system initially designed to treat victims of the expected bombing. Doctors and nurses were directly employed and paid by the government, often at higher rates than before. The increased need for medical care for injured service personnel and civilians created, as in the last war, a shortage of key staff. Again, more women gained training as doctors than before or after the war and more were employed by EMS, though few at more prestigious levels.[14] The EMS took over voluntary and public hospitals and established new ones in buildings of variable suitability. Access to non-war-related civilian health care was curtailed by the recruitment of doctors for war service, and long-stay patients, including many older people, were decanted from city centre to rural and suburban hospitals to provide space for victims of the war. The reorganization alerted the Ministry and the British Medical Association (BMA, which represented doctors) to deficiencies in existing services. The need for health care reform was constantly discussed and reforms proposed.[15]

Ministry officials became convinced of the need for a comprehensive health service for the whole population, for which there had been growing pressure before the war. Again, the poor physical condition of many recruits to the services and fear of the loss of young men at war, together with the condition of children evacuated from poor neighbourhoods, further stimulated demands to build a healthier nation. In October 1941, the Minister of Health, Liberal Ernest Brown, announced that immediate reorganization was impossible, but a comprehensive hospital service accessible to all would be introduced after the war. Local authority Medical Officers of Health (MOHs) and GPs working with poorer people supported reform enthusiastically. Maternal and child health and welfare services expanded further during the war, partly due to demand from mothers with infants evacuated to rural areas and small towns where services were sparse. Additional health and welfare centres, maternity homes and nurseries were staffed by volunteers, often from the

WVS.[16] In 1943 a survey by the independent research organization Mass Observation found widespread enthusiasm for a free national health service, though many Conservatives, including Churchill, opposed a state-managed service, while Labour strongly supported it. A succession of proposals for post-war reform emerged but the shape of possible reform remained uncertain in 1945.[17]

As in the last war, the health of most people not directly affected by bombing and war service improved. This was partly due to improved access to health services, also to full employment, better diets due to higher incomes, rationing and adequate supplies, and restrictions on supplies of unhealthy imported foods, including sugar. From 1939 to 1945 the infant death rate fell by a further 20% as more mothers received expert ante-natal care and delivery, more support from local health centres and access to cheap milk, orange juice and other supplements.[18] Deaths among older children also fell, mainly due to prevention of infectious diseases. Deaths from TB, which killed mainly adults, and other respiratory diseases, including bronchitis, influenza and pneumonia, fell significantly following the development and more extensive use of effective drugs plus improved living standards.[19] For similar reasons, after the discovery of penicillin, maternal mortality declined between 1938 and 1945 from 4.22 deaths per 1,000 births in England and Wales to 2.33, with similar falls in Scotland and Northern Ireland. The development of blood transfusion services during the war, by a woman medical researcher, Janet Vaughan, following her struggle against substantial opposition to a woman in the profession, helped reduce deaths in childbirth due to haemorrhage. Vaughan later became Mistress of Somerville College, Oxford.[20]

Women's Work

A higher proportion of British women were mobilized for the war effort than in the previous war or than in other belligerent countries with the possible exception of Russia, and more experienced the war at close quarters. More were in paid employment than before the war, but, as Janet Vaughan's experience suggests, prejudice and discrimination against women workers continued, including in the professions. At the peak in 1943, approximately 7,250,000 were in civilian work, the services or civil defence, 46% of all women aged 14–56, 90% of able-bodied single women aged 18–40, 80% of married women in the same age group without children under 14. Approximately 8,770,000 women were full-time 'housewives', many caring for evacuees. Due to labour shortages, the marriage bar was lifted in most occupations and generally did not return after the war. The number of female civil servants increased 1,214% between 1939 and 1945, from 14 to 54% of the total. Women in skilled jobs in industry increased by 128%, from 28 to 39%. In commerce, banking, insurance and finance the proportion of women rose from 31 to 63%.[21] A minority continued in all these occupations after the war. Married middle-class women were more likely to serve as volunteers, as the conscription laws allowed.

In manual work, again, munitions quickly employed over two million women. Concerning women taking normally male jobs in industry, as in the previous war, employers and unions agreed that they should receive the same rate for the job as men. Again, this was due not to the unions' support for the principle of equal pay but to their determination to ensure the long-term security of male pay rates. Male workers and employers could be patronizing or openly hostile to women workers. Employers, as in peacetime, resisted women's claims for equal pay where it was lacking and for equal access to training or promotion.[22]

As labour became increasingly scarce, in September 1941 the Ministry of Labour held a conference of women to discover how to encourage more women into the workforce. They were told that married women, especially, were concerned about low wages, poor working conditions, long hours and lack of childcare. Limited improvements followed, including reduction of women's daily working hours in industry to ten and encouragement of employers to provide part-time work and childcare.[23] In 1938 only about 10% of under-5s in England, Wales and Scotland, generally the poorest, attended publicly funded day-care.[24] Most working mothers, as before the war, left their children in the care of grandmothers or other relatives, neighbours or paid carers. From April 1941, despite much reluctance and opposition, the Ministry of Health felt it had no alternative but to establish and fund nurseries and registered childminders to draw more women into work. Under pressure of war, publicly funded childcare reached its highest-ever level in Britain. By July 1943 there were 1,345 war nurseries with 59,000 places, a year later

72,000 full-time places and 138,000 part-time places in day nurseries and nursery classes of elementary schools.[25] Children up to age 5 were eligible if their mothers were employed in work of national importance; parents contributed 1s. per day for a full-time place including all meals. Most nurseries were open from 7 am to 7 pm. They opened first in places where women's work was urgently needed and they filled up quickly. There were residential nurseries for evacuated children. Some employers provided day-care.[26] The problem remained for working mothers of providing meals and supervision for school-age children after school and in school holidays. The extension of school meals partially helped. A very few local authorities provided after-school and holiday play-schemes, otherwise mothers had to rely on relatives and other private arrangements.[27]

Mothers of young children were not conscripted, but the absence of a male breadwinner and the small service allowances forced many into employment despite the difficulties. By April 1943 the labour shortage was so acute that women previously exempt because of domestic responsibilities were directed into part-time work, often in shops, where staff shortages added to the queues and stresses of wartime life. In 1943, roughly 700,000 women, about 10% of the female workforce, were employed part-time, mostly married women working morning or afternoon shifts in essential occupations. Before the war, part-time casual work as cleaners, daily domestic workers or shop assistants was commonplace, but regular part-time work was rare in industry or in white-collar/blouse work. In wartime it became essential in many occupations to attract women workers. It appealed to women because it left them time for childcare and household duties and the often hours-long queues for rationed goods. Considerate employers altered start and finish times to enable married women to leave early or even recruited volunteers to fetch groceries for workers during working hours. Absenteeism among full-time women was almost twice as high as among men, especially on Saturday mornings, often for shopping. Absenteeism among part-timers was much less. Some shared childcare and food preparation, handing over at lunch time. But part-time employees were not eligible for bonuses or overtime payments, and few earned enough to pay for childcare or domestic help, while the total workload, in and out of the home, was heavy.

Survival was especially difficult for unmarried or separated single mothers or widows with small pensions, who needed a full-time income unless they had strong family support.[28] Again, the best option for many of them was live-in domestic service, for which there was considerable demand due to the exodus of single women servants.

Equal Pay

Recruitment of women for war work intensified the equal-pay campaign. Women's campaigns did not die in wartime. They were invigorated by the indispensability of women to the war effort and the government's continuing opposition to their demands. Early in the war, Conservative MP Irene Ward formed the Woman Power Committee of women MPs to urge government to employ more women in skilled work. It also campaigned against the Personal Injuries Act, 1939, which allowed unmarried male civilians 7s. per week more in compensation (total 21s.) for war-related injuries than unmarried women, on the grounds that it was compensation for pay, which was normally unequal. Mavis Tate, Conservative MP, and Labour MP Edith Summerskill protested in the Commons that the cost of living was equal for men and women, demanding equal compensation. When this failed, they and leading women's associations organized rallies and deputations and in 1943 the government complied. Also in 1943, it invited leading women's associations to a National Conference of Women, raising campaigners' hopes. Bevin and the Chancellor lavished praise on women for their war effort but refused equal pay. The response was the establishment of the highly active Equal Pay Campaign Committee (EPCC) in January 1944, uniting women's groups and among the pressures behind the establishment of the Royal Commission on Equal Pay in 1944.[29] As we will see in the next chapter, it reported in 1946.

There were strikes by working women demanding equal pay, more than in the previous war, especially in male-dominated industries, including engineering, where one worker in three was female by 1943. Some strikes were successful.[30] They were supported by the unions, again due less to enthusiasm for gender equality than because, as in the last war, they feared employers would permanently re-designate as less skilled and lower-paid the jobs taken by women, as many employers indeed tried. A British Institute of Public Opinion (BIPO) poll in 1940 found that 68% of respondents favoured 'equal pay for the same work'. Real change was slight: women's average weekly wages in manual work were 47% of men's in 1938, 52% in 1945, though the averages disguised greater variations by 1945. There were similar differentials among male workers, those in occupations 'essential' to the war effort faring best.[31]

Social Reform

Pre-war women's organizations remained active through the war, including campaigning for improved social conditions, though membership dropped due to evacuation, war work and other war circumstances. Some women transferred their energies to the WVS.[32] Women contributed substantially to the extensive body of proposals for social reform that emerged during the war, building on pre-war campaigns, intensified by wartime conditions. In September 1939 women's associations established the Women's Group on Public Welfare, which, chaired by Labour MP Margaret Bondfield, the first woman Cabinet Minister 1929–31, recruited women to inform people, especially women at home, of their rights to welfare, health and other services and to press government and official bodies to extend those rights. They investigated the circumstances of children and mothers whose problems had been exposed by evacuation and in 1943 published *Our Towns: A Close-Up* advocating reforms, including better housing, nursery schools for all children from age 2 and domestic training for schoolgirls.[33]

Improved housing was a major focus of women's campaigns. In May 1942 a Women's Housing and Planning conference was organized at the Royal Institute of British Architects in London by prominent women's associations, determined that plans for post-war housing should take account of women's views and needs.[34] The Ministry of Health established the Design of Dwellings Committee to improve home design and the layout of suburban estates. It included seven women, including three from the WIs and two from the WCG. The Women's Advisory Housing Council, formed by campaigners, issued a detailed questionnaire. More than 40,000 women of all classes responded, as summarized in a report to the Committee. Most wanted houses with sufficient living space and a garden, an upstairs, tiled bathroom and hot and cold running water; large, bright, soundproof rooms with rounded corners for easy cleaning; kitchens with conveniently placed, built-in cupboards and work surfaces, gas and electric cooking appliances and ventilated larders, all designed to improve family living standards and women's homeworking conditions. In 1944 the Committee endorsed many of their recommendations, proposing national minimum standards which were introduced by the Labour government after the war.[35]

Another area of social reform promoted during the war, following inter-war discussions, was education. R.A. Butler, the Conservative President of the Board of Education, was keen to reform secondary education. He introduced the only major piece of wartime social legislation, the Education Act, 1944, to be implemented after the war. It raised the school leaving age to 15 (implemented 1947), to rise to 16 as soon as practicable (implemented 1973), and abolished all-age elementary schools, dividing state education at age 11 into 'primary' and 'secondary' sectors, without further specifications. It abolished secondary school fees in state schools and increased grants to universities and students. The Act passed smoothly through parliament until women MPs introduced an amendment granting equal pay to teachers. Moved by Conservative Thelma Cazalet Keir, this passed the Commons by 117 to 116 votes. The following day Churchill diverted his attention from the war to insist this was a matter of confidence in the government and the amendment must be withdrawn, just as, in 1936, Baldwin had similarly forced reversal of a vote for equal pay in the civil service, to the fury of the staff associations, as described in the preceding chapter.[36] Both Baldwin and Churchill were probably impelled by unwillingness to raise the costs of state services or to support equal pay in principle, which would lead to further demands in the public sector and further cost rises. Protesting that the amendment hardly threatened the war effort, the House gave in, but Churchill, under pressure from women, appointed a Royal Commission on Equal Pay, which reported after the war, described in the next chapter. The women MPs won another amendment abolishing the marriage bar in teaching, which the Board of Education accepted because it anticipated a teacher shortage in the reformed post-war system.

The most influential and popular of the wartime reform proposals was William Beveridge's 1942 report on reform of the social insurance system which had developed through the earlier part of the century.[37] Beveridge proposed a thorough overhaul, integration and extension of old age and widows' and orphans' pensions, health and unemployment insurance and other benefits, and the introduction of new benefits, all universal for the whole population, not just for those on lower incomes as before, all to be fixed at a 'subsistence' level, i.e., adequate to live on as most existing benefits were not. Beveridge proposed that pensions and other benefits should be funded by weekly contributions from all workers in a national insurance system, to ensure that they unquestionably had a right to the benefits because they had paid for them and could no longer be stigmatized as dependants on wealthier taxpayers. Workers at all levels were included to ensure that state benefits could no longer be disparaged as designed only for the poor, as was too often the case. Beveridge hoped by this means to increase social cohesion, encouraging the better-off to feel common interests with poorer people and an obligation to support them, to benefit society as a whole.

Married women not employed outside the home presented difficulties because they could not pay contributions yet needed pensions and other benefits. Beveridge believed they should receive these by right, funded by their husbands' contributions. For this reason, he has been criticized by some feminists for believing that married women *should* stay at home, funded by their husbands as dependants in a 'male breadwinner welfare state'.[38] It is clear from a careful reading of Beveridge's report that he represented wives not in paid employment not as dependants but as 'partners' of their husbands, deserving benefits funded by their husbands because they 'must be regarded as occupied on work which is vital though unpaid, without which their husbands could not do their paid work and without which the nation could not continue'.[39] They should also be assisted with publicly funded domestic help to cover their essential work, including caring for children, when sick. These views echoed those of Eleanor Rathbone, a friend of Beveridge and an Independent MP from 1929 until her death in 1946, and many women activists, as discussed in chapter 2.[40] Beveridge did not believe that wives *should* stay at home, but, realistically, that very many of them did so, given the difficulties of combining work inside and outside the home and the shortage of affordable childcare, while the marriage bar excluded them from work in many occupations. Its wartime decline was not yet evident in 1942. Beveridge feared, presciently, that if wives' benefits were funded directly by the state rather than by their husbands' contributions, they would be denigrated as dependants upon hard-working taxpayers, not as equal citizens as he hoped would result from his proposals.

Married women in paid work would contribute and receive benefits, both at lower rates than their husbands because, Beveridge argued, being normally better paid, husbands should bear the housing costs. He also proposed insurance benefits for divorced and separated wives, funded by their former husbands' contributions, and funeral allowances and universal, state-funded family allowances, as Rathbone and others had long demanded. Old age pensions for the first time should be paid on condition of retirement, from age 65 for men, 60 for women, but with higher payments for each year worked beyond the minimum, to encourage older people who were able to keep working, to combat the costs of the ageing society with which Beveridge was still much concerned, as described in chapter 2.

Beveridge recognized that certain groups, especially many long-term disabled people and unmarried women who gave unpaid, full-time care to aged or disabled people, could not be fitted into the national insurance scheme because they were not in paid work or partnered with someone who was. Regretfully he recognized that the only option for these groups was means-tested benefits. He was highly critical of these because they were stigmatizing and inefficient at meeting need because the stigma or lack of awareness of their rights always prevented substantial numbers of eligible people from applying. This continues to be true, but Beveridge could see no alternative to proposing a, hopefully humane, means-tested benefit system, called National Assistance, to replace Public Assistance (which had modified the Poor Law in 1929). Beveridge's report was immensely popular, selling an unprecedented 600,000 copies. He worked hard to promote it in the press, on the BBC and on cinema newsreels. Churchill tried unsuccessfully to suppress it, while it was welcomed by Attlee.

Marriage, Sex and Family

The war unavoidably affected family life. The number of marriages rose from, in 1938, 17.6 per 1,000 of the population in England and Wales, 16.5 in Scotland, 13.4 in Northern Ireland to 22.5, 21.2 and 15.1, respectively, in 1940 – in all three countries the highest rates since official records began, surely driven by impending wartime separation. Numbers fell in 1943–4, then, not surprisingly, rose again in 1945–8, as the men returned.[41] The early surge in the number of marriages did not lead to an equivalent rise in births. The birth rate fell early in the war, reaching the lowest levels since official records began, 13.9 per 1,000 population in England and Wales in 1941, 17.1 in Scotland in 1940. Births in Northern Ireland stayed close to low pre-war levels. Then, surprisingly, they rose in all three regions, reaching 17.7 in England and Wales, 18.5 in Scotland and 22.8 in Northern Ireland in 1944.[42] This was the beginning of a sustained rise – the so-called 'baby-boom' – confounding pre-war projections of indefinite decline. During the war, the rise was attributed to wartime conditions; decline and population ageing were expected to return post-war.[43] In 1944 the government appointed a Royal Commission on Population to clarify what was changing and why and to propose policy responses. It reported in 1949, as discussed in the next chapter.

Again, births to unmarried women rose between 1939 and 1945, from 4.2 to 9.14% of live births in England, in Wales from 3.7 to 7.9%, in Scotland from 6 to 8.6%, in Northern Ireland from 4.7 to 5.4%.[44] Almost 300,000 more 'illegitimate' children were born in England, Wales and Scotland than in the six years before the war.[45] As in the last war, this sparked condemnation of young women liberated from parental control, 'running wild', 'going out for a good time', especially in this war with overseas, especially American, especially Black, servicemen. Married women with husbands absent at war aroused suspicion too. The Bishop of Norwich chastised 'women and especially young girls in town and village alike' for their casual relationships with soldiers.

But in this war, statistics challenged the moralizers. As we saw in chapter 1, from 1938 parents were obliged to record their date of marriage on birth certificates and in 1939 the Registrar General reported, to great surprise and shock, that almost 30% of first children born 1938–9 were conceived out of wedlock, based on births within eight-and-a-half-months of the parents' marriage. Some births might have been premature, but he believed they were balanced by parents misrepresenting their marriage date to hide premarital conception. He later reported that premarital pregnancies fell between 1939 and 1945, from 60,346 to 38,176, while 'illegitimate' births rose from 26,569 to 64,743, suggesting that the latter were often due to marriages delayed or halted by the war. It is unknown how many children were legitimized by the parents' marriage when the father returned from war.

The statistics indicated that during the war younger women were less prone to sexual irregularities leading to childbirth than their seniors. The number of pre-marital conceptions plus 'illegitimate' births among women under 20 in England and Wales declined from 12.1 to 10.7 per 1,000 between 1939 and 1943, returning to pre-war levels by 1945. Among those aged 25–30, they rose from 26.6 in 1939 to 46.5 in 1945, at ages 30–35, from 15.8 to 33.2.[46] The Registrar General concluded that the wartime rise in unmarried motherhood was not due to lax morals, but

> is almost unquestionably to be found in the enforced degree of physical separation of the sexes imposed by the progressive recruitment of young males into the Armed Forces ... rendering immediate marriage with their brides increasingly difficult – and in the case of many quite impossible. ...
>
> .... Taking the six war years as a whole the average increase of 6% in the total number of irregularly conceived births will hardly be regarded as inordinate, having regard to the wholesale disturbance to customary habits and living conditions in conjunction with the temporary accession to the population of large numbers of young and virile men in the Armed Forces of our Dominions and Allies.[47]

A notably more sober – and convincing – assessment than some contemporary polemic.[48] As ever, women faced most of the blame for immorality despite evidence that the blackout increased their risk of harassment and sexual assault in the streets.[49] And, as ever, some unmarried motherhood was due to rape, still not discussed in public. It is unlikely that there was significant change in sexual behaviour during the war, rather some behaviours became more visible, though war conditions may have given some men opportunities for greater sexual aggression.

Clearer evidence later emerged of who the unmarried mothers were, the realities of their lives and how they differed from those of men. The official historians of the wartime social services, Sheila Ferguson and Hilde Fitzgerald, reported:

> it would appear that the women who bore illegitimate children during the war belonged to all classes, types and age groups. Some were adolescent

girls who had drifted away from homes which offered neither guidance nor warmth and security. Still others were married women with husbands on war service who were unable to bear the loneliness of separation. There were decent and serious, superficial and flighty, irresponsible and incorrigible girls among them. There were some who had formed serious attachments and had hoped to marry. There were others who had had a single lapse, often under the influence of drink. There were, too, the 'good time girls' who thrived on the presence of well-paid servicemen from overseas and the semi-prostitutes with little moral restraint . . . Some of the unmarried mothers of the war were of a 'new type' and surprised the moral welfare workers to whom they were referred. Their spirit of independence was considerable and there was little of the sinner or penitent among them.[50]

Pregnant wives of husbands absent at war could be particularly desperate. They could not disguise the fact that their absent husband was not the father. They could not have the child adopted legally because any child born to a married woman was legally the child of her husband and his permission was required. The Forces' Welfare Services gave sympathetic help to husbands and wives[51] and the NCUMC helped many women, for the first time receiving government funding for this purpose.[52] Unmarried mothers of 'coloured' children faced particular hostility and difficulty in finding lodgings and foster care, while white British women who married Black Americans faced even greater discrimination in the United States.[53]

Wartime conditions made life even harder for unmarried mothers who did not have family support or adequate incomes. There were fewer foster-mothers than before the war, as women could find better-paid work, and fewer voluntary and local authority welfare workers, who were diverted to urgent war work.[54] The outcome was, as the founder of the NCUMC wrote, a 'fever of adoptions' by desperate women 'often arranged with the minimum of care and the maximum of irresponsibility'.[55] Babies were offered in newspaper advertisements, until legal regulation of adoption was tightened further in 1943, while lurid press reports of sales of babies continued. In 1944 George Orwell and his wife Eileen Blair (the writer George Orwell's real name was Eric Blair) adopted a baby straight from hospital, arranged by Orwell's sister-in-law, Dr Gwen O'Shaughnessy, though his wife was sick and died of cancer nine months later. The boy, Richard Blair, was brought up by Orwell's sister, Marjorie Dakin.[56] Public sympathy for the mothers and children grew, alongside the opprobrium, but they received little help from public services.

There were excited press reports especially of the immorality of women in the armed services. To investigate, the government appointed a committee chaired by Violet Markham, long active in voluntary work and support for women's rights.[57] In the First World War, she took part in an investigation into reports of immorality among the Women's Auxiliary Army Corps stationed in France, which concluded that they had no foundation.[58] Her report in 1942 rejected the latest outcry equally firmly:

> Rumours that illegitimate pregnancy was both common and on the increase in the Services have been rife. This is the kind of rumour that starts in every war . . . We can . . . with certainty say that the illegitimate birth-rate in the services is lower than the illegitimate birth-rate among the comparable civilian population.[59]

The Ministry of Health then funded unmarried servicewomen who could not return to their families to live in hostels, providing more generous support than to civilians, including advice on future work and training. This was kept secret during the war. The number of women involved was never revealed and all records were destroyed after the war. But for the first time a government department was closely involved with helping unmarried mothers and their children, providing more than the bare necessities of food, shelter and maternity care, a wartime experience which contributed to the post-war reform of services whose inadequacy had been clearly exposed. In all these respects, many women had a very different war experience from men.

Conclusion

The Second World War, like the First, created advances in gender equality, some more lasting than others. Again, women's work opportunities grew and conditions improved, including the permanent decline of the marriage bar, spurring campaigns for further advance after the war, especially for equal pay. Women and their families gained from wartime social reforms, including to health services. They campaigned for further reforms after the war and supported proposals including those of Beveridge. Again, they were very active as volunteers in helping war victims, including those impacted by the blitz. As in the last war, moralizers, male and female, were convinced that the war created opportunities for 'immorality' among women, though not among men, which evidence disproved. War experiences encouraged women to continue campaigning for greater gender and social equality after the war.

FOUR

Making the 'Welfare State', 1945–1951

The end of the war in 1945 was followed by a general election which brought Labour into government with a large majority for the first time. Further gradual shifts towards gender equality were immediately evident. The election yielded the largest number of women MPs so far, though still a small minority: 24 out of 640 MPs in total, 21 Labour, one Conservative, one Liberal, and Independent Eleanor Rathbone. Opinion polls suggested that most women in all classes voted Labour, attracted by its proposals to improve social welfare and social and economic conditions.[1] There was one female Cabinet Minister, Ellen Wilkinson, Minister of Education, but she died in 1947, and no further women were appointed to the Cabinet.

Labour indeed improved social conditions for most people with the development of what was later known as the 'welfare state'. In particular, the National Health Service (NHS), introduced in 1948, at last gave all women and men access to all forms of health care 'free at the point of use' as its creator, Aneurin Bevan, Minister of Health, put it. As we have seen in chapters 1 and 2, this was especially needed by poorer women and long demanded by women campaigners. Substantial numbers of high-quality council houses were built, managed by local authorities, and the first New Towns, meeting many of women's demands, providing low-density, well-designed, well-equipped, affordable housing, easing the stress of housework, reducing overcrowding and poor living conditions. Pensions and social security benefits improved. Family allowances were introduced on Beveridge's recommendation, but they were not presented as payment to women for their hard work in the home, as Eleanor Rathbone proposed, but as 'children's allowances', intended to encourage births to redress the expected post-war decline, so they were not paid to the first child in any family. And, as with the first maternity benefits in 1911, described in chapter 1, they were initially to be paid to the father until, again, women protested successfully, including Rathbone shortly before her death in 1946, and they were paid directly to mothers. These allowances and other benefits, including pensions, were all less generous than Beveridge had proposed, below the subsistence level he recommended, to his great disappointment, and poverty was not eliminated as he had hoped.[2] In 1948 the National Assistance Board (NAB) was established, as he had proposed, providing means-tested benefits for those in need, also less generous than he wanted but better than anything before and especially helpful for many lone mothers. By 1951 over one million pensioners applied to the NAB for supplements to their inadequate state pensions to enable them to 'subsist', mostly women, who still tended to be poorer than men at all ages.[3]

Many of Labour's welfare measures were less generous than expected because it prioritized economic growth and full employment. From its foundation it believed that full employment at fair rates of pay was the best means to raise working-class living standards, as it proved to be.[4] It planned to expand state welfare further when economic growth was fully achieved. Consequently, in addition to the lower benefits, it built fewer council houses than planned, though still a substantial number, and no new hospitals or schools. In 1946 it implemented a reformed state secondary education system based on the 1944 Education Act. The Act had not specified details of selection for secondary education and Labour implemented the recommendations of the Hadow Report of 1926 for a tripartite division between grammar schools 'for the academically most able', technical schools for those with appropriate skills and secondary modern schools for the remainder, selected by examination at age 11. Some psychologists argued that innate ability was evident by this age and the system would provide the best opportunities for all. But fewer girls than boys passed the new 11+ exam to attend grammar schools because, in a school system that had long been and remained gender-divided, there were fewer existing grammar schools for girls, who had not previously been expected to want or to receive academically demanding education, and due to funding limitations Labour built very few new schools. To gain entrance to the limited number of girls' grammar schools, they had to achieve higher grades in the 11+ than boys, though this was little known at the time. More middle-class than working-class boys and girls passed the exam. The great majority of girls and working-class boys received a basic education at secondary modern schools and left at 15 without qualifications.

Work

Labour achieved substantial economic growth and full employment at decent rates of pay for the first time in peacetime in modern Britain. This was a major achievement, supported by both Beveridge and Keynes, but they and the Labour politicians meant full employment for men. They did not necessarily oppose women's employment but did not think it realistic to expect most women to work full-time all their adult lives when they had responsibilities in the home, as men did not. The outcome was improved opportunities for regular work and pay for men, improved living standards for most working-class families and a narrowing of national income inequalities, especially because social and economic improvements were funded by exceptionally high taxation of the better-off.

Women's post-war work experiences, as ever, were more complex. During the war the Ministry of Labour forecast a post-war labour shortage and planned to keep as many women at work as possible.[5] But the government wished to sustain the rising wartime birth rate, fearing a post-war return to decline, and it wanted younger women to give up work to raise families. This was also influenced by psychologists, who had become increasingly prominent during and since the inter-war years. John Bowlby, Donald Winnicott, Melanie Klein and others were widely publicized and influential in arguing that the mothers of young children should not leave home to work because the care of children other than by their mother – 'maternal deprivation' as they called it – damaged their physical and mental health, potentially causing what they called 'juvenile delinquency' and rising crime. Much of their 'evidence' was drawn from studies of total separation of young children from their mothers in unusual wartime circumstances, including evacuation, or in orphanages, but they were widely believed.[6] The rise of social psychology was seen as progressive for increasing knowledge about human behaviour, but its powerful recommendations reinforced traditional gender norms about family responsibilities.

Childcare experts challenged the psychologists, recognizing from their experience that children could be well cared for by others, but mothers of young children experienced strong cultural pressure against taking employment. Affordable childcare became scarce when the government, despite women's protests, closed the wartime nurseries to discourage mothers' employment and refused further funding for childcare.[7] By 1951 only 1% of Britain's under-5s received publicly funded day-care, mainly 'social cases': children of unmarried mothers, widows, deserted or divorced wives who needed employment if they lacked other support, or mothers too sick, mentally or physically, to provide care, but places were too few even for these mothers in need. Social welfare support was more generous for such families than before the war, but not adequate for all their needs. It helped that rationing continued to 1954, though it gradually declined from 1948, along with government-controlled supplies of consumer goods, as it prioritized exports to assist economic growth. Women in the Labour Party pressed for investment in nursery schools, without success. As before the war, and more recently, employed women made their own arrangements with relatives, especially grandmothers, and friends; mothers who could afford it paid for care at home or in private nurseries.[8]

Most married women did not work outside the home due to lack of childcare, cultural pressures and other barriers. Yet growing numbers of married women did work, full- or part-time, due to need or to help their husbands fund improvements to family life, providing holidays and consumer goods including cars, or saving for mortgages to buy a home, gradually accessible to many for the first time. Some women were attracted by the prospect of an independent income and companionship away from the monotony of the home and found paid work fulfilling. The Ministry of Labour encouraged older women without dependent children to remain in or return to employment after the war, due to the continuing labour shortage. It launched a 'Women in Industry' campaign, with ads in the press, on buses, trains and billboards, and appeals on cinema newsreels and BBC broadcasts and from mobile vans on loudspeakers, along with door-to-door canvassers urging women to continue giving 'patriotic service'. It was not intended to draw women into 'men's jobs', but into 'work which it has always been usual for women to do', including the textile industries, retail and laundry work.[9]

A strict gender division of labour revived. The post-war expansion of social, health and education services created more work long judged suitable for women. There was a severe shortage of teachers as the baby-boom increased school intakes and more children stayed longer at school following the reforms, while the government aimed to reduce class sizes. Ex-servicemen and -women were subsidized to take training, as many did, and the Ministry of Education worked to bring back former teachers who had left to raise families.

The marriage bar was abolished in most occupations, including teaching. This faced opposition in some occupations, including the civil service, where men still feared it would harm their promotion chances. Prime Minister Attlee and colleagues in the government supported abolition when the economy so urgently needed more workers and in 1946 implemented it throughout the civil service, while assuming that women would resign on their first pregnancy.[10] Senior officials and Cabinet Ministers agreed that married women would not get any special treatment and 'firmness would be shown' towards those whose 'domestic responsibilities were found to interfere with efficient discharge of their duties'. They remained unsympathetic to women struggling to combine careers and caring responsibilities.[11]

The Foreign Office decided in 1946 to admit women to the diplomatic service for the first time, despite much internal opposition, but it operated a marriage bar for all grades of female staff until 1973. It was widely believed, including among some people otherwise supportive of gender equality, that it would be 'unsuitable to have a husband as a sort of dependent upon a female diplomat'.[12] The marriage bar also survived in banking until the 1960s and there was reluctance to abandon it throughout the private sector, but shortage of labour left no option in many occupations. Some manufacturing businesses tried to boost recruitment by installing nurseries and laundries on site or making workers eligible for nearby factory-owned housing.[13] Abolition of the marriage bar increased opportunities for women, to limited degrees, gradually eroding the previous cultural prohibition against middle-class married women's employment.

By contrast, more working-class women chose to stay home, at least while their children were small, as male employment and pay and family living standards improved. They were relieved to escape the 'double burden' of work in and out of the home, made more onerous by the need to spend time queuing for essentials due to shortages. A new, cross-class pattern emerged of women employed until their first pregnancy, taking a break for child-rearing, returning later, often part-time.[14] A minority remained in employment following childbirth. They were assisted by rare, generous employers providing maternity leave. The London County Council (LCC), impelled by labour shortage, offered four weeks leave at full pay and nine weeks at half pay for women, including teachers, with at least one year's service, on condition they returned to work for at least three months following leave. Maternity leave became increasingly standard for teachers over the following decades due to the shortage. There were growing demands from women's organizations for state legislation to make maternity leave obligatory in all occupations, unsuccessful until 1975.[15] The government tried to encourage women to return to live-in domestic service, to enable more mothers to work, but few women would return to this traditional employment of poorer women when they could afford not to, as increasing numbers could; an unknown number worked casually providing housework as 'dailies'.[16]

Part-time work was easier to combine with domestic responsibilities and it suited many employers who were not required to give part-timers paid holidays or other benefits normal for full-time workers. Full-time work predominated in the Lancashire and Yorkshire textile areas which had long employed substantial numbers of women; part-time work was more frequent elsewhere, most common in manufacturing where shift work was normal, least in offices. The number of employed women increased by at least 300,000 in each year from 1947 to 1950, 11.5% worked part-time in 1951, mostly 'returners' aged over 40.[17] As before the war, much casual work, such as by cleaners, childminders and landladies, was under-recorded. The proportion of women in paid work was highest in the affluent south-east of England, perhaps because more women could afford to pay childminders, low in Wales. Mothers working part-time often sought evening shifts – four hours from 5.30 or 6 pm – when husbands could look after children, though this could be exhausting for both partners, each working non-stop through the day.

Equal pay remained rare despite continuous women's campaigns. After the war as before, the National Union of Women Teachers (NUWT) campaigned for it in collaboration with the National Association of Women Civil Servants (NAWCS), the cross-party Status of Women Committee of Women MPs and a range of women's organizations, including the

Equal Pay Campaign Committee (EPCC), which remained very active. The two unions and other groups also campaigned on other aspects of inequality. The NUWT focused on unequal taxation of married women, who did not receive the married persons' tax allowance payable to their husbands, so paid more tax; on their lower occupational pensions since they were determined by pay and years of employment, both generally lower for married women; and on access to part-time work and paid maternity leave, with little success on all these issues. Discrimination against married women remained widespread, bolstered by complaints that they kept ex-servicemen out of employment.[18]

The continuing labour shortage forced employers, including the government, to look abroad for workers, first from Ireland, then refugees in Europe and finally, reluctantly, colonials, initially from the Caribbean, first, in 1950, women from Barbados to work as nurses and hospital domestics in the NHS, then men to staff public transport. This increased racial diversity and racism, neither of which were new in Britain, and it grew further in the following decades.[19] Since its foundation in 1948 the NHS has depended upon immigrant labour and expertise at all levels, male and female, fewest at the highest levels, especially in its early years.

The Royal Commission on Equal Pay

The Royal Commission on Equal Pay reported in 1946. It found that gender pay differences varied across occupations and from place to place for no obvious reasons. In the civil service men and women normally entered at the lowest levels on the same rates but their pay diverged during their twenties as more men were promoted. Generally in the public sector, pay inequalities averaged 50% at the bottom levels, 10% at the top, where there were few women. Recruitment and promotion were as severely unequal as pay. In some professional occupations equal pay formally existed, including universities, architecture, medicine, the law and among MPs. But in 1946 just 7,198 medical practitioners out of 44,341 were female, 325 of 9,375 architects, about 164 of 17,102 solicitors, few academics and, as we have seen, very few MPs.[20] Few women held senior positions in any of these occupations and little had changed by the 1950s. Unequal pay continued to be defended on the grounds that men supported families. This was, as always, broadly true, but was not the case for many men and many women supported dependants. The Treasury insisted that the economy could not sustain a costly pay rise for female civil servants, while the Council of Women Civil Servants, representing women in the top grades of the service, asked why, given the Treasury's concern for the economy, it did not employ exclusively low-paid women civil servants?

Employed women were roughly equally divided across 'white blouse', middle-class secretarial and clerical work, retailing, hospitality and other services, and manufacturing. In all of them pay differences were hard to explain and remedies hard to propose due to the strict gender division of labour, and complex gradings and systems of payment, especially in industry. The Ministry of Labour estimated that in 1945, on average, earnings of women in industry were 53% of those of men, but the Royal Commission noted that such averages disguised great variations in women's earnings even in similar occupations. It concluded that in engineering and clothing, two major employers of women employing about one million and 309,000 respectively in 1945, men and women received 'widely unequal sums for doing equal amounts of work so closely similar that it would commonly be described as identical'.[21]

The Commission found it difficult to establish when gender pay differences were due to genuinely higher skills and responsibilities required of men or to discrimination against women in comparable work. In the 'white blouse/collar' public sector, especially the civil service, local government and teaching, men and women most clearly did identical work, often for different rates of pay, and pay rates were clearly spelled out. Consequently, as we have seen, women in these occupations actively campaigned for equal pay and were strongly unionized, and the unions supported equal pay even when they had a majority male membership.

The British Employers Confederation asserted to the Commission its support in principle for equal pay when men and women did identical work, but that, unfortunately, this rarely occurred because men were more efficient, more flexible, more ambitious, took less time off, were physically stronger, less tolerant of monotonous work, could better manage other men, were more committed to a career and so deserved investment in training which women were said to be reluctant to undertake. They provided no evidence for these assertions and evaded suggestions from the Commission that in wartime women had been as productive as men in occupations defined as 'male' in peacetime. Trade unions were overwhelmingly male, but more women were unionizing and Trades Union Congress (TUC) representatives, having consulted affiliated unions, were more sympathetic to the need for change – change to equal pay for 'equivalent' work since restriction to 'equal' work would seriously limit the occupations to which it could apply. It asserted the need to increase women's access to training and that there was greater similarity in the work performed by men and women in industry than employers admitted. They encouraged and exaggerated dissimilarity in order to maximize their use of cheap female labour.

Union attitudes were shifting. They had long supported inequalities on grounds of the family responsibilities of men but thought this no longer justified now that average male wages had risen well above basic subsistence. The TUC now demanded 'the rate for the job' regardless of gender. They recognized that, even when granted equal pay for equivalent work, women would often take home less pay than men because they tended to work fewer hours due to home commitments, but they argued that women should have choice in such matters. They also advocated improved conditions of work in the home, with improved housing and social service support, to ease the double burden. How widely these views were shared across unions and their members is unclear, but it was a clear shift in the views of union representatives. The TUC opposed legislation for equal pay because they opposed government intervention in wage bargaining, arguing that equal pay in the private sector should be achieved by greater unionization of women, collective bargaining and a gradual process of evaluation to establish equivalence between male and female jobs.

The Commission also heard from several women's organizations, including the London and National Society for Women's Service (later renamed the Fawcett Society, still campaigning for equal pay) and the Fabian Women's Group, all advocating equal pay for equivalent work. An array of medical specialists and psychologists gave contradictory opinions. Some insisted that menstruation and the menopause had no effect on women's work capacities, others that both reduced efficiency; some that women were frequently absent from work due to sickness, others that they were not.

Following a thorough analysis of the almost universal gender inequality in pay across the UK, the Commission concluded that it could not be explained in rational economic terms, as a measure of men's higher work capabilities, but owed much to 'assumptions drawn from the sociological background' together with the oversupply of female labour in the limited range of occupations open to them. They were convinced that women were fully capable of most occupations. They made a strong argument for 'equal pay for work of equal value', believing that few men would resent this. But they concluded that speedy implementation would harm postwar economic recovery and should be delayed. Three of the four female members of the Commission disagreed and recommended immediate mandatory equal pay. Labour was supposedly committed to this by a vote of its annual conference but, repeatedly until they lost office in 1951, Labour spokesmen stated that they supported the principle but, until the economy strengthened sufficiently, implementation would delay recovery. Women continued to campaign, and MPs of all parties demanded implementation of equal pay.

Other Gender Inequalities

One move of the period towards gender equality, following decades of women's campaigns, was the British Nationality Act, 1948: British women who married men of another nationality were no longer required to adopt his nationality and lose their rights of British citizenship but could choose which nationality to hold.[22] Women kept protesting against other inequalities. The Married Women's Association (MWA) was founded in 1938 by mainly middle-aged, middle-class married women aiming to remove the unequal property rights of husbands and wives and achieve equal partnership in marriage. The problems included the unequal tax allowances which favoured husbands, that men too often evaded paying maintenance to their wives and children after formal separation as required by law, and that wives lost all rights to family property, including the home, following separation. These were not resolved for some decades.[23] Women also campaigned unsuccessfully on other issues, including the harsh treatment of prostitutes compared with their male customers: 'solicitation' was illegal, taking advantage of it was not, and deprived women were still trafficked into the trade and exploited by greedy men.

Family Life

Despite fears, the 'baby-boom' continued after the war. This was not due to many women having more children: average family size remained about two. Rather a higher proportion of men and women now married and had at least one child. After the war there was a more even gender balance in the population as male life expectancy grew and fewer men emigrated alone, and full employment and higher incomes may have encouraged more men to feel they could afford to marry. This may also have influenced the unprecedented decline in the marriage age. Ages at first marriage in England and Wales fell to historically low levels from a norm over the previous 300 years of 27 for men and 25 for women to 22.6 for women and 24.6 for men by 1971.[24] Marriages lasted longer because they started earlier, average life expectancy lengthened for both sexes and divorce remained difficult and expensive, though the number of divorces and separations increased, as we will see.[25] Infant death rates were now low. In 1951, 14% of all births within marriage were premaritally conceived, according to official statistics, more than before the war, indicating that post-war Britain was less sexually repressed than is sometimes suggested.[26] Younger marriage ages may have owed something to 'shotgun marriages', as they were known, due to pregnancy, sometimes enforced by parents. Births registered as 'illegitimate' in England and Wales fell from 6.6% in 1946 to 4.8% in 1951.[27]

Pessimism about the birth rate continued. The influence of eugenics had not gone away, including from the Royal Commission on Population, which reported in 1949. In familiar terms it warned that 'a disproportionately small number of the nation's children come from the higher income groups', creating a 'tendency towards lowering the average level of intelligence of the nation'[28] – a situation, they believed, that was potentially exacerbated by immigrant workers. It recommended higher family allowances and improved social services to encourage more births and help women combine childcare with the greater freedom and independence they aspired to, including through paid work, which the commissioners believed had driven the pre-war birth decline. But the recommendations were ignored. The government was unwilling to encourage the 'freedom and independence' of women of childbearing age.

Unmarried mothers continued to be excluded and stigmatized, but they made some gains from the post-war welfare state. Beveridge had proposed a further investigation into the most effective means of supporting them through the benefit system, supported by the NCUMC and other voluntary organizations. The Labour government did not take this up or introduce a benefit specifically for unmarried mothers because they feared it would be unpopular with voters. But the mothers and children were better supported by improved social services and benefits.[29] The NCUMC worked hard to inform mothers of their new rights. Like other low-income women, they and their children benefitted from the NHS, and they became eligible for the first time for a maternity grant, introduced in 1911 for the wives of male contributors to National Insurance, as described in chapter 1, now paid to all mothers and raised from £4 to £12.10s. (£12.50), plus 13 weeks maternity benefit of 36s. (£1.76) per week, as recommended by Beveridge.

Local authorities now had a duty to care for single mothers and their children under the National Assistance Act, 1948. They appointed social workers to support them or subsidized voluntary organizations, including the NCUMC, to do so. They were also obliged to provide lodgings for the homeless and many more Mother and Baby Homes or Hostels were established. Mothers were no longer required to register for work if they had a school-age child at home and claimed benefits, though not all authorities observed this. The NAB could make additional means-tested payments, including for household equipment or clothing, to those in need. Unmarried mothers living with their parents could now claim benefits for themselves and their children regardless of the parents' income. The 1948 Act also required local authorities to take responsibility for the care of frail older and disabled people, removing some pressure from female relatives who were the majority of carers. Benefits were still low, and many lone mothers felt the need to earn money to gain more comfortable living conditions, but the system was more supportive than anything before, removing some of the inequality and stigma long experienced by unmarried mothers and their children compared with other families.

Labour hoped to stay in government long enough to substantially expand the welfare state, but middle-class voters, many of whom had voted Labour in 1945, were increasingly alienated by high taxes, rationing and controls.[30] An election was unavoidable in 1950. Labour won with a majority of just five, with an exceptionally high turnout of 84%, then called another election in 1951 hoping to increase their majority. They won over 230,000 more votes than the Conservatives but fewer seats, after another high turnout, 82.5%. They piled up votes in working-class constituencies. The elections suggested that Britain was deeply divided by class. Labour gained more votes from working-class women, who were grateful for the NHS and other welfare gains, than from men, but fewer middle-class female votes than in 1945.[31] Having lost the election, Labour could not complete the welfare state and further improve social conditions as they had hoped.

Conclusion

Under Labour, women made some gains in gender equality, including in the labour market, despite continuing discrimination, but much inequality remained. Gender equality was not a high priority for the government, which was more committed to achieving socio-economic equality. Older women were encouraged to work due to the labour shortage, but not to take work conventionally defined as 'male'. Younger women faced exceptionally strong opposition to their employment, driven by the government's commitment to raising the birth rate. But more women were employed, assisted by the decline of the marriage bar enabling the employment of more middle-class women, who could afford childcare. But the workforce remained strictly gender-divided and women had limited opportunities, including for equal pay, despite their campaigns and the recommendations of the very thorough survey of the situation by the Royal Commission on Equal Pay. Working-class women faced less pressure to work when improvements to work and pay for men augmented family incomes. They benefitted considerably from welfare measures, especially the NHS and improved housing.

There were some gradual shifts towards gender equality, including women gaining equal nationality rights on marriage, but much inequality remained and campaigns continued, including for equal pay and equal work opportunities assisted by provision of childcare and paid maternity leave.

FIVE

'Never Had It So Good'? 1951–1964

There was just one woman Cabinet Minister during the 13 years of Conservative government that followed: Florence Horsbrugh was Minister of Education for one year, 1953–4. In 1951 the number of women MPs fell to 17: 6 Conservative and 11 Labour, then returned to their peak of 25 in 1959.

Women gained one long-sought equality goal in the political system, part of wider campaigns to improve women's representation in public office. In 1958 the first women were appointed to the House of Lords. Lady Rhondda (who inherited her father's peerage but not his right to sit in the Lords, as women could not) had campaigned for this since women gained the right to be elected to the Commons. She lived to see the change enacted but died before the first Baronesses were appointed.[1] Lord Astor, husband of Nancy, the first woman elected to the Commons in 1919, as described in chapter 2, introduced Bills to admit women to the Lords almost annually from 1924 to 1930, but they all failed. Women's organizations persistently pointed out the number of countries where women were admitted to the upper house following enfranchisement, including Australia, New Zealand, the United States and Ireland, without effect. That was until 1958 when legislation initiated by the Conservatives enabled the appointment of life peers, female and male, to the previously wholly hereditary House. Women still could not inherit a seat in the House, though this continued for men. The probable reason for the change was that attendance in the Lords was declining as hereditary peers aged, and it was becoming less effective. Women were probably included because the Conservatives wanted their votes. Four women were appointed in the first year, one Conservative, one Labour and two non-party crossbenchers to a House of 908 members. Then no more were appointed until 1963 when 18 more women became Baronesses, mostly Conservatives.[2] In the post-war years governments took more initiatives in the slow advance towards gender equality, Labour more than Conservative governments as we will see.

Work and Pay

Increasingly, young women expected to work after marriage, at least until their first pregnancy. A survey in the mid-1950s by psychiatrist Eustace Chesser of about 700 single women found that over 60% of those aged 20 or below and almost half aged 21–30 wanted to work after marriage.[3] The gap between marriage and leaving employment on first pregnancy was often short, though most expected to return to the labour market at some point. Owing to the falling marriage age, women now spent more years of later life in work. But they still experienced severe inequalities at work, which now affected more women and aroused more concern and further campaigns. Trade unions, including, still very actively, the NUWT and NAWCS, continued to campaign for equal pay, alongside other women's organizations, including the EPCC. Neither union was recognized as a bargaining or consultative organization by employers as male unions were. The civil service remained reluctant and slow to appoint or promote married women after abolition of the marriage bar in 1946. Throughout the 1950s most female civil servants were single. For teachers, conditions varied from place to place because in some local authorities teachers were in short supply and they felt greater need to employ married women. The NUWT was also still concerned that breaks in service and part-time work reduced women's pensions, and they continued to argue that married women should not be treated as dependants of their husbands for taxation purposes, which reduced their net incomes. They also continued to demand easier access to part-time work, provision of childcare and the introduction of maternity leave. Given the continuing shortage of teachers, the union argued that equal pay and increased support for married women would attract more staff.[4]

Campaigners, including the EPCC with which 50 women's organizations were now affiliated, helped to fund the film *To Be a Woman*, directed by Jill Craigie, wife of Labour MP Michael Foot, which described the working lives of women, in and out of the home, and the unfairness of pay inequality. It was widely shown in 1951–2, supported by demonstrations, mass meetings, petitions to parliament, letters to MPs, encouraged by the Labour-controlled LCC – again in the lead in advancing gender equality – granting equal pay in 1952.[5] The Treasury remained opposed to funding equal pay in the public sector and the Conservative government prevaricated, despite promising it in the 1951 election campaign. In 1954 Labour promised to implement it when it returned to government. This perhaps persuaded the Conservatives in 1955, with an election due, to announce the introduction of equal pay in the civil service and local government, gradually over six years.[6] After further pressure, this was extended to teaching and in 1956 to other public sector work in the NHS and gas and electricity corporations. It only applied to grades which employed men and women for the same work, not to workers doing similar work of equal value. Nor did it cover gender equality in appointments or promotion. It was another partial advance. The EPCC disbanded, its main aim achieved, but it urged women to campaign for equal pay in the private sector, where there was no significant change by the end of the decade.

Difficulties and controversies around women combining work in and out of the home persisted and grew as more women sought to enter or re-enter employment after marriage and/or motherhood. Scarcity of affordable childcare continued to restrict their options. The number of local authority places in England and Wales fell from 40,000 in 1950 to 28,000 in 1955 and 21,500 in 1961, and they were increasingly restricted to families in severe need.[7] There were few employer-run nurseries: 55 in factories at the end of 1960, about 12 in hospitals, mainly for the use of much-needed nursing staff. Working women continued to look to friends and family, still mainly grandmothers, for childcare, though, as more families moved to the growing suburban estates of council houses or owner occupation where day nurseries were rare, this became more difficult because relatives no longer lived nearby and the distance from home to work grew.[8] In these circumstances some fathers provided more childcare and greater help with housework when their working hours allowed.[9]

Official statements made clear that it was not Conservative government policy to assist mothers to work if they did not need the income, though there was little sign of help for women in need. Margaret Wynn's survey of fatherless families estimated that by the mid-1960s in Great

Britain there were 175,000 widows bringing up 260,000 dependent children, and roughly 250,000 separated wives and 55,000 divorced women with children, many of them living in very precarious economic circumstances and needing to work.[10] Divorced women suffered especial stigma and discrimination. Ferdynand Zweig's interviews with employers in the early 1950s, for his study of *The Worker in an Affluent Society*, revealed that some refused to employ divorced women, even innocent partners in divorce proceedings.[11] None of these lone mothers could be sure of accessing childcare to enable them to work sufficient hours to earn adequate pay. Through the 1950s and 1960s women's organizations campaigned for their financial security.

The cultural idealization of the 'traditional family' with the mother at home remained widespread, reinforcing the difficulties of working mothers. Bowlby and other psychologists continued to insist on the damaging effects of separating young children from their mothers and hostility to working mothers persisted in the press and elsewhere. An article in the popular magazine *Picture Post* in 1956 quoted a child psychiatrist making the extreme claim that separation of mothers from infants under 5 'may cause more lasting and irreparable damage to the child even than underfeeding it through poverty'.[12] The phrase 'latchkey kid' became widespread, a disparaging reference to children believed to have to let themselves into empty homes after school while their mother was absent at work, leaving them vulnerable to harm. Some men promoted the belief that 'real men' were the sole support of their families. Such views were now less universal and opinion was shifting but slowly concerning mothers of young children.

The growing importance of these issues in British politics and culture, and the increasing body of social science research improving understanding of them, is indicated by several contemporary surveys of women's work, some initiated by the government, facilitated by the growth of social sciences in universities at this time. In 1956, *Women's Two Roles: Home and Work*, by sociologists Alva Myrdal and Viola Klein, discussed ways for women to combine paid employment and care for the family, largely repeating proposals for which British women had long unsuccessfully campaigned. They included extended maternity leave of one to two years, work training for older women, shorter working days for women and men to bring 'a fairer distribution of work and leisure between the sexes', better-planned housing, more services, including day nurseries, and for employers to adjust work conditions to women's needs. Like many women previously, they argued that society should value equally all of women's 'productive efforts', paid and unpaid, in and out of the home and at all levels, 'whether they educate children or spin cotton is of minor concern in this connection'. They argued that society was creating new dilemmas for women, making their choices harder. Theories of 'maternal deprivation' were 'a new and subtle form of anti-feminism'. They concluded that women were increasingly adopting the best way to negotiate the difficulties of combining home and work: working until the first pregnancy, then caring for the family at home until the children were old enough to enable their return to work. The book was successful and spread these ideas among a younger generation. Simone de Beauvoir's *The Second Sex*, translated into English in 1953, also encouraged feminist discontents with gender inequalities.

Viola Klein looked further into the issues in 1957 in a survey of 'how ordinary men and women feel' about working wives, finding men increasingly supportive.[13] She concluded that:

> The outstanding impression gained from this survey is that women's lives, today as much as ever, are dominated by their role – actual or expected – as wife and mother ... there is no trace of feminist egalitarianism ... nor even is it implicitly assumed that women have the 'right to work' ... men appear on the whole to be less conservative in their outlook in these matters than they are usually assumed to be ... the majority of women seem to get moral support from their husband in their decision to take a job ... the idea of marriage as a partnership is widely accepted today.

'Moral support' did not seem to extend to active support with such tasks as housework, though she found that among husbands with wives working full-time, only 14% expressed disapproval, just 4% when they worked part-time. The men valued their wives' contributions to improving family living standards, relieving them of some pressure. Ferdynand Zweig, around the same time, found working wives very positive about the assistance of their husbands, ranging from cleaning windows and preparing meals to walking the children to school and managing their baths and bedtimes when their wives worked evening shifts.[14]

A larger survey carried out for the government by Audrey Hunt shortly after concluded that the husband's contribution was rarely more than occasional washing-up, though more than one in five helped with cooking, one in seven with washing, ironing and mending.[15] Their contributions to housework and childcare still varied considerably according to family circumstances and personal inclinations.[16] It was never a cultural norm that men, like women, should play a substantial part in home care, but always some did so, probably more through the 1950s and 1960s, not least because more wives were at work. Wives expressed gratitude for any assistance they received. The fact that the government funded this survey suggests the significance in contemporary politics of questions concerning women's employment and what impeded or facilitated it.

Women experienced greater problems with employers. Questioned by Klein, private employers expressed extreme unwillingness to adapt to the needs of married women, less so concerning manual or lower-level work, probably due to labour shortage. Hospitals and local authorities increasingly arranged part-time working, often with a variety of start times, to attract women with experience of nursing, midwifery or health visiting, all occupations short of labour. By the mid-1960s one-third of all NHS nurses worked part-time. The civil service also introduced part-time working for married women at the lowest levels (only), as typists, telephone operators and bookkeepers. They held 34,000 jobs, just 5% of the workforce.[17] Some employers were attracted to part-time work for women because it was low-paid and, unlike full-time work, required no commitment to provide superannuation or sickness or holiday pay. Women returning to work typically could only find work that was less skilled, lower-paid and more precarious than they had held before maternity.

Similar employer attitudes emerged from a survey for the Ministry of Labour in 1959 of 50% of all women who had graduated in science and engineering in Britain in 1954 and 1956 – just 708 – and a sample of employers in relevant industries. It was motivated by concern about labour shortage in these occupations. Of the graduates, 74% were employed in teaching or other public services including the NHS. The minority working in industry were concentrated in research posts. They felt they had lesser prospects of promotion than their male colleagues and were undervalued. Many employers said they considered women scientists 'particularly good at detailed work', but 60% paid higher rates to men. They justified this by stating that men had dependants to support and had a longer career commitment, though this was not supported by interviews with the women. For similar reasons, 24% of employers allowed women no opportunities for promotion and others limited the level to which they could rise because they believed there would be difficulties if women had authority over men. Only 28% of managers surveyed wholly favoured employing women.[18]

A follow-up study three years later was undertaken by Nancy Seear and colleagues at the London School of Economics (LSE) at the request of a group of industrialists who feared that women's scientific and technical training was being underused in industry. The researchers reported that the 1961 census showed that of 249,000 economically active people with qualifications in science and technology just 18,300 were female. Another report had concluded that by 1965 there would be a shortage of 28,000 people trained in these fields. The LSE team surveyed senior girls in 17 schools and found that a substantial minority were interested in such training but had great difficulty finding information about occupations not traditionally defined as female and serious discouragement from all quarters about entering them. Science and technology were seen as essentially male interests. Females did not have equal access to education in these subjects and there was a severe shortage of female science teachers and laboratory facilities in girls' schools in a strongly gender-divided school system. In 1954–5 there were 1,969 state scholarships to university in science, chemistry and physics, only 154 of which went to girls. University appointments officers frequently told girls who managed to graduate in sciences that their only employment opportunity lay in teaching. Employers and teachers expressed their conviction that women could not perform well in the sciences. An acute shortage of trained scientists through the 1950s brought no change.

Seear and her colleagues found that young women were aware of the barriers and:

> Competing mainly with men was not a prospect which attracted many of them. They were chary of entering into a situation in which they would have to push in order to win promotion . . . not one girl expressed enthusiasm for breaking down prejudice simply because it was there.[19]

Many opted for teaching because it was socially acceptable and could be combined with domestic roles due to the hours and holidays. Entering university was difficult. In 1960 just 4% of 18–21-year-olds attended university in the UK, only 25% of them females, who overwhelmingly studied arts subjects. Two-year teacher training colleges catered predominantly to females.

The LSE study also revealed prejudice against women as managers: 'Women have emotional crises and can't take being kicked' was one employer's response. Most girls expressed distaste for working in industry, of which they had a negative image. Interviews with women in industry found that most planned to take a break for childrearing but believed it would be difficult to get retraining on their return, and that in general their skills and talents were underused. The report concluded that:

> Prejudice runs like a scarlet thread through all the pattern of this study . . . so far we have not gained so much as a toe-hold . . . in the industrial world. The question is not whether women should be allowed better opportunities, but rather whether as a community we can afford to continue to waste their trained powers . . . of course there are difficulties (such as women's family responsibilities) . . . but these are not the fundamental difficulties. From this survey the basic problem seems to be prejudice.[20]

Hunt's much larger survey in 1965 for the Ministry of Labour confirmed these findings.[21]

In the 1950s and 1960s more women, including wives and mothers, from a wider range of backgrounds sought employment in a wider range of occupations, in all of which they encountered severe gender inequalities driven above all by sexist prejudice. We know more about their experiences at this time, and the attitudes behind them, than before because one growing occupation for highly educated women was social research and they focused upon this topic, perhaps influenced by the fact that their own prospects for promotion to the highest levels in universities were remote.

Gender Inequality in Education

Gender inequality, together with inequality by class and race, was pervasive in education and, as we have seen, influenced employment opportunities. Through the 1950s girls were more likely than boys to leave even grammar schools at 15 without qualifications and to take jobs generally regarded as suited to secondary modern students. Many parents still believed that education was wasted on girls whose best career was marriage and motherhood, a view many girls internalized, and it was upheld by the government. A White Paper on Technical Education in 1956 stated that it aimed to help every boy and girl reach their potential. It urged more positive help for girls to increase their knowledge and expertise in an age of technological change – not to improve their work opportunities, but to help them care for their families by improving their expertise in the home.[22]

By contrast, the 1959 Crowther Report, *15 to 18*, found only 12% of young people still in full-time education at age 17, 6% at 20, concluding that education for both genders and all classes was inadequate in quality and duration, harming the economy. It proposed encouragement of able girls to gain qualifications before marriage to improve their employment opportunities in later life, taking for granted that married women would work. It noted that 33% of 18-year-old boys received day release from work for further education or training, but only 8% of girls; 36% of boys got apprenticeships, only 6% of girls. Apprenticeships were concentrated in primarily masculine occupations, including building and heavy engineering. The report recommended raising the school leaving age to 16, especially to help girls.[23] The government responded that it would comply – in the future. That future turned out to be 1973, as arranged by the 1964–70 Labour government. Conservatives in the 1950s showed little enthusiasm for improving female education or work opportunities. The British Federation of Business and Professional Women (BFBPW) and the British Federation of University Women (BFUW) both worked to improve girls' opportunities in school education, including in science and technology, with support from many head teachers. The Women's Engineering Society established bursaries and scholarships to enable girls to study engineering. There was little response from the government.

Unequal Opportunities for Graduates

Female graduates in all subjects experienced gender inequalities. This was demonstrated in 1957 in Judith Hubback's book *Wives Who Went to College*. She lived in north London, a Cambridge History graduate in her mid-thirties with three children, married to a senior civil servant. She had married young, given up teaching on the birth of her first child, then found occasional opportunities to publish press articles, work for the BBC and tutor girls for university entrance. After ten years spent largely at home, she felt frustrated by the lack of opportunities for talented, well-trained women like herself. She undertook a postal survey of over a thousand graduate mothers to discover how widespread such experiences were.[24] She found them overwhelmingly regretful that they could not spend more time in useful and satisfying work outside the home.

She recommended more part-time professional work and training for women returning to work or taking up new careers in their thirties and forties, repeating the frequent complaint that the country could not afford to neglect so much highly skilled womanpower. The book was widely reviewed and commented upon in the press and elsewhere by supporters and by virulent opponents of her views arguing that she proved that degrees were wasted on women, wasting taxpayers' money. Others, including some graduate women, argued that higher education was an end in itself and beneficial to families and society even if the graduate never re-entered the labour market. Hubback discussed the book widely, including on radio and TV, suggesting how extensively the topic was believed to matter. She sought to persuade married women graduates to reconcile themselves realistically with unavoidable compromises, recognizing the benefits of both family and working life, however restricted. Each woman should work out her own best solution for herself and her family.[25] Hubback did not expect gender equality any time soon.

She inspired one woman to establish a part-time employment agency especially for graduate wives.[26] The number of such agencies increased, as did, gradually, training for returners, including part-time and correspondence courses and handbooks providing practical advice.[27] They were encouraged by the continuing shortages of teachers, doctors, nurses and social workers in the expanding welfare state. In 1960 the Minister of Education launched a search for 50,000 teachers, urging local authorities to do everything possible to enable women to combine teaching with family responsibilities, including expanding day-nursery places, as many, but not all, did. Fast-track training was provided for graduates.[28] The number of part-time teachers increased. Teaching became by far the most frequent destination for female graduates in all subjects due to its exceptional compatibility with marriage and children. But this was not true everywhere and part-timers might be put on short-term contracts, treated disdainfully by full-timers and denied promotion. Some local authorities limited the number of headships open to women.

Working-Class Women

In 1954 social researcher Pearl Jephcott explored the experiences of working-class married women in work. She was based at the LSE with Nancy Seear and studied Bermondsey, a working-class area of south London where over half of all married women were in paid work. In this district they had always worked to support their families, as unskilled factory hands, casually employed cleaners or homeworkers. By the 1950s, for most women in Bermondsey opportunities and lifestyles had improved dramatically from the poverty and stress of the past. Early-morning office cleaning remained popular among mothers looking for part-time work that fitted with family responsibilities, but, in contrast to pre-war studies of working-class wives, Jephcott found smartly dressed, house-proud women in excellent health, able to take their pick of well-paid (by past standards) part-time jobs. She and her team mainly surveyed workers at the large Peek Frean biscuit factory, a major local employer of women. It and other local factories ran four daily shifts to accommodate married women workers.

The women benefitted from their husbands' newly secure, better-paid employment, many of them dockworkers whose previously notoriously insecure conditions were massively improved when in 1948 the Labour government established the National Dock Labour Board which introduced a good, guaranteed minimum wage. The wives now worked not to rescue their families from starvation but to further improve their already improving lifestyles, including with better food, clothing, furniture, consumer goods like TVs and holidays by the sea, as most regular workers now benefitted from paid holidays. As Conservative Prime Minister

Harold Macmillan claimed in 1957, 'most of our people have never had it so good'. They gained also from greater availability of better-designed, affordable rented housing, mostly supplied by local councils. Jephcott noted that many of the women enjoyed going to work to socialize with other women and escape the grind and loneliness of housework and childcare. Some had been advised by their doctors to find work to help them recover from depression. They gained pleasure and confidence from contributing to the family budget, which they felt raised their status with family and neighbours.[29] They could not compete for work with men and did not have equal pay by any measure, but they did not expect such equalities, and this did not appear to trouble them.

Professional Work

Concerns grew that encouragement to enter or re-enter teaching narrowed the career horizons of educated women. These were already limited because married women found it difficult to re-enter the senior civil service, university posts, the law and higher levels of business management, whatever their experience and skills. Numbers of female doctors grew gradually but remained restricted by the quotas limiting their entry to medical schools, despite campaigns by the very active Medical Women's Federation. Women who succeeded in entering medicine were more likely to continue working as mothers without a break than in any other profession, often working part-time while their children were young. They benefitted from the relative flexibility of General Practice in which over 50% of working mothers in medicine were employed in the early 1960s. It had the great advantage that surgeries were often based in the GP's own home.[30] Hospital medicine was more demanding and less compatible with family life. Even fewer mothers than single women reached its highest levels.

By the mid-1960s women accounted for fewer than 1% of chartered surveyors, accountants, auctioneers, estate agents and electrical and mechanical engineers, and only about 3.5% of practising lawyers. In universities they represented about one-sixth of junior lecturers, 2% of professors. Very few held managerial posts in industry or occupied the boardrooms of big business. Banks were reluctant to appoint married women, arguing that they lacked ambition and were unreliable, or to promote any woman. Lloyds Bank in the 1950s had a management training college but women were not admitted. Barclays Bank appointed its first female manager in 1958 following pressure from the BFBPW.[31] At the highest levels of the civil service, where part-time work was unavailable, women made up 7% in 1950, 8.4% in 1968, and they were predominantly single. Maternity leave, career breaks and flexible working were rare in all these occupations, which had no difficulty recruiting well-qualified men.[32] Women made up only one in twenty earners in the top salary range of £2,000–£3,000 per annum in 1967.[33]

Despite unequal opportunities in most occupations, before or after marriage, the number of married women in employment steadily increased, especially returners in their thirties and above. The 1961 census recorded 35% of married women in employment. The proportion aged 45–54 doubled between 1951 and 1966 from 25% to 50%. Two-fifths of wives of manual workers were in paid work, under one-third of wives of professional men, managers or employers. Most women workers were still in low-level clerical and allied occupations in business and services: 55.7% in the 1951 census, 60.1% in 1961.[34] The small minority of married women in full-time professional work might add little to the household income due to the costs of childcare and domestic help. Their husbands' salaries supported the family, and the wives benefitted from self-fulfilment from their work. Families in which both husband and wife had full-time careers were rare and criticized as much as praised.

Mothers at Home

Many women graduates opted to remain at home, some undertaking freelance work. They were deterred by the difficulties of getting a good job, or in some cases happy to support their husband's career, as a clergyman, diplomat, senior manager, university leader or doctor, perhaps working as receptionist if his GP surgery was based in the home. They might have little choice if he frequently changed his place of work and they had to move house. They often found interest and fulfilment, as women long had, in voluntary work. New organizations emerged to bring together and support married women, including the National Childbirth Trust, established in 1960 to support and advise new parents and help women who chose to give birth at home. The National

Housewives Register was formed also in 1960 to bring 'housewives' together for companionship, intellectual exchange, leisure activities and local campaigns. The Pre-School Playgroups Association was founded in 1961 to provide opportunities for mothers and small children to get together, enjoy themselves and learn new skills in the absence of pre-school provision. All three grew from local to national organizations, giving women a variety of roles, paid and unpaid, often giving them experience and confidence to enter employment or training as their children grew older.[35] They could also draw them together to campaign on issues that concerned them.

Another survey in the early 1960s of married women by a married woman revealed the discontent of many women confined to the home. Hannah Gavron studied north London housewives for her sociology PhD, published posthumously as *The Captive Wife*.[36] She committed suicide, according to her son despairing of the obstacles she encountered to equal independence with men, including domination by her husband and resistance in the publishing industry to publication of her book.[37] Her research revealed that many other women felt isolated and unhappy: 35% of the working-class wives and 21% from the middle class believed they had married too young, mainly to break free from their families and, in the case of working-class women, to escape monotonous, low-paid work. Most felt their marriages were more egalitarian and companionate than their parents', though 62% of the working-class wives – but only one middle-class wife – did not know their husbands' earnings. Of the middle-class women, 90% had received training above school level and 77% intended to return to work. Only 29% of the working-class wives had acquired skills useable in the workplace; 87% intended to return to employment.

Few of the wives 'saw their lives dominated by the role of wife and mother'. They were all aware of the conflicts between the roles of mother and worker, but saw no conflict between those of wife and worker. Gavron concluded that the worlds of education and work were too exclusively geared to the male life cycle. Schools should prepare females for the life pattern that was becoming normal for most of them, and they should have access to training and education in later life. Klein's 1957 study also found that almost two-fifths of women surveyed mentioned the 'depressing effect of unrelieved household activity', which Klein linked to the fact that many of them now led isolated lives in new housing estates on the outskirts of cities, far from relatives and old friends, especially when children were at school and the husband at work, leaving them alone all day, longing to escape to work.[38]

In the 1950s, advertisers began to present positive images of working mothers in women's magazines and elsewhere.[39] It gradually became more widely accepted that married women's work was a normal feature of modern societies to which the culture and the economy should adjust, though criticism continued, including of the consumerism fuelled by their earnings. Labour Party publications attacked the Conservatives' 'crude materialistic appeal' to the advantages of owning refrigerators, washing machines and other items, failing to see that the washing machine especially, far from representing selfish, individualistic consumerism, liberated women from the exhaustion of the weekly wash, and other modern appliances eased domestic work. Women understandably resented such attacks and female support for Labour declined.[40]

Inequality in Marriage

Women still experienced gender inequality at home as well as at work. The MWA continued to lobby MPs and Ministers and to hold public meetings advocating equal rights in marriage and raising the status of married women, whether they worked in or out of the home. The NCW, among others, argued that husbands should be legally obliged to give their wives part of their incomes to spend as they liked in return for the essential support they received from their wives' unpaid work in the home. The long campaign begun by Eleanor Rathbone continued, now looking to the husband not the state to reward hard-working wives.

The MWA argued that the economic dependence of wives caused resentment, stress and marriage breakup. But access to divorce remained a major inequality between marriage partners. Women continued to campaign for reform of inequalities in the divorce law in England and Wales. They and others demanded reform because marriages broke down but often the partners did not meet the limited conditions for divorce or, wives especially, could not afford it, still often leading to unmarried cohabitation with a new partner, which was still generally thought shameful, including by many cohabitees. Husbands might extort favourable financial terms from wives in return for agreement to divorce. The opposition argued, as they always had, that divorce was already too easy. After a peak following wartime disruption, the number of divorce petitions fell from 206,678 in 1946–50 to 146,353 in 1956–60 in England, Wales and Scotland, though still substantially above pre-war levels.[41]

Following pressure, the government established a Royal Commission on divorce. Its report in 1956 expressed widespread divisions on divorce and the family. Nine of the eighteen commissioners opposed change. They felt 'grave anxiety' that marriages were breaking up which in the past would have survived because:

> Greater demands are now made of marriage, consequent on the spread of education, higher standards of living and the social and economic emancipation of women. The last is probably the most important. Women are no longer content to endure the treatment which in past time their inferior position obliged them to suffer. They expect of marriage that it shall be an equal partnership and rightly so. But the working out of this ideal exposes marriage to new strains. Some husbands find it difficult to accept the changed position of women: some wives do not appreciate that their new rights do not release them from the obligations arising out of marriage itself and, indeed, bring in their train new responsibilities.[42]

They recognized the reality of cultural change but resisted it. The Report exposed the continuing deep cultural divide concerning family relationships. Traditional ideas were still powerful, but not all-powerful. Nine Commissioners and the final recommendations were more moderate, proposing marriage counselling to enable reconciliation before attempting divorce and enforcement of maintenance orders after separation, which was embodied in subsequent legislation. Both were widely supported by women, but most Conservatives opposed easier divorce and there was no change in divorce law. It remained difficult for many people to obtain, and campaigns for reform continued.

The Justice System

Women's organizations continued their campaigns for gender equality in the justice system, with limited results. The NCW and others worked especially to increase the number of female magistrates, which rose from 3,700 in 1948 to 4,199 in 1962, alongside over 10,000 men. Women campaigned against the ruling that a court could not proceed if there was no male magistrate present, though it could proceed without a woman. From 1955 the government ruled that one man and one woman should sit in every court. This led to increasing numbers of women magistrates through the 1960s.[43]

Angry Young People

Public awareness of inequalities of class, race and gender was increased by criticism on stage, in literature and on film by a disparate group of writers described in the media as 'Angry Young Men', including John Osborne, John Braine, Colin Wilson and Alan Sillitoe. There were also Angry Young Women, who showed greater interest in gender inequalities. Shelagh Delaney's *A Taste of Honey* was first staged in 1958, filmed in 1961, both immediately successful. The play was set in a desolate flat overlooking a gasworks and slaughterhouse in Salford, Manchester, where 16-year-old Jo lived with her feckless, drunken mother. When mother went off with a salesman, Jo had a brief affair with a Black sailor, became pregnant and was abandoned. She was rescued and supported with her child by a gentle young homosexual, until her mother drove him away. The play challenged racism, homophobia, the stigma of unmarried motherhood and many disadvantages still suffered by poorer young women, realistically with no happy ending.[44]

Another female contribution was Nell Dunn's novel *Up the Junction* (1963), about working-class life and sex near Clapham Junction in south London. It confirmed many of Pearl Jephcott's findings in another district of south London. Unlike many writers challenging convention in the 1950s and early 1960s, Dunn was a Chelsea heiress whose marriage was celebrated at the Ritz hotel. In 1959 she and her husband moved to working-class Battersea. She worked in a chocolate factory while her husband, Jeremy Sandford, studied the plight of homeless families. *Up the Junction* portrayed working-class women, mostly in their early twenties, with whom Dunn worked and whom she befriended. She showed that 'affluence' had not eliminated class divisions, class identity or insecurity, nor did she romanticize working-class life past or present in one of the less glittering sectors of London, with shabby terraces, outdoor toilets, railways and smoky air.

But life there was not miserable. Work was plentiful for young men and women. If a job or an employer did not suit, it was easy to leave and find another. Young working-class women could afford the contemporary fashions for piled-up 'beehive' hairdos, pointed 'winkle-picker' shoes and American pop music, consumption represented as fun, not as symptoms of moral decay, while living in familiar environments with their families. Women of all ages were represented as sexually active and certainly not deferential to men, deriding them, well aware of the violent tendencies and unreliability of too many of them, suggesting that little had changed in relations between the sexes. The sexual awareness of older women portrayed by Dunn challenged contemporary assertions of unprecedented moral decay among the young, of which there was no evidence. She also showed the downside of sex, describing an illegal abortion.[45]

Some of the inequalities experienced by better-off women were expressed from the late 1940s until her suicide in 1963 by poet, novelist and short-story writer Sylvia Plath, first in the United States where she grew up, then as a graduate student at Cambridge, later an unhappy wife and mother in London, suffering recurrent depression. Her many publications express the sexism, loneliness and obstruction of their career ambitions she and other women experienced, intensified by her difficulty in getting published in popular magazines. In an article in the Oxford University newspaper *Isis* in 1956, she exposed the sexism she encountered at Cambridge, including a male scholar exclaiming, 'But really, talk about philosophy with a *woman!*' and another: 'As soon as a women starts talking about intellectual things she loses her feminine charm for me.'[46]

Wolfenden and Sexuality

There was growing concern about female prostitution. It was legal, though soliciting, judged to be a public nuisance, could result in a fine. Prosecutions rose from 2,966 in 1938 to 9,756 in 1962 and complaints grew. Homosexuality also began to arouse public discussion. All forms of sexual activity between men in public or private were criminal offences, not between women who were still assumed not to indulge in such disgusting behaviour. In 1938 there were 134 recorded cases of sodomy and bestiality in England and Wales, 1,043 in 1954; of 'gross indecency' between men, 316 in 1938, 2,322 in 1955.[47] By the mid-1950s about 4% of the male prison population was convicted of homosexual offences. Issues around homosexuality were publicized following the defection to Russia of the spies Guy Burgess and Donald Maclean in 1951, whose homosexuality was held to explain their treason by making them vulnerable to blackmail. In 1952 the mathematician Alan Turing, highly influential in the development of computer science, awarded the OBE for cracking the Enigma code at Bletchley and helping to win the war, was arrested for homosexual offences. He accepted a hormone treatment 'cure' in place of prison. As a result, he became impotent, grew breasts, suffered depression and committed suicide in 1954. In 1953 the prominent actor John Gielgud was arrested and fined £10 for importuning in a public lavatory, unleashing press criticism of the leniency of the penalty. At his next appearance on stage, he was greeted with standing applause, suggesting a certain public support for homosexual rights. In 1954 came the sensational trial of Lord Montagu of Beaulieu and Peter Wildeblood, Diplomatic Correspondent of the *Daily Mail*, who were imprisoned for inciting two RAF men to commit 'unnatural acts' in private.

Prejudice against homosexuals was deep, but there were hints of change and more open discussion of sexual issues. The American Alfred Kinsey's *Sexual Behaviour in the Human Male* was published with much publicity in Britain in 1948, followed by *Sexual Behaviour in the Human Female* in 1953. The publications encouraged parts of the widely read popular press to discuss everyday sexual behaviour more explicitly than before, arousing predictable disapproval in some quarters, welcomed, with relief, in others. A Mass Observation survey suggested that the latter might be more representative.[48] Kinsey revealed that 37% of his sample of white, middle-class American males had experienced sex with another man. Quiet campaigning for reform of homosexual law in Britain was led by the Sex Education Society, led by medical practitioner Norman Haire until his death in 1952 after which the organization flagged. In 1954 the Moral Welfare Council of the Church of England published a report by clergy and doctors, *The Problem of Homosexuality*, which asserted that it was indeed a sin, but sins were not necessarily crimes and reform should be considered.

The Conservative Home Secretary decided that laws on homosexuality and prostitution should be reviewed. In 1954 a committee was appointed chaired by Sir John Wolfenden, Vice-Chancellor of Reading University, whose son was homosexual, to examine the legal treatment of homosexuality and prostitution. The Wolfenden Report on Homosexual Offences and Prostitution was published in 1957. It concluded that, despite the official numbers, there was little sign that these activities were increasing. Prostitution was possibly more visible – though less so in many areas than a hundred years previously – but the main cause of more convictions was police zeal in pursuing offenders, especially in London and other cities, particularly following the appointment of an ardent Roman Catholic as Director of Public Prosecutions in 1944, then a zealous Metropolitan Police Commissioner in 1953.[49] The report echoed contemporary cultural conventions in regretting 'the general loosening of former moral standards' and 'the emotional insecurity, community instability and weakening of the family'.[50] Less conventionally, it recommended decriminalizing male homosexual behaviour in private (only), arguing for a distinction between sin and crime, public and private morality. Criminal penalties should apply only when male and female sexual behaviour caused a public nuisance. It denied that homosexuality was a disease but recommended further research into its causes and the possibility of effective 'treatment' to be offered to perpetrators of homosexual offences.

Most of the popular press reacted to the proposals on homosexual law reform with horror. The *News of the World* claimed they would lead to 'the most dreadful corruption and pollution', though the now left-leaning *Daily Mirror* and the liberal *News Chronicle* supported decriminalization.[51] R.A. Butler, now Home Secretary, inclined to agree with the proposals, but believed they were too far ahead of public and Conservative opinion, and the Cabinet opposed them. The Homosexual Law Reform Society (HLRS) and the Albany Trust, a research and counselling service for homosexuals, were formed in 1958 to campaign for implementation. No government action followed.

The Street Offences Act, 1959, implemented Wolfenden's recommendations on prostitution, criminalizing soliciting in public and increasing the maximum penalties. This was strongly supported by responses to opinion polls and by most of the press. 'Tarts will no longer cling to every lamp post', commented the *Mirror*.[52] Many women opposed it because, like past legislation controlling prostitution, the women were punished while male customers went free. Butler agreed but was over-ruled by the Cabinet. The Wolfenden Report justified this because 'the simple fact is that prostitutes do parade themselves more habitually and openly than their prospective customers and do by their continual presence affront the sense of decency of the ordinary citizen'.[53] Prostitutes then moved off the streets and risked greater exploitation by male pimps. There was little public sympathy for women whom even the *News Chronicle* described as 'hardened professionals not driven to it by want but choosing it for gain'.[54] Convictions for prostitution declined to 2,726 by 1960, but prostitution did not. Strip clubs and cafes associated with vice and organized crime grew as alternative locations.[55] This brought condemnation but no government action. The Conservatives lost the election of 1964 and Labour returned to government.

Conclusion

Under the Conservatives women gained some long-term objectives, in particular equal pay in the public sector (only), though not equal employment opportunities, and representation in the House of Lords, though as a tiny minority in a large male-dominated House. Cultural changes in the 1950s and early 1960s led to certain gender and other inequalities becoming more publicly identified, discussed and challenged than before, notably homosexuality, though strong opposition persisted and there was no progress towards equality. There was similar lack of progress to equal divorce rights. Research provided more detailed information about women's unequal opportunities in education and at work at all levels and the reasons underlying them, including the negative attitudes of employers, also about the attitudes of married women themselves to their experiences at work and at home. Literary and dramatic representations of inequalities increased public awareness, and increased knowledge encouraged further women's activism, which continued over a range of issues, including reform of taxation. Movement towards gender equality continued to be gradual, owing more to cultural change than to Conservative government initiative.

SIX

A Permissive Society? 1964–1970

Labour returned to government from 1964 to 1970 led by Harold Wilson, initially with a majority of just four seats. Wilson aimed to further expand and modernize the economy and the welfare system, continuing the reforms of the post-war government, following what Labour called the 'Thirteen Wasted Years' of Conservative rule. This seemed all the more justified when they discovered that the previous government had unexpectedly left a very large deficit in the public finances, owing much to tax cuts, and it limited Labour's capacity to implement further reform.

It was still strongly committed to class equality but, again, made no explicit commitment to gender equality, though it was vigorously advocated by female Labour Party members, MPs and Baronesses, especially Baroness Edith Summerskill, as she now was. And one of the government's first measures was the Married Women's Property Act, 1964, granting wives ownership of an equal share of the housekeeping income provided by their husbands and freedom to spend it as they wished. It was drafted and introduced by Edith Summerskill, following the long campaign by the MWA and others for equal property rights in marriage. It was a limited advance but important because it established the principle of equal rights in marriage. Campaigns for further reforms continued.

Wilson called a second election in March 1966 and his majority rose to 98. Initially there was, again, just one female Cabinet Minister, Barbara Castle, Minister of Overseas Development, 1964–5, of Transport from 1965, then Minister of Employment from 1968, when she was joined by Judith Hart as Paymaster-General for one year. The number of female MPs crept up to 29 in 1964. In 1966 more women voted Labour than Conservative,[1] though the number of female MPs slipped to 26: 19 Labour, 7 Conservative.

Family Life

The exceptional post-war marriage rise continued. At the peak, in 1966–70, 82% of the UK adult population had married at least once. The mean ages at marriage reached their lowest point in 1971 at 24.6 for men, 22.6 for women.[2] The number of divorces in England and Wales rose from 137,392 in 1956–60 to 284,449 in 1966–70, before major divorce reform was implemented, as we will see.[3] Divorce was still difficult and expensive, especially for women, but perhaps more people could now afford to divorce as well as marry due to rising incomes. Also expectations of marriage appeared to be rising, and more women seemed unwilling to tolerate disappointment in relationships and increasingly ready to opt for independence.[4]

This contributed to growing numbers of single-parent families, overwhelmingly headed by mothers, beginning a major long-term trend. Unless they had independent wealth or family support, they faced the danger of severe poverty due to women's continuing difficulty in finding affordable childcare or adequately paid work. The benefit system improved somewhat under Labour, though it remained far from generous. It was widely believed that poverty had been largely eliminated since 1945 except among older people. Then in 1965 two social scientists at the LSE, Brian Abel-Smith and Peter Townsend, launched their research report, *The Poor and the Poorest*, causing widespread shock by revealing much more poverty than was generally assumed, not confined to older people.[5] It became known as 'the rediscovery of poverty'. Using the government's measure of need for means-tested National Assistance benefits, they found that 14% of the UK population (7.5 million people) were poor. A high proportion of these, as expected, were retired. Most were women, who still outlived men, in greater poverty, but this gender difference was little noticed at the time. The greatest shock was that two million of those in poverty were children, obviously in poor families, often with single mothers.[6] This finding especially was widely publicized and led to the foundation in 1965 of the Child Poverty Action Group (CPAG) to campaign for improved child benefits to eliminate poverty, as it still does.[7] The government was slow to respond, mainly due to financial constraints and its decision to prioritize raising the still very low old age pensions. But in 1969 it established a

Committee on One-Parent Families to investigate the conditions of this growing social group and recommend policies to assist them. It reported in 1974 when Labour was again in government as discussed in chapter 7.

Another emerging trend was that births to unmarried parents rose from 5% of all births in 1950–2 to 8.2% in 1971.[8] In 1971, 45% of 'illegitimate' births were jointly registered by the parents, suggesting that they had stable, often cohabiting though not officially recognized, relationships.[9] Nationally, the number of births began to decline from 1968, unexpectedly ending the post-war boom, perhaps another sign of women seeking independence. This became easier following the introduction of the birth control pill in the early 1960s, the easiest form of contraception ever known and highly effective. The culture was still changing, fuelling pressure for further change in gender relations.[10]

Education

As part of the Wilson government's aim to extend the welfare state, Anthony Crosland took charge of education. He had long been committed to equal access to good education and equal opportunities for all regardless of class, and critical of the socially selective tripartite system at secondary level. He was impressed by sociological studies demonstrating that this benefitted the white middle classes, especially males, though the social scientists, and Crosland, paid more attention to class than to gender or race inequality, which were at least as substantial.[11] He issued a circular requesting local authorities in England and Wales to submit plans to reorganize secondary schools on 'comprehensive' lines, abolishing 11+ selection and replacing grammar and secondary modern schools with single schools for all abilities. Technical schools had always been few due to financial constraints preventing the foundation of new schools, and shortage of qualified teachers. Scotland had long had a more socially inclusive secondary school system. Crosland could not order local authorities to comply because they still had considerable independence concerning education policy, but by the early 1970s most authorities had introduced comprehensive schools. Unlike grammar schools, most comprehensives were mixed-sex and girls' opportunities began to improve, though slowly because conventional views about gender differences in aptitude and career opportunities were slow to shift. Physics was still represented as an unsuitable subject for girls.[12]

Crosland also funded the development of thirty degree-awarding 'polytechnics' out of local authority technical colleges, alongside the autonomous universities. The number of universities was growing with the foundation of new universities, bringing about a total of 38 universities in Great Britain by 1970, including seven new foundations in England and one, Stirling, in Scotland. With more places available, opportunities for girls to enter universities grew, though they remained a minority of students and concentrated in arts and social sciences. By 1970–1 there were 182,600 females in full-time higher education in the UK, 274,200 males, still fewer than in many other high-income countries.[13] Under Crosland also, ten Colleges of Advanced Technology were granted university charters to assist the government's aim to improve technological skills and modernize a flagging economy. Polytechnics were developed for similar reasons. They focused on science and technology and, unlike most universities, provided part-time courses for people of all ages, enabling them to develop their skills and, hopefully, democratizing higher education. Part-time education, usually in the evening, after work, was the best route for people to compensate for an inadequate school education. Polytechnic student numbers rose from around 33,000 in 1962 to 215,000 in 1970–1, predominantly male.[14] Planning also began for a favourite Wilson project, a 'University of the Air', later named the Open University, designed to extend post-school opportunities and further democratize access to higher education by broadcasting part-time degree-level classes on radio and TV, supported by correspondence with tutors, printed materials and summer schools. It opened in 1969 and increasingly attracted older women 'returners' seeking skills and expanded employment opportunities.[15]

In another respect the government expanded educational opportunities and assisted some working mothers. In 1967 the Plowden Report on *Children and their Primary Schools*, initiated by the government, proposed an expansion of nursery education, initially in poor areas, from children's earliest years and compensatory education for older children[16] – all part of the programme of improving opportunities which had modest success in the short time before Labour lost the 1970 election.

Work

Education reforms did not, at least in the short run, improve women's opportunities in the labour market. Full employment – for men – continued to improve family living standards, but there was increasingly widespread awareness in the later 1960s of the inequalities limiting women's opportunities, and greater discussion of the causes, cultural and economic, aroused at least partially by the surveys previously discussed. The (Donovan) Royal Commission on Trade Unions and Employers' Associations, appointed by Wilson's government, reported in 1968 and, surprisingly in a male-dominated field, argued strongly that attitudes towards the training and employment of women were one of the (many) enduring weaknesses of British management. It stated that 'the facts are so disturbing and the implications – both social and economic – so important that they must be singled out for discussion'. It reported that female access to apprenticeships remained 'extraordinarily limited'. Girls performed as well as boys in O-level examinations, but then only 7% entered apprenticeships, mainly in hairdressing, compared with 43% of boys. Forty-nine per cent of male workers in industry were classified as skilled, only 29% of women. In 1966, 538,000 male workers were granted day release for training, only 87,000 women. Based on their interviews with managers and trade unionists and evidence from another survey by Nancy Seear (initiated by the Commission), the Commission concluded that, although family commitments did create obstacles to women's work and training, this was much less the case for older women returners, yet:

> Lack of skilled labour has constantly applied a brake to our economic expansion since the war and yet the capacity of women to do skilled work has been neglected ... forecasts of the size of the working population indicate that there will be a very limited increase between now and 1981. Women provide the only substantial new source from which extra and especially skilled labour can be drawn during this period ... Many of the attitudes which support the present system of craft training and discrimination against women are common to both employers and trade unionists and deeply engrained in the life of the country. Prejudice against women is manifest at all levels of management as well as on the shop floor. Among the professions there are to

be found demarcation rules and rules for qualifying for practice which are no less strict and no less open to question than those practised in many crafts.[17]

The Commission's chair, Lord Donovan, was a former Labour MP, a High Court judge and Lord of Appeal.

Nancy Seear's survey for the Commission, conducted in 1966, found no evidence of change since her 1962 survey, discussed in chapter 5. She commented that: 'Even the most ardent feminist will agree that there is no great upsurge of protest by women against the existing situation.' This did not necessarily mean that they approved of it: 'Human beings are remarkably adaptable and most people once they have recognized a brick wall for what it is decide not to bang their heads against it.' She believed the biggest obstacle was that:

> in subtle and not so subtle ways an atmosphere is created and sustained which still makes it appear peculiar or comical for women to be both feminine and using their capacities to the full. This attitude thrives ... while BBC commentators make facetious asides about women in science and managerial jobs, while the press and public chatter nervously about how to address a lady judge, while a girl in a mixed comprehensive school can be told that 'technical drawing is only for boys'.[18]

Belittling women's capacities and opposition to their promotion indeed remained pervasive, including in the professions. In 1964, responding to the continuing shortage of schoolteachers, the LCC proposed making part-timers eligible for senior appointments, but met strong opposition from full-time, generally male, staff. Still in 1973, only 7% of women working in primary schools were heads compared with almost 30% of men. At secondary level three times as many men as women were school heads.

In medicine the numbers of active married women grew, from approximately 9,000 in the early 1950s to roughly 13,000 (about one-fifth of qualified doctors) twenty years later. Women still remained in continuous work in medicine more than in other professions. In 1963 almost two-thirds of medically qualified women with children under five were working (17% full-time, 46% part-time) and about four-fifths of mothers of school-age children.[19] Progress was difficult, though there were efforts to make part-time practice easier and more acceptable. Rosemary Rue, a senior medical officer in Oxford, herself a mother, established a scheme in the mid-1960s to enable talented female doctors with children to find flexible pathways to senior medical ranks. She organized salaried placements, matching female trainees with consultants in their preferred specialties, in hospitals close to the women's homes, non-residential, for four and a half days per week. It was highly successful and much copied. It persuaded the Department of Health in 1969 to issue an official memorandum on the re-employment of women doctors which urged hospitals to provide part-time postgraduate training and create part-time registrar and consultant posts to attract women into understaffed specialties. The results were, at best, uneven. The government had recognized the need, as an official put it, 'to educate the medical profession to accept married women who are only able to work part-time', but they could not win over most of the profession and ensure equal opportunities for women.[20]

The situation in social work was similar, despite being generally perceived as a female occupation. In 1966 Bromley Technical College started a two-year diploma course in social work aimed at married women, taught from 10.15 am to 3.20 pm to fit with school hours. Like similar courses elsewhere, it was successful in attracting women. But they then had difficulty finding permanent part-time posts, though these had been recommended in 1959 by the otherwise very influential Younghusband *Report on Social Workers in Local Authority Health and Welfare Services*.[21] The dominant view in the profession remained that social work was a full-time occupation and those unable to comply should consider voluntary work. Requests for flexible working were resisted. Throughout the 1960s men became increasingly predominant in senior positions.[22]

From the mid-1960s women campaigned with mounting vigour for greater equality in the labour market, including for equal pay. Perhaps in response, and to the findings of the Donovan Commission, in 1967 the Labour Party appointed a committee to investigate discrimination against women. It reported in 1972 when Labour was no longer in government, but, as we will see in the next chapter, after it was re-elected in 1974 it introduced what became the Sex Discrimination Act, 1975, building on the committee's recommendations. Also in 1967, Labour arranged negotiations between the Confederation of British Industries (CBI) and the TUC to try to devise a way forward on equal pay. This only revealed that little had changed since 1946. The CBI would only commit to 'equal pay for equal work', dismissing the TUC's preference for 'equal pay for work of the same value' as too open-ended and imprecise. The breakdown of the talks convinced the TUC at last to support legislation on equal pay, which, as we will see, followed in 1970. There were signs that the government was becoming more aware of the need for action on gender inequalities.

Also in the very active year 1967, women established the Women's Taxation Action Group (WOTAG). They campaigned to end the joint taxation of married couples, which increased the wife's tax burden by adding her earnings to those, generally higher, of her husband for income tax purposes. They also proposed tax relief for employment of help in the home, to encourage highly qualified married women back to work, arguing that the costs of employing domestic help and childcare took most of a professional woman's salary, reducing the incentive to work. They gained some favourable press comment, but Labour Ministers were not persuaded. They were focused upon the needs of low-income people and argued that only the small minority of couples with joint incomes above £5,000 paid significantly more tax under joint assessment. They overlooked the injustice of treating the wife's income as an extension of her husband's. This was partially modified in 1971 when the Conservative government granted couples the option of separate assessment.[23]

Labour showed no inclination to grant tax relief to the better-off for childcare and domestic help. Initially it was more concerned about racism following the defeat in the 1964 election of the sitting MP for Smethwick in the Midlands, Patrick Gordon Walker, in an aggressive racist campaign blaming Labour, unjustifiably, for unduly favouring immigrants in the allocation of council housing and other services. 'If you want a nigger neighbour vote Labour', chanted the racists. This led to the first Race Relations Act in 1965, outlawing discrimination against women and men on grounds of race, colour, ethnic or national origin in public places or on public transport, but not in the important areas of employment or housing where racism was severe for men and women.

Towards the 'Permissive Society'

The Race Relations Act was just one in an exceptional succession of liberal reforms introduced by this government from 1967 to 1970. They included some significant moves to advance gender equality, mostly long supported by women's and other campaigning groups, of which this government was more supportive than its predecessors, especially Roy Jenkins in the key role of Home Secretary from 1965 to 1967.

Abortion

An early example was the legalization of abortion for the first time in western Europe. The Abortion Law Reform Association (ALRA) sprang into action soon after the 1964 election. Founded in 1936, as described in chapter 2, it flagged after the war as its leaders aged and died, but when Madeleine Simms was appointed leader in 1961 it became another very active campaign group. It commissioned polls revealing higher than expected support for legalization. The press, popular and serious, discussed abortion more openly than before and more papers supported it. The growing body of female columnists highlighted how illegal 'back-street' abortions still damaged many women unable to afford private operations: 'As having an abortion has become so much a matter of having £200 and the right address, it seems grossly unfair that it should be denied to the have-nots', wrote Anne Batt in the *Daily Express* in 1965.[24] In 1965 National Opinion Polls (NOP) found 66% of doctors supported legalization, only 10% opposed; in July 1966 that 75% of women favoured it and only 20% opposed; in 1967 that Catholic women were no less likely to have had an (illegal) abortion than others and 44% supported legal abortion 'if the woman is unable to cope with any more children'.[25] But Catholic and other Christian opposition became increasingly organized and outspoken, principally in the newly formed Society for the Protection of Unborn Children (SPUC). The Church of England was officially opposed.

Attempted legislation started in the Lords where a Bill won a second reading in November 1965, but it was delayed by the March 1966 election. Then in July 1966, Liberal MP David Steel accepted ALRA's invitation to introduce a Bill in the Commons to legalize abortion, which passed its second reading by 194 votes, creating an explosive public debate, including vicious personal attacks by SPUC.[26] An amendment allowing doctors to refuse to perform abortions on conscience grounds mollified some opposition, but it remained strong. The medical profession was divided, though many doctors with experience of the death and damage resulting from the large, and, it was suspected, growing, numbers of illegal abortions supported legalization. It was opposed by disabled campaigners, who feared that easier abortion would prevent the birth of disabled people capable of viable lives.

The debate focused on the grounds for legal abortion. There was no question of women being allowed to choose: a doctor must decide. The main issue was whether it should be allowed strictly on health or on broader social grounds, which arguably lay outside the competence of most doctors. Narrowly defined health grounds won; abortion was allowed if the mother was judged likely to take her own life, but not if she felt too overburdened to rear a child. The Bill was guided through parliament by Labour MPs, ensuring it received sufficient time and space for debate. The Cabinet was divided between strong supporters and opponents, including Catholics and those who feared legalization would lose Labour votes. The government remained officially neutral, but this became less credible as it repeatedly extended the time available for debate to counter opposition delaying tactics, until it finally passed both Houses following lengthy debates.[27] Abortion became legal, up to 28 weeks' gestation, with permission from two doctors. The dissension enforced compromise, and the legislation was imperfect and, in some respects, unclear about the grounds on which abortion was permissible, but it was a breakthrough, a significant extension of women's rights.

Opposition to abortion has never gone away. Almost immediately, opponents tried, unsuccessfully, to amend the law, encouraging rumours in the press of private nursing homes providing abortion on demand and women flocking for abortions from countries where it was illegal. Bills to restrict abortion rights were brought, unsuccessfully, to parliament in 1969, 1970, 1975, 1977, 1978 and 1979–80.[28] The number of legal abortions increased from 22,100 in 1968 to 75,400 in 1970, evenly divided between married and unmarried women, most aged over 20.[29] It is unknown how this compared with numbers of previous illegal abortions.

The law applied in Scotland but not in Northern Ireland, where Catholics and Protestants united in opposition to abortion as on little else except resisting other liberal reforms. Into the twenty-first century, abortion was only permitted when there was serious risk to the health and life of the mother and Northern Ireland had the harshest criminal penalty for abortion in Europe: life imprisonment for a woman convicted of undergoing an illegal abortion. An unknown number of women travelled from Northern Ireland to Britain for abortions, also from the Republic of Ireland, though Irish nationals were not allowed free access to the NHS. Not until 2019, when the devolved government of Northern Ireland was suspended due to internal disputes, could the Westminster government over-rule the opponents and abortion was legalized, though it remained difficult to obtain. In the Republic also it was legalized in 2019 following the unexpected positive outcome of a referendum on the issue.

Birth Control

Women had long campaigned for free birth control services on the NHS. Local authority health and welfare centres could still provide advice free of charge, but only if the pregnancy put the health of a married woman at risk, as established in 1931, described in chapter 2. Charities, notably the Family Planning Association (FPA), still provided free services and demand kept growing. The FPA worked hard through the 1950s and 1960s to publicize its work, to improve public knowledge about birth control and campaign for more state provision. From 1960 the press became excited, and moralists alarmed, about the revolutionary new birth control pill, apparently more effective than other methods, and about the sexual liberation of women that could follow this easy, reliable form of contraception.[30] Brook Advisory Centres, also charities, were founded throughout Britain from the early 1960s specifically to provide sexual advice, and later, when they could, the pill and contraceptive devices for young unmarried people to counter the inadequacy of sex education in schools, which they worked with some success to improve. They helped young unmarried people to better understand their sexuality and sexual relationships, helped them manage their sexual feelings and experiences, prevented unwanted pregnancy and protected young people against the all-too-frequent attacks of moralizers, of which the centres, predictably, were themselves targets. They provided a valuable and effective service into the twenty-first century.[31]

Kenneth Robinson, Minister of Health 1964–8, wanted to extend free services, but this required legislation, and opposition, especially from Catholics and some fundamentalist Protestants, held the government back. Labour MP Edwin Brooks introduced a Private Member's Bill to extend state services, largely drafted by the Ministry of Health. It allowed, but did not require, local authorities to provide contraceptive advice and supplies free of charge to anyone regardless of age, marital status or any other limitation. The Family Planning Act passed easily through parliament in 1967, with little fuss even about supplying birth control to unmarried people, including teenagers, while sections of the press shrieked 'Sex on the Rates!' Its passage was probably helped by contemporary fears about world and national population growth and potential overpopulation. But fewer than 25% of local authorities complied.[32] By 1969 the Minister of Health, now Richard Crossman, believed the pill should be free for all women on the NHS, but his officials opposed this on grounds of cost, and some did not believe routine birth control was a health issue. It did not become wholly free on the NHS until Labour was again in government in 1974. It remained hardest to obtain in Northern Ireland. In 1971 Labour MP Phillip Whitehead introduced an amendment to the Family Planning Act to make male contraception, vasectomy, available at local authority discretion. This became law in 1972.[33]

Homosexual and Lesbian Rights

As we have seen, a major, long-established gender inequality was the criminalization of sex between men. Sex between women, lesbianism, was never criminalized though nor was it culturally acceptable or publicly discussed. Its existence was ignored or denied, or it was disparaged, like most female activities regarded as less significant than 'deviance' among men. Lesbians gathered in a few clubs and pubs and began to campaign for acknowledgement and respect. In 1963 they initiated the first explicitly lesbian social and political organization in Britain, called the Minorities Research Group to avoid undue police interest. They published a magazine, *Arena Three*, provided counselling and means of contact for isolated lesbians and worked to inform public opinion and promote independent research, generating a number of regional groups but with limited public impact.[34]

Male homosexuality had been seen as a major cultural threat for centuries and men had campaigned, discreetly, for legalization since earlier in the century. In the 1950s it became increasingly a public issue as we have seen in chapter 5. Homophobic prejudice remained deep but there were hints of change and more open discussion stimulated by the Church of England's support for reform of homosexual law and the Wolfenden Report. When the Conservatives failed to respond, the Homosexual Law Reform Society (HLRS) was established in 1958 to campaign for legalization. It became increasingly active when Labour returned to government. Homosexual rights were then more widely and sympathetically discussed. Two films, *Victims* (1963), starring Dirk Bogarde, and *The Trials of Oscar Wilde* (1964) with Peter Finch, both prominent stars, presented sympathetic portrayals of homosexuality. In 1964, several prominent women journalists asked the HLRS for help with articles 'opening up' the subject to discussion.[35] In May 1965 Labour MP Leo Abse tabled a motion in the Commons to reduce criminalization of homosexuality, as proposed by Wolfenden. Ministers feared the timing was unfortunate given the small majority, the impending election and the risk they already ran with voters by abolishing capital punishment, which controversially became law in 1965. They refused to support Abse's motion, anticipating its return at a more convenient time. It was defeated in the Commons.

Two days earlier, the newly liberal Lords, with growing numbers of life peers and peeresses, approved a Bill brought by Lord Arran to decriminalize homosexual acts between adult men in private. Arran's homosexual older brother had been driven to suicide. He faced fierce opposition from two Conservative Lords Chancellor, including Lord Kilmuir warning about 'buggery clubs', demanding 'Are your Lordships going to pass a Bill that will make it lawful for two senior officers of police to go to bed together?' They did, supported by the Archbishops of Canterbury and York and a majority of bishops. Polls suggested that most people, regardless of age, gender or class, now agreed, 63% in an NOP poll for the *Daily Mail*. The Bill was introduced in the Commons by Conservative MP Humphrey Berkeley, supported by Jenkins as Home Secretary, and passed its second reading easily in February 1966, but the election intervened, and Berkeley lost his seat, due to opposition to his Bill it was believed.

After the election Arran reintroduced his Bill in the Lords, who again passed it easily. Abse introduced it in the Commons, assured of Jenkins's support. Leading Ministers, including Wilson, resisted, partly because, as Crossman put it, 'working-class people in the north jeer at their Members at the weekend and ask them why they're looking after the buggers at Westminster instead of looking after the unemployed at home'.[36] The parliamentary party was fiercely divided on all liberal reforms, but there was an influx of younger, more liberal Labour MPs in 1964 and 1966. The proportion of university-educated Labour MPs rose from 39% in 1959 to 46% in 1964 and 51% in 1966, and surveys showed the close association between higher education and cultural liberalism.[37] Crossman supported homosexual and abortion reform and persuaded Wilson not to risk these controversies dragging on to the next election.[38]

The draft legislation modified the Wolfenden proposals with a tighter definition of 'in private' – a couple could be prosecuted for having sex when someone else was in the same building – and exemption from the reform of the armed forces whose leaders feared the spread of homosexual activities. The merchant navy was also excluded after lobbying by the National Union of Seamen.[39] The maximum penalty of life imprisonment for anal sex was repealed but the penalty for 'gross indecency' – effectively any visible act perceived as homosexual, including men kissing in public – rose from two to five years' imprisonment. The age of consent was fixed at 21, as Wolfenden had recommended, not the heterosexual age of 16, for fear that young men would be seduced by older men, as though young women would not. The Sexual Offences Act passed the Commons in a twenty-hour, all-night session, at 5.30 am, by 99 votes to 14 with many absences and abstentions. Crossman and the Chief Whip encouraged Labour MPs to vote 'Yes', despite official government neutrality. Conservative MP Gerald Nabarro attacked the 'depravity' of Labour MPs, prophesying, perhaps accurately, that 'the long hair of Mr Wilson's intellectuals on the back benches would strangle him' at the next election. It passed the Lords even more easily, becoming law in 1967.

The new law was far from 'legalizing homosexuality' as some claimed and campaigners were not euphoric, but they recognized it was a start, at last the beginning of decriminalization, and that public prejudice remained so strong that it was wise to keep quiet about defects in the law. The Archbishop of Canterbury reassured the Lords that it 'would still leave by far the greater number of homosexual crimes and convictions unaltered'. Indeed, prosecutions for such 'acts of gross indecency' as men holding hands in public increased, from 420 in 1966 to 1,711 in 1974, a police response to the change in the law.[40] Activism for further change grew with the formation of the Campaign for Homosexual Equality (CHE) in 1969 and the Gay Liberation Front (GLF) in 1970. As discussed in chapter 7, they campaigned peaceably throughout the 1970s and beyond for legal and social equality for lesbians, gay men and bisexuals.

The Act applied only in England and Wales, and in Scotland the legal ban was no longer enforced. In 1969 the Scottish Minorities Group (later the Scottish Homosexual Reform Group, SHRG) formed to campaign to extend the law to Scotland. Bills failed until in 1979 the SHRG brought a case in the European Court of Human Rights (ECtHR). Probably to avoid a long, expensive and possibly unsuccessful legal battle, in 1980 Margaret Thatcher's Conservative government extended the law to Scotland, despite continuing opposition mainly from the Scottish churches. It was more fiercely opposed in Northern Ireland, where the fundamentalist Protestant Rev. Ian Paisley led a 'Save Ulster from Sodomy' campaign. Gay rights groups became active and in 1980 a gay man brought a successful case in the ECHR, arguing that the law violated his right to a private and family life. The law changed in Northern Ireland in 1982. The Isle of Man and Jersey followed only in 1992.

Divorce

Then, at last, came comprehensive divorce reform, promoted by Gerald Gardiner, Lord Chancellor 1964–70. The Archbishop of Canterbury appointed a committee whose report in 1966, *Putting Asunder*, accepted that secular divorce law should no longer be dictated by religious belief. It recommended 'breakdown of marriage' rather than matrimonial offence as the test for divorce, as reformers had long advocated, as we have seen. It took the government two years to draft legislation, with external consultation. The Archbishop, Michael Ramsey, wanted thorough discussion to prevent opposition mobilizing in the church. Women's groups insisted that reform must include sound financial provision for divorced partners, which was agreed by supporters of reform.

The government was preoccupied with financial problems, violence in Northern Ireland, crises in Rhodesia and Vietnam, but campaigners kept divorce on the political agenda. The Divorce Law Reform Union (DLRU) was reinvigorated, assisted by women's groups, the Methodist Church, progressive Catholics and the Church of England, though Ramsey retreated as support grew for divorce by consent, which he believed went too far. Jenkins became Chancellor of the Exchequer in November 1967 and was replaced as Home Secretary by James Callaghan. Callaghan held conservative views about the family and was not a strong supporter of divorce reform, though he had supported the partial decriminalization of homosexuality, and a government divorce reform Bill went forward in 1969.[41] It passed easily through parliament and came into force in 1971.[42]

Divorce was now easier and cheaper to obtain. Applicants for divorce, male and female, now had to prove the marriage had broken down and give one of five reasons: adultery, unreasonable behaviour, desertion, separation for more than two years if both agreed to the divorce, or at least five years if they disagreed. Supporters of no-fault divorce were disappointed with another compromise. The accompanying Matrimonial Proceedings and Property Act[43] allowed each divorced partner an equal share of family assets, as women demanded. The laws applied only in England and Wales, extended to Scotland in 1975. They were forced upon Northern Ireland in 1978, opposed by Paisley. Divorce remained difficult to obtain there and there continued to be fewer divorces there than elsewhere in the UK.

In Great Britain the number of divorces rose rapidly after the law was implemented in 1971, most brought by women, discussed in later chapters. The reform enabled some cohabiting couples at last to divorce and remarry. In 1972 a lawyer observed in the divorce court:

> A succession of elderly persons of eminently respectable appearance . . . all had lived apart from their lawful spouse for more, usually much more, than the stipulated five years. In almost every case the story was essentially the same: the youthful wartime marriage, the long separation in service . . . the drift apart, the formation of a new relationship, the birth of children, the woman taking the man's name, the passionate desire to legitimize those children and

so on. In each case the decree was granted: in each case the elderly couple's faces reflected happiness and quiet domestic comfort.[44]

The number of such cases is unknown. The reform brought gender equality in marriage and divorce closer, but it was still incomplete.

Equal Pay

Labour's final reforming breakthrough was the Equal Pay Act, 1970. It was initiated by Barbara Castle, as Minister for Employment and Productivity from April 1968. Women in the Labour Party, trade unions and women's organizations campaigned with increasing intensity for equal pay in the 1960s. Seventy per cent of new union members between 1964 and 1970 were female, as the public sector expanded, influencing union policy. In the mid-1960s came a flurry of strikes by women for equal pay and equal treatment at work. During the 1966 election, an alliance of women's organizations demanded equality at work, including in pay, taxation, pensions and other benefits.[45] The European Community (EC, as the EU was then known) in its founding Treaty of Rome, 1957, committed member states to 'maintain the principle of equal remuneration for equal work as between men and women workers', following pressure from women across the participating countries. Labour Party leaders were anxious to meet EC standards where possible because they planned to seek admission to it, though they did not succeed. As we have seen, discussions in 1967 between the CBI and TUC got nowhere.

The cause progressed when Ray Gunter, who had no known interest in gender equality, was replaced at the Ministry of Employment and Productivity by Barbara Castle. She faced two strikes which, she later commented, 'fired my determination to force the macho male chauvinists in the Treasury to accept the principle of equal pay'.[46] The first was the strike of women sewing machinists at Ford's motor-manufacturing centre at Dagenham in June 1968, much mythologized and the subject of the film *Made in Dagenham* in 2010. The strike was not directly about equal pay but about a job evaluation scheme which women workers believed undervalued their work and skill in relation to men. The male trade unionists at Dagenham turned the issue towards equal pay as a condition of their support because they did not want the job evaluation, which favoured them, reopened. Castle intervened and the women achieved something closer to equal pay – a rise from 85 to 92% of the men's rate – without revisiting the job evaluation, and the men and women returned to work. The strike led to the formation of the National Joint Action Committee for Women's Equal Rights composed of women's groups and trade unionists. It adopted a charter calling on the TUC to campaign for equal pay and equal opportunities, launched at a big rally in Trafalgar Square in May 1969.

The second dispute arose from a pay demand by male engineers. The men agreed a settlement which paid women employees less and the women protested. The men switched to supporting equal pay until it became clear that they would receive lower pay than they wanted, at which point they agreed the deal which disadvantaged women. Castle 'knew then that left to themselves the unions would never do anything serious about equal pay and that the government had to legislate'.[47]

But her time was consumed by tussles with the unions over the government's policy of controls on prices and incomes, which are discussed later in this chapter. Equal-pay legislation came about because 'once again it was the women who made the running'.[48] In spring 1970, with an election imminent, women Labour MPs, led by Lena Jeger, who had pressured the government on a series of gender inequality issues, tabled an amendment to the government's Prices and Incomes Bill demanding that pay controls should not prevent moves towards equal pay. Castle argued that the government would probably be defeated on the amendment unless she announced equal-pay legislation. The Cabinet felt forced to agree. She rushed the Equal Pay Bill through parliament before the election, later admitting it was prepared in a hurry: 'It was far from perfect, but it established the principle on which later refinements could be built. I knew that if we lost the election our Tory successors would be forced to proceed with it.'[49] As they were when Labour indeed lost the election. The Act required equal rates of pay for the same or similar work, to be assessed by job evaluation schemes. Compliance would be voluntary until 1975 to allow time for evaluation. Claims of non-compliance could be made to an employment tribunal and successful claims compensated by up to two years' back pay. The Act overlooked women's unequal access to promotion or appointment to higher-paid work. It was further, partial, progress towards equality.

Women remained concentrated in low-status, low-paid work. Employers still argued that they were not victims of discrimination for it was rational to withhold training or promotion when women would leave to raise a family. Some evaded the new law by re-grading posts where men and women did the same work for unequal pay: a shoe store re-graded male shop assistants as 'managers', though they continued, like the lesser-paid women, to sell shoes. Ancillary workers, such as cleaners or porters, were dismissed or 'outsourced' to agency employment, enabling employers to evade 'like-work' issues among their own employees. There was gradual progress. In 1970 the median earnings of adult women full-time workers were 54% of males', by 1983 66%, following further legislation, discussed in chapter 7.

Conclusion

Women's struggle for gender equality continued, becoming more militant with the emergence from 1969 of what became the Women's Liberation Movement (WLM). In part it emerged out of the Campaign for Nuclear Disarmament (CND), the Vietnam Solidarity Campaign and various socialist organizations, created by representatives of the growing numbers of highly educated, independent women reacting against the sexism of otherwise radical males in such groups and the extent of continuing inequalities. By 1969 there were 70 local women's liberation groups in London. The first Women's Liberation Workshop was held in Oxford in 1970 and drew 600 delegates. The WLM became increasingly prominent in the 1970s, as we will see, along with other very active new social movements, especially the GLF and anti-racist movements.[50]

Women and homosexual men gained real, if incomplete, improvements in equality from an exceptional succession of liberal reforms under the 1964–70 Labour government, for many of which, including equal pay, they had long campaigned. Continuing cultural change transformed the experiences, including the number of single mothers, and attitudes of men and women. Research further extended knowledge and understanding of the extent of gender inequalities, especially in employment, and the motivation behind them, above all prejudice and discrimination, further stimulating women's activism. For the more conservative-minded, this government ushered in a 'permissive', excessively individualistic, society, destroying established values, undermining 'traditional' morality. Still in the twenty-first century the legislation of the late 1960s was blamed for the growth of single parenthood, youth crime and most of what were perceived as society's ills, causing the 'Abolition of Britain', according to *Daily Mail* journalist Peter Hitchens,[51] 'Broken Britain' in the rhetoric of David Cameron, Conservative Prime Minister 2010–16. Some believed it explained why Labour lost the 1970 election. There may be some truth in that, but undoubtedly this government contributed more to progressing gender equalities and showed greater awareness of them than its predecessors, though much remained to be done.

SEVEN

The Seventies, 1970–1979

The 1970s has a dismal reputation, still promoted by the political right, as a decade of financial crises, unemployment and industrial and political conflict driven by militant trade unions and the overspending and incompetence of the Labour government of 1974–9. It was a period of international financial difficulties, causing the first significant unemployment in Britain since the war, and of growing trade union membership and activism. But it is rarely noted that the mid- and later 1970s saw income inequality between rich and poor in Britain at its narrowest point of the century and state welfare benefits and services at their peak. Income and wealth inequalities remained substantial and poverty was never eliminated, but living standards continued to improve for many people.[1] Food banks and widespread starvation were unheard of. Two-thirds of households owned a washing machine by 1972, which eased housework, but not everything improved. Domestic standards and expectations also rose and the time women, employed or not, spent on housework hardly changed between the 1940s and 1970s.[2] Childcare remained scarce and expensive. Most husbands still contributed little to housework or childcare. Gender roles in marriage appeared to be shifting gradually, but a Gallup poll in 1973 found that still only two in three wives knew their husband's take-home pay.[3] Continuing gender inequalities led to further intense campaigns for change and to significant legislation contributing to their further, gradual decline. This was partly due to the militancy of the newly formed WLM while the GLF campaigned equally actively for further changes to the law and culture to achieve equality for homosexuals. And, again, progress owed much to a supportive Labour government.

From 1970 to 1974 Edward Heath led a Conservative government less responsive to these campaigns. His Cabinet again contained only one woman, Margaret Thatcher, as Minister for Education. Labour returned to government for the rest of the decade and advanced some of the policies for gender and other equalities that had emerged before 1970.

Changing Families

Labour's 'permissive' legislation of the 1960s stimulated change. The number of divorces shot up when the 1969 divorce reform was implemented in 1971, from 285,449 in England and Wales in 1966–70 to 812,403 in 1976–80; in Scotland 20,280 and 45,340, respectively, most following petitions by wives. Divorce was now less stigmatized, while the number of marriages declined.[4] It had long been argued that easier divorce would reduce unmarried cohabitation, but the opposite occurred. Cohabitation became more culturally acceptable, part of wider changes in attitudes and practices of sexuality and family life. The number of cohabiting couples in England and Wales is unknown before 1979, when its growth led to the collection of official statistics. Three per cent of women aged 18–49 in Great Britain were officially estimated as cohabiting in 1979, rising to 5% in 1985 and 9% in 1991; most never married.[5] The number of marriages fell substantially, from 82.3/1,000 men and 97.9/1,000 women in England and Wales in 1971 to 46.6/1,000 and 64/1,000, respectively, in 1981. The average age at marriage rose gradually, from 24.6 for men and 22.6 for women in England and Wales in 1971 to 25.4 and 23.1, respectively, in 1981,[6] with similar changes in Scotland. As increasing rates of divorce made marriage appear more precarious, people perhaps became more cautious, delaying marriage or choosing a trial period of cohabitation, while others consciously rejected official sanction for a committed partnership.

Births continued to decline from 16.9/1,000 population in 1966–70 in England and Wales to 12.2 in 1976–80; in Scotland 17.9 to 12.7; 21 to 17.5 in Northern Ireland.[7] Births to unmarried parents fell more gradually, from 21.5/1,000 women aged 15–44 in England and Wales in 1970 to 19.6 in 1980. More were registered by both parents, 45.5% in England and Wales in 1971, 58.2% in 1981, suggesting that more were in stable relationships, often cohabiting.[8] There were growing numbers of unconventional households, including gay couples, male and female, and complex families of divorced or separated and re-partnered parents, all increasingly openly acknowledged and accepted in the community, though severe criticism of 'immoral' behaviour continued.

Single-Parent Families

There were growing numbers of single-parent families, most headed by mothers. Concern about the increase in the 1960s led the Labour government in 1969 to appoint a committee to advise how best to respond. The Committee on One-Parent Families was chaired by Sir Morris Finer, a respected barrister. Members included prominent social scientists, educationists and social work specialists: four women and eight men. They carefully researched the experiences of single-parent families, taking evidence from a wide range of organizations, the most thorough exploration of the issue of the century. The Committee reported after Labour returned to government in 1974. DHSS statisticians informed it that in 1971 there were 620,000 one-parent families in Britain with over one million children. One hundred thousand families were motherless, 520,000 fatherless, 90,000 mothers were unmarried, 190,000 separated, 120,000 divorced and 120,000 widowed.[9]

It became especially concerned that 'with only a few individual exceptions, fatherless families are considerably worse-off financially than two-parent families'.[10] They were disadvantaged by the continuing unequal earning power and work opportunities of women compared with men, and the committee argued that these inequalities should be eliminated. It devoted much less attention to motherless families, 'who tend to be financially better off than fatherless families because of the higher earnings men can command'.[11] They also tended to last for a shorter time because single fathers were more likely to form new partnerships than single mothers. A problem for fatherless families was the failure of some fathers to pay due maintenance. The Committee recognized that this was often because they had to support second families and could not afford both. It also recognized that mothers could be put under excessive pressure by the Supplementary Benefits Commission (SBC, which had replaced the NAB in 1966, supposedly to give more humane support) to pursue fathers in the courts for maintenance, which was stressful, especially if the separation was due to male sexual violence, and rarely successful. It recommended that the SBC should pay an allowance to the mother and itself take legal action against the father if necessary, and a Family Court should be established to take responsibility for matrimonial and affiliation cases.

Supplementary benefit was the main source of income for one-third of mother-headed families. Most mothers lived on benefits plus part-time work due to their childcare responsibilities. The Committee proposed a guaranteed maintenance allowance (GMA), sufficient to take the family off supplementary benefit, tapered if the mother worked or had other income, up to the level of male average earnings when eligibility would end. It would include a childcare allowance and a fixed allowance for dependent children up to age 19, payable to all lone parents regardless of income. The Department of Health and Social Security (DHSS) opposed the idea due to cost. If lone fathers applied for benefits, unlike mothers they were required to register as job seekers. It was assumed that they, unlike mothers, should and could always support their families through reasonably paid full-time work, and afford childcare.

The Committee surveyed lone mothers' low earning capacity, limited employment opportunities and difficulties obtaining training to improve their skills and earning power and in finding childcare. It recommended that mothers of young children should be free to choose whether to take paid work and that flexible working and leave of absence to deal with caring responsibilities should be available to all families, especially lone parents, along with rights to maternity leave. The report argued that pervasive gender inequality hit lone mothers hardest: 'As a society we pay lip service to the ideal of equality for women while practising discrimination in the very area where it hits most.'[12]

It also surveyed lone parents' difficulties in accessing good, affordable housing. They, especially unmarried mothers, were more likely than two-parent families to share a home, usually with relatives. They all had greater difficulty than two-parent families in gaining council housing. The Committee received evidence that this was often due to prejudice and discrimination. Consequently, lone mothers too often paid high rents for inferior accommodation and were at particular risk of homelessness. The Committee acknowledged improvements since the 1964–70 Labour government had introduced national rent and rate rebate schemes and agreed with the recommendation of a 1974 circular by the Labour government, *Homelessness*, that local authorities should take responsibility for housing the homeless. It concluded that housing was 'the largest single problem of one-parent families . . . second only to financial difficulties and to a considerable extent exacerbated by them'.

It declared: 'Discrimination against lone parents in the allocation of council housing on grounds that they are "less deserving" than others should cease.'[13] Housing need should override other qualifications. The SBC and housing authorities should also help lone-parent families furnish their homes when needed.

The unanimous report described the inadequacy of social and other services for single parents and recommended improvement. It urged 'the utmost priority' for the introduction of Labour's proposed Child Benefit scheme, an improved replacement of family allowances, and that the maternity grant be paid to all mothers without contribution conditions. It recommended introduction of the GMA to give lone parents, 'whether mothers or fathers', the choice whether or not to take paid work, though 'Whenever possible children under three should not be parted from their parents for long periods.'[14] Employers should be more flexible about working hours and conditions, 'but the fundamental issue is the need to raise the pay and status of working women'. The Equal Pay Act was a start, but women should have wider employment opportunities 'so that they are no longer concentrated in a narrow range of low-paid jobs'. Employment rights should be equalized between full- and part-time workers, including a minimum period of notice, remedies for unfair dismissal and maternity leave of 'at least' 3 months paid, 3 months unpaid. Also 'radical changes are required in the sphere of curricular and careers guidance for girls in secondary schools' and employers should offer young women the same day-release opportunities as young men, extend them for both and make adequate arrangements for the training of women workers. Training arrangements should be flexible enough to allow for family responsibilities.[15] Social workers should be better trained to understand the needs of lone-parent families and there should be 'considerable expansion' of day-care services, giving priority to lone parents, taking account of their work commitments. There should be more play groups in deprived areas. Childminders and schoolteachers should be trained in awareness of the needs of children of lone parents and of pregnant schoolgirls, providing home tuition for the latter when needed.

It was a comprehensive list of recommendations with potential to reduce gender inequalities for all women, not only single mothers. Unfortunately, publication of the report in 1974 coincided with an international economic crisis, known as the 'oil shock', as Middle Eastern oil-producing countries quadrupled oil prices following war between Egypt and Israel. In Britain it caused rising inflation, unemployment and cuts to services, worsening the situation of many poorer one- and two-parent families. Barbara Castle, now Minister for Health and Social Security, read the report and approved of much of it. But, she later wrote, 'my heart sank' at the cost, which she knew the Cabinet would not accept in current circumstances.[16] She decided to focus on the party's proposed Child Benefit scheme.

The government preferred to help all families in hard times rather than risk unpopularity by singling out one-parent families. The Treasury thought the Finer proposals too expensive and advised Castle to reject the GMA. James Callaghan became Prime Minister when Wilson resigned in 1976. He opposed spending on Child Benefit and the Finer recommendations and removed Castle from the Ministry. But, after tense debates in the Cabinet, he gave in to pressure from the CPAG and other campaigners and Child Benefit was phased in from 1977 to 1979. It was worth £4 per child per week by 1979, more generous than family allowances, designed to reduce poverty in all families. It was paid for all children in every family and partly funded by replacing the child tax allowance in place since 1911, which benefitted only better-off taxpayers, as the CPAG had advocated.

A group formed to campaign for implementation of the Finer proposals, the Finer Joint Action Committee (FJAC), composed of 28 groups involved with issues of welfare and poverty, including the NCUMC, the CPAG and the homelessness charity Shelter (also formed in the mid-1960s). They unsuccessfully supported implementation of the GMA but persuaded the government to grant children in one-parent families an additional 50p in Child Benefit.[17] Single mothers also benefitted from the 1977 Housing (Homeless Persons) Act, which made them eligible for council housing if they became involuntarily homeless due to marriage break-up or any other cause, for which women's groups had campaigned for some time.[18] These changes eased the difficult lives of many single mothers.

The Women's Liberation Movement

Throughout the 1970s, gender inequalities were challenged by the growing WLM, more publicly and noisily than by any women's campaigns since the suffragettes, on whom the WLM consciously modelled itself. It described itself as the 'second wave' of feminism, in the belief that women had been largely inactive since the 'first wave' partially gained the vote in 1918. This mistaken but widespread belief arose largely because, until the early 1970s, women's history was neglected and there was little published research on women's movements since the suffrage campaign. Since 1918 women's activism had been quieter, arousing less publicity, but was extensive and often effective, as we have seen, but this was little known in the 1970s. The WLM was born at an Oxford conference of the radical History Workshop movement in 1969, among women infuriated by men radical enough to attend the event who sneered at women's history. Writing women into history became one of the WLM's objectives and achievements, notably the work of historian Sheila Rowbotham who initiated the first meeting.[19] It modelled itself on the public activism of the suffragettes and, like the growing number of other contemporary radical movements, preferred direct public action to patient lobbying and was critical of, or hostile to, conventional party politics, not expecting it to deliver significant improvements to equality.

Similar movements emerged in other countries, including the US, but the UK WLM was among the leaders and further to the left than much US feminism. A national conference met annually from 1970 to 1978, attendance peaking at 3,000 in 1977. Feminism became public and flamboyant again, notably when women dramatically interrupted the televised Miss World beauty contest at the Royal Albert Hall, London, in 1970, shouting 'We're not beautiful, we're not ugly, we're angry.' This followed a similar demonstration against a Miss America contest in New York in 1968. At this event women threw bras, nylons, false eyelashes and other items into a bin, challenging the false images they believed these consumer items imposed on women. They intended to burn them but did not. This seems to have given birth to a hostile media image of feminists as 'bra-burners', ugly, dungaree-wearing man-haters, as prevalent in the UK tabloids as in the US. Like previous negative stereotypes of feminism, it was an image which sometimes alienated even women sympathetic to gender equality, making them reluctant to identify as feminists.

The WLM was a movement mainly of younger unmarried women operating alongside but, initially at least, with little apparent contact with the many established organizations of older women which remained active. The international character and impact of this new wave of women's activism was signalled in 1977 when the UN instituted an annual International Women's Day on 8 March to promote women's rights. The movement in Britain brought hidden issues into public view and new groups of women into activism, reflecting and advancing cultural change.

Black and Asian women created the Organisation of Women of Asian and African Descent (OWAAD) in 1978 and Southall Black Sisters (1979), Brixton Black Women, Liverpool Black Sisters, Baheno Women's Organization in Leicester, and groups elsewhere in Wales, Scotland and England. They campaigned against restrictive immigration laws, virginity tests imposed on women immigrants, domestic and sexual violence, and discrimination in employment and other spheres, which these women experienced due to both race and gender. They resisted marginalization by male-dominated anti-racist organizations and felt equally excluded by the white-dominated WLM. This stimulated their growth and they aroused the WLM's sensitivity to race. OWAAD organized the first national Black women's conference in 1979; 250 women attended.[20] Lesbian women also felt sidelined. They protested at WLM conferences and increasingly organized to promote their interests. There was continuing neglect of the many disadvantages of older women, especially low pensions and poverty. They were overlooked by young and middle-aged women. Age discrimination was as pervasive in the culture as gender and race discrimination, and older women did not yet organize on their own behalf.

Another problem suffered disproportionately by women, domestic violence, had been exposed intermittently since the 1860s when Frances Power Cobbe campaigned against 'wife torture'.[21] But still in the 1970s it was rarely publicly discussed and upholders of the justice system, including police, refused to take it seriously, insisting that 'domestic disputes' were private, beyond their powers to intervene. This was publicly challenged by Erin Pizzey who in 1971 started a support group in west London for married women with children, not as a WLM activist but because she thought her local WLM group too unconcerned with the needs of mothers like herself. She was not a feminist, she wrote in her memoir, because her affluent parents (her father was a diplomat) were both violent towards her and her siblings as children, convincing her that women could be as vicious as men. Her concern about domestic violence, especially its effects on children, grew partly from personal experience reinforced by victims revealing their experiences at her meetings. Her home became a refuge. Soon forty women and children were crammed into four small rooms and Pizzey was threatened with prosecution for overcrowding. Publicity brought a private donation enabling them to take a larger house in Chiswick, west London, which also became overcrowded. The resulting publicity about 'battered wives', as they were known, and the failure of the police to support them, along with demonstrations by Pizzey and her supporters, gained her a grant from the DHSS, under Castle, in 1974 to support the families. Shortly after, her book *Scream Quietly or the Neighbours Will Hear* brought further publicity, and the Women's Aid Federation (WAF) was formed to promote the campaign. Volunteers founded more refuges and Pizzey and her allies squatted in empty buildings, joining a wider contemporary squatting movement protesting at rising housing costs and homelessness.[22]

Pizzey opened up a serious issue and showed the way forward, but she had a tense relationship with the WLM and increasingly with WAF. Activists felt she wanted too much control and personal publicity. In 1975 she stormed out of WAF's annual general meeting and severed her connection with the Chiswick refuge. WAF drew close to the WLM, whose supporters founded and staffed refuges throughout the country, raising funds from charities, private donors and central and local government, revealing the shocking dimensions of a long-hidden problem. By 1980 there were about 200 refuges. The WLM campaigned for legal reform. In 1974 a Private Member's Bill, introduced by Labour MP Jo Richardson, led the Commons to appoint a Select Committee on Violence in Marriage. This noted that the law allowed courts to grant injunctions prohibiting men from molesting their female partners (and occasionally vice versa), on pain of imprisonment, and could order them to leave the family home, but it was rarely implemented. Women did not always seek protection from the justice system, fearing reprisals from their partners and rejection by the police and the courts. Police were still reluctant to act and lacked powers to arrest perpetrators who breached injunctions.

The Domestic Violence and Matrimonial Proceedings Act, 1976, which followed, made domestic violence a specific offence for the first time. Courts could punish violence against a partner, married or unmarried, or a child, and exclude violent partners from the family home; from 1978 magistrates' courts could issue personal protection orders and exclusion orders, though not to unmarried partners.[23] The law was imperfect but better than anything before. Then the 1977 Housing (Homeless Persons) Act removed a barrier to victims leaving violent partners by obliging local authorities to house them and others who were involuntarily homeless, also following women's campaigns, as we have seen. But, as we will see, domestic violence did not end or even evidently diminish, remaining severe into the next century.[24] Still, police did not always take complaints seriously and WAF and women's refuges continued to support victims until they were severely reduced following Conservative public spending cuts from 2010. Domestic violence continued to be a serious issue and focus of women's campaigns despite the legislation.

The WLM also raised awareness of sexual violence, including rape, another long-standing form of violence much stigmatized but rarely publicly discussed, mainly against women, though the GLF publicized attacks on gay men. There was no evidence that it was increasing in any form, but the incidence appeared high, and victims often failed to complain, especially about rape, fearing reprisals from the perpetrator, feeling shame or that they would be disbelieved and denigrated. With good reason. Police and the courts still did not always treat reports of rape seriously but blamed the victim, for drunkenness or wearing 'provocative' clothing, rather than the perpetrator.[25] The first rape crisis centre opened in north London in 1976 providing counselling, refuge and support, established by feminists, funded by charities and a radical local authority. Sixteen centres plus rape crisis phone lines were established across Britain by 1981. From 1977 women's 'Reclaim the Night' marches walked through streets at night asserting their right to walk unmolested after dark, in response to another all-too-frequent experience of women, which also continued into the twenty-first century, discussed in chapter 10.

One outcome of publicizing sexual violence was more frequent, explicit and sensational coverage of rape trials by the popular press, distressing the victims and creating further obstacles to their coming forward. In response, the Sexual Offences (Amendment) Act, 1976, introduced by Labour backbencher Robin Corbett, guaranteed anonymity in reports of court proceedings for victims alleging rape, but not for the perpetrator.[26] Yet it continued to be a major hazard for women still in the early twenty-first century, as described in chapter 10. Only one attack in five was reported to the police because the victims were traumatized, feared reprisals or publicity, were uncertain of support and feared blame from police or the courts, still all too realistically. The legal changes in the 1970s made clear that domestic violence and rape were punishable crimes, some perpetrators were punished, and the issues were made public, but these problems severely affecting women did not disappear or even noticeably decline to the present, so far as can be judged from the available evidence.

The WLM also campaigned, with little success, for men to share domestic work and for 24-hour nurseries to assist parents required to work 'unsocial' hours, including low-paid women night-time office cleaners, and they protested about such work conditions. They also unsuccessfully sought abortion on demand, without the obligatory agreement of two doctors which was hard to obtain in some, especially strongly Catholic, areas. Groups were formed to promote equal opportunities in specific occupations, including Women in Media, Women in Publishing. New feminist journals included *Spare Rib*, founded in 1972. A successful publisher, Virago, was established and run by women from 1973, reprinting as low-cost paperbacks books by neglected women authors and publishing new works by and about women past and present, providing an outlet for the growing work on women's history in the 1980s. The WLM also liberated women's creativity in many other spheres, including theatre, film and fashion.

The WLM had some real achievements, but as it grew, so did divisions, including race and class tensions in a mainly white, middle-class movement of younger women from which many, especially working-class, women felt excluded.[27] The final WLM conference in 1978 descended into chaos following conflict between 'revolutionary feminists' who opposed co-operation with men, and the rest, yet pressure for progress to full gender equality continued.

Inequality at Work

Action on gender inequality was still much needed, including in the workplace. Under Heath's Conservative government, MPs introduced a succession of Bills aimed at reducing gender discrimination at work. One drafted by Nancy Seear (now a Baroness and a prominent Liberal) led to a House of Lords Select Committee in 1972 which heard how little the attitudes of employers and managers were changing. The CBI and the Engineering Employers' Federation still argued that training most women was not worthwhile due to their short stay in the labour market, while insisting that they opposed discrimination and prejudice. They asserted that it hardly existed in industry. But the largely male Institute of Personnel Management provided clear evidence that it did exist and accounted for the small numbers of women in top positions, including in personnel management. They were supported by a memorandum from the Department of Employment on 'Sex discrimination in employment and training', which provided statistics demonstrating women's continued concentration in low-paid, low-skilled sectors.

Baroness Edith Summerskill asked the TUC representatives before the committee why they had done so little to achieve gender equality. They pointed out how difficult it was for even well-intentioned union leaders to influence their branches in these matters. Mrs Marie Patterson was Women's Officer of the Transport and General Workers' Union (TGWU) and in 1975 became the fourth female President of the TUC, two signs that trade union attitudes to women were shifting, but slowly, as she informed the committee. She described the resistance to the process currently under way to persuade bus driver branches of the TGWU to accept female drivers. The think tank Political and Economic Planning (PEP) drew upon research it sponsored in 1966–71 on women in top jobs to provide evidence of discrimination in promotions and appointments to top professional posts, including university professorships. They argued that discrimination was hard to prove, but the disparity between the numbers of women at the top and bottom levels of most professions left discrimination, conscious or unconscious, as the only likely explanation.

The Labour government from 1974 implemented some of the policies it had developed before it lost the 1970 election. The Sex Discrimination Act, 1975, tackled some inequalities by outlawing, in principle, discrimination in employment, education, advertising and the provision of housing, goods or services. Women were now allowed to make financial arrangements, including holding mortgages, on the same terms as men, and at last married women no longer needed their husband's agreement to undertake hire purchase or other financial arrangements even when they had independent earnings. The Equal Opportunities Commission (EOC) was established to investigate complaints and support women claiming discrimination, as it did. The legislation persuaded medical schools to remove the quotas restricting women's entry: by the early 1990s, women increased from a small minority to over 50% of students. It put pressure on other professions and institutions and encouraged women to enter them. The proportion of female lawyers rose from 4% in 1971 to 27% in 1990.[28] Most male-only Oxford and Cambridge Colleges admitted women, and women students at Oxford and Cambridge increased from 15 and 10%, respectively, in 1975 to over 50% by the 1990s. In 1975 also the Equal Pay Act came fully into force, though pay equality remained distant.[29]

Twice as many women as men joined unions in the 1970s, partly because the number of female public sector workers, in a highly unionized sector, increased to almost four million by 1979. Labour increased state funding for public services as it brought the post-war welfare state to its peak provision of funding and services, increasing women's opportunities. More workers from Black, Asian and Minority Ethnic (BAME) groups engaged in disputes and joined unions, and unions became more responsive to their needs. A much-publicized example was the strike in 1976 of more than 130, mainly Asian, female staff at the Grunwick photo-processing firm in Willesden, north London, challenging pay and conditions, including forced overtime and the owner's refusal to allow them to join a union. They were supported by the TUC and by white workers, feminists and Labour politicians.[30] The strike lasted for two years but failed, signalling the limits to union power and the strength of opposition to it. The militantly right-wing owner, supported by increasingly assertive right-wing political groups, was intransigent. Such groups were growing, part of a rising international neoliberal tide.[31] At Grunwick, 130 workers were sacked, none were reinstated, despite a government-appointed committee headed by Lord Justice Scarman recommending that they should be, and no union was recognized.

Responding to women's activism and union membership, in 1975 the TUC adopted the Charter for Working Women. This demanded equal pay, equal opportunities at work, 18 weeks' paid maternity leave, a minimum wage, increased family allowances and an end to discrimination against women in the administration of social security and income tax.[32] Labour was anxious to conciliate the unions to prevent strikes and conflict and introduced the Employment Protection Act, 1975, largely drafted by the TUC. This extended employee rights to appeal against unfair dismissal and trade union rights to recognition by employers, and established an Advisory, Conciliation and Arbitration Service (ACAS) for neutral settlement of disputes. In victories for female trade unionism, introducing rights already normal in the EC, which Britain joined in 1973, it became illegal to dismiss a woman because she was pregnant (long commonplace, and it continued) and statutory maternity leave was introduced at last. It granted female employees with two years' full-time service or five years part-time (working at least 16 hours per week) the right to eleven weeks' leave before the birth and three weeks after, at 90% of normal pay for six weeks, then statutory sick pay, and the right to reinstatement up to 29 weeks after the birth in similar, though not necessarily the same, work as before. These were inferior to the rights of women in many other EC countries and those proposed by Finer, the TUC and many others, but were further real, though imperfect, improvements to British women's employment rights and incomes.[33]

More women joined the labour force through the 1970s, though a high proportion, mainly mothers, still worked part-time with fewer employment rights than full-time workers. More women became ambitious for careers, though fulfilment remained difficult. Increasingly opposition was expressed to girls/women being conditioned to believe that housework was their responsibility, whatever else they might aspire to in their lives. Ann Oakley's influential sociological study *Housewife* (1974), arising from her own experience as a married mother of two, argued that 'the housewife role must be abolished . . . gender roles must be abolished'. Mothers should stop training their daughters in housework because it was 'directly opposed to the possibility of self-actualization'.[34] The WLM supported the international 'Wages for Housework' campaign for its recognition as real work, unaware of how widespread this view had been among British feminists long before, led by Eleanor Rathbone as we saw in chapter 2. The new movement was established in 1972 and was very active in Britain and internationally throughout the 1970s and 1980s, continuing into the twenty-first century. Wages for Lesbians and Black Women for Wages for Housework were also established in Britain. It later developed internationally into a campaign for payment for all forms of caring, for farmers caring for the planet as well as carers for people. Some feminists, however, resisted what they saw as encouragement to women to be housewives and inviting capitalism into the home. Having grown up in the post-war welfare state with higher expectations than earlier generations, they were encouraged by the legislation for equal pay and against sex discrimination at work to believe that they had a right to paid employment if they wished and to equal opportunities, beliefs that inspired campaigns for further equalities, including gender equality in responsibility for housework.[35]

Women's opportunities were limited partly by their continuing under-representation in higher education. Still, more girls than boys left school without qualifications, though the proportion of female university students in a growing student population rose from 28% in 1971 to 38% in 1979.[36] They were still concentrated in arts and social sciences, few in the natural sciences, fewer still in engineering and few women held academic posts, especially at the higher levels. Women remained the great majority of students in teacher training colleges.[37] More older women compensated for their limited opportunities by attending universities, including the Open University, but women still had fewer opportunities than men to gain further training at work.

About 45% of married women were employed in 1970, 60% in 1980. In 1977, 5% of mothers of children under five were in full-time employment, 22% part-time.[38] By the end of the 1970s one in four mothers re-entered work within a year of giving birth, one in six within six months, often assisted by maternity leave. Part-time work expanded especially fast, mainly at lower levels. By 1977 more than two-thirds of all female employees, 70% of wage-earning mothers, worked part-time.

Working mothers were not always motivated by aspirations to independence and equality. Many were driven by high inflation following the 'oil shock', and by male unemployment. In 1975 unemployment in Britain rose above one million for the first time since the war, where it remained until 1979. It was mainly due to the 'oil shock' and other international pressures and especially affected the manufacturing and mining sectors, which were declining. There were growing, often part-time, though low-status and low-paid, opportunities for women in the expanding service sector, including hospitality. Their work might be the family's main protection against poverty, especially in lone-mother families. It was estimated in 1971 that about two million women were the chief earners in their household. Their need for employment made them vulnerable to exploitation. Employers benefitted from employing mothers part-time for low pay with no rights to benefits such as holiday pay. If they worked fewer than 16 hours per week they had limited protection from unfair dismissal and did not qualify for maternity leave and pay. Low-paid homeworking revived in certain industries.

Part-time working was still most common in unskilled jobs; the much smaller numbers of women in the professions and management were more likely to work full-time. Even in the largely female public sector professions, such as social services, women seeking part-time work and flexible hours had access only to low-status jobs at low pay.[39] On average part-time women workers earned 58% of men's full-time hourly rates in the early 1980s, 80% of the average hourly wages of full-time women workers.[40] For much part-time work it was difficult to prove pay discrimination because no men did comparable work. The Low Pay Unit, a voluntary body established to defend low-paid workers and press for improvement, pointed out that in only 3% of occupations dominated by men were weekly average earnings below £40 compared with 75% of jobs typically held by women.[41] In 1978 the TUC again called for government action to end low pay and provide greater health and safety protection for the growing numbers of female homeworkers. It began to unionize homeworkers and gained some improvements in their conditions.

Access to training gradually expanded for women returners. The Sex Discrimination Act forced employers to open male-only courses to women and the Labour government increased funding for initiatives targeting older returners. New Opportunities for Women (NOW) provided short courses aimed at building women's confidence and skills for professional employment, and Wider Opportunities for Women (WOW) provided placements in manual and semi-skilled jobs. They tended to focus on traditional women's work – education, clerical work, typing, catering – but they could be helpful. New women's organizations pushed for equal opportunities in many highly skilled fields, including publishing, media, banking and finance, medicine, dentistry, the civil service, management and architecture. Women's share of these occupations crept upwards, though they remained fewest at higher levels. By 1980 women accounted for almost 25% of practising doctors, 17% of dentists, 27% of the senior civil service and 21% of newly qualified accountants. The number of female solicitors doubled to over 7% in 1977 and they became over 8% of barristers.[42] Fewer women sought to enter teaching. Demand for teachers fell with the birth rate, training budgets were cut, and other opportunities opened.

Lack of childcare remained a major obstacle to mothers in all occupations. Local authority childcare remained sparse. The number of nursery places fell further in the 1970s to approximately 30,000 in 1977 – enough for one in thirty pre-school children overall. Numbers varied from place to place, highest in inner cities and districts with traditions of women's work. In Islington, north London, there was one place for every 16 children under five, in Oxfordshire just three council nurseries with 95 places in an area with roughly 40,000 under-5s.[43] Women pressed for more places with little effect. WLM groups established nurseries, some gaining funding from sympathetic local authorities. High-earning women could still pay for care at home, though they complained about the cost. But most mothers could not afford this and took their children to paid childminders, a much cheaper option, or relied on relatives – still grandmothers very often – or friends. Women in the growing numbers of multi-generational South Asian households benefitted most from family care. They had a high rate of return to work and much need for the earnings given the poverty prevailing in their communities.

The Labour government commissioned a report published in 1978 on services for the children of working mothers. It assumed that significant numbers of mothers of under-5s were working and would continue to do so, and proposed that the government should 'take a fundamental look' at how it supported them, and that serious investment was required in pre-school day-care, nursery education and after-school and holiday care for older children.[44] The government was not persuaded at a time of heavy retrenchment in government spending due to financial crises, but this was not the only reason. The Home Secretary, Merlyn Rees, wrote to Prime Minister Callaghan in July 1978 expressing the familiar objection that following the report's recommendations 'would raise important questions of principle about the extent to which the Government ought to finance programmes designed to make it easier for women to go out to work'.[45] Some attitudes never changed.

No action followed. Employers provided workplace creches only when they had difficulty recruiting full-time female staff. The Pre-School Playgroup Association expanded fast in the 1970s to meet the needs of children and mothers for activities and company but was of limited help to most working mothers though it provided work for a minority. The stress and difficulty of finding affordable childcare was greatest for single mothers. In 1971 150,000 of them were at work, half employed full-time, and the numbers continued to grow. Nationally, 5% of all primary earners in households had earnings below £20 per week, in lone-parent families 70%. The Finer Committee noted the shortage of pre-school and after-school care provided by local authorities, although, by law since 1946, children of lone parents had priority for such care. It recommended enforcement of this requirement. Nothing changed. Supportive of women's rights though Labour was in many respects, it was persistently unresponsive to the need for childcare and gave very limited support to working mothers.

Gay Liberation

Campaigns for equal rights for male homosexuals were equally active. The British GLF was formed in autumn 1970, following the Stonewall riots in New York after police raided a gay bar, though it had roots in the longer history of campaigns for homosexual rights in Britain and the somewhat greater openness following reform in 1967. Two students organized the first meeting, at the LSE, attended by nine people. A few months later, 400–500 attended weekly meetings. Like other 'new social movements' of the time, the GLF defined itself as a revolutionary collective organization challenging oppression, rejecting the caution of older groups like the Homosexual Law Reform Society. It aimed to be a mass movement organizing public events: 'Gay Days' in London parks; 'zapping' gatherings of opponents, like a rally by the fundamentalist Christian Festival of Light in 1971. Also in 1971, lesbians invaded the WLM conference platform, believing that it marginalized them.

The GLF ran the first Gay Pride march in London in 1972 involving 1,000 people. They supported campaigns by women's and anti-racist groups and marched with the TUC against Heath's restrictions on unions. They supported miners on strike in 1984 with a 'Pits and Perverts' campaign, in 2014 made into a successful film. In 1972 they launched the weekly *Gay News*. The GLF encouraged individuals to 'come out', acknowledging their sexuality publicly. The term 'Gay' (Good As You) became international. But the GLF also experienced divisions: lesbians felt their interests were ignored by male homosexuals, as did members of minority ethnic groups, some of whom faced exceptional prejudice within their communities.

The cultural 'coming out' encouraged by the GLF left a lasting legacy while other groups expanded. The Campaign for Homosexual Equality (CHE) became the largest gay organization in Britain by 1972, preferring orthodox lobbying and appeals to the law. Lesbians organized separately, publishing *Sappho* magazine from 1972, holding regular meetings and forming Action for Lesbian Parents in 1976, seeking rights to custody of their children, which they could lose due to their lesbianism if they left a heterosexual partnership.[46] Local counselling and befriending services and helplines for gay men and women grew, especially in London and larger cities. The London Gay Switchboard, established in 1974, received 200,000 calls in its first year. By 1976 all major political parties and professions, Jewish and Christian faith groups, theatre and cinema organizations, had gay support groups.[47]

Lesbian and gay experiences and the location of services and support groups varied from place to place within Britain, shaped by the local economy, culture, population, local events and the attitudes of local government, as were most forms of inequality, though the variations are not always on record or easy to trace.[48] Brighton was known as a 'seaside "Gay Mecca"' since at least the 1930s, and still in 2024.[49] Leeds became a centre for lesbian politics, especially following a traumatic series of murders of women in the area by Peter Sutcliffe, from 1975 to 1981, arousing anger at misogyny and violence against women and fuelling radical lesbianism in the city.[50]

Polls suggested that public support for homosexual rights was gradually growing, but homophobia persisted everywhere, promoted especially stridently by Mary Whitehouse, a prominent conservative activist and passionate critic of the 'permissive society'. In 1977 she brought a successful prosecution against *Gay News* under the ancient Blasphemy Act, for publishing a poem, 'The Love That Dares to Speak Its Name', in which a Roman centurion expressed homosexual fantasies about the crucified Christ.[51] A week later a gay man was murdered in north London, another in Liverpool the following year. An opinion poll for *Gay News* in 1975 found general support for the 1967 legislation but little for further change.

Open transgender campaigns also emerged for the first time alongside other new movements, demanding social acceptance for a condition not previously discussed in public, for improved medical treatment and abolition of legal disabilities concerning marriage and birth certificates for those who changed gender. The campaigns had little success but provided support for transgender people and publicity for their difficulties, though it was still very limited. They gained some respectability when, in 1974, Jan Morris, a respected author and travel writer, published an unprecedented account of her male-to-female transition.[52]

Conclusion

There was no gender revolution in the 1970s but a steady growth in understanding of the range and effects of inequalities and real if incomplete improvements due to Labour legislation and pressure from women, especially in the WLF, including on women's pay, education and work opportunities and legal rights and protection against physical and sexual violence. But women continued to experience disadvantages such as lack of childcare and limited employment opportunities. Inequalities were more openly and frequently discussed and analysed. Many young women grew up with higher expectations, encouraged by parents as it became harder to assume that marriage was their only future, as divorce increased. There were even more gradual shifts in the rights, experiences and cultural acceptance of gay men, lesbians and, especially, transgender people, who gradually became publicly visible for the first time, though all of these groups continued to face profound hostility from some. All gender groups continued to demand greater rights.

EIGHT

The Lady's Not for Equality, 1979–1997

The UK's first woman Prime Minister, Margaret Thatcher from 1979 to 1990, was emphatically not a feminist and she permitted few, reluctant, moves towards gender equality. It is unlikely that the Conservative Party would have elected as leader an explicit feminist who was not a conventional Conservative – surely an impossible combination – though some women took her success as a hopeful sign that equality of opportunity was approaching, without supporting her politics. Her election as leader in 1974, after Heath lost two general elections, was widely surprising, including among Conservatives. It owed much to the absence of strong male candidates.

Nor did racial inequality decline or gay rights advance significantly under her rule or that of her Conservative successor, John Major from 1990 to 1997, while social and economic inequalities soared. Such advances as there were owed little to government action, which rather held them back. Thatcher was convinced that inequalities were natural and desirable, incentivizing people to work hard and strive to do better. She believed sincerely that women's inequalities in the workplace were not due to discrimination but to women's own lack of effort, that she had achieved success through her own efforts and others could do likewise. She told a group of children in a TV programme in 1982:

> I think most of us got to our position in life without Women's Lib and we got here, not by saying 'you've got to have more women doing so-and-so' but saying 'look we've got the qualifications, why shouldn't we have as much chance as a man?' And you'll find that so many male bastions were conquered in that way, whereas Women's Lib, I think, has been rather strident, concentrated on things that don't really matter and, dare I say it, being rather unfeminine. Don't you think that?[1]

She was generalizing from her own unusual experience. Daughter of a shopkeeper in Grantham, Lincolnshire, she gained a place at a grammar school, then, in 1943, a scholarship to Somerville College, Oxford, to study chemistry, which, as we have seen, was unusual and discouraged among girls. After graduating she worked as a research chemist, then stood, unsuccessfully, as a Conservative candidate in the elections of 1950 and 1951. In 1950 she was the youngest Conservative candidate in the country. In 1951 she married wealthy Denis Thatcher who funded her to study for the Bar, for which she qualified in 1953, the year her twins were born. She failed to be selected for the 1955 election but in 1959 was elected for Finchley, north London, which she represented for the rest of her career.[2] It was an unusually successful career for any woman at that time, especially one born in the lower middle class, success she evidently thought all women could emulate. John Major also came from a lower-middle-class background, but did not go to university and worked his way up through a successful banking career before taking up politics. He claimed to support gender equality and gave it some limited assistance.

Thatcher in Power

Only one other woman was appointed, briefly, to the Cabinet throughout Thatcher's 11 years in office: the unelected Baroness Janet Young was Chancellor of the Duchy of Lancaster, October 1981–April 1982, then Lord Privy Seal to June 1983. The number of women MPs slowly increased: in 1983, 13 Conservatives and 10 Labour, in 1987 more than ever before, 17 Conservative, 21 Labour, two Liberals and one for the Scottish National Party, a modest contribution to the international rise in elected women in the 1980s. In 1991 women represented 38.5% of members of the Finnish lower house, 20.4% in Germany, both with proportional representation (PR) electoral systems which assisted diversity in representation and certainly benefitted women.[3] They made up just 9% of Westminster MPs, elected under the UK's first-past-the-post system. By the late 1980s there was growing pressure from women in the Labour Party and the TUC for positive action to increase the number of female MPs. Emma Nicholson, Vice-Chairman (*sic*) of the Conservative Party, 1983–7, soon to defect to the Liberal Democrats, complained repeatedly about local parties' reluctance to select women and the leadership's lack of interest in this inequality.[4]

Margaret Thatcher was unresponsive. Women volunteered as candidates for all parties, but were still rarely selected for winnable seats,[5] as Thatcher herself had experienced in the early 1950s.[6] In other respects, much was changing in British culture and politics. Under her premiership more women voters shifted from Conservatism, dividing between the opposition parties, part of a growing international 'gender gap' in voting as men were more attracted to increasingly influential neoliberalism, hostile to a powerful central state, while women resisted its effects, especially welfare cuts. There were no MPs from ethnic minority backgrounds until four Black MPs were elected in 1987, all for Labour, one, Diane Abbott, female.[7] Thatcher was well aware of another cultural change, the growing influence of TV and press scrutiny in politics, especially of an unusually prominent woman. Before the election she took elocution lessons to lower and project her voice and avoid the 'shrillness' with which female speakers were stereotyped, while otherwise presenting a stereotypically middle-class female image. She was advised on hair and clothing styles, things not required of male politicians.

Families

Thatcher strongly promoted her vision of the 'traditional family', based on life-long marriage, gender division and intergenerational support. She wrongly believed the latter to be in decline. Nevertheless, divorce continued to rise to unprecedented levels; more children than ever before were born to unmarried, cohabiting parents; more openly gay partners, female and male, lived together, increasingly with children. Despite much government rhetoric about 'preserving' the family, never had families changed so much so fast or so many unconventional families lived openly together.[8] Births outside marriage rose from 11.5% of all UK births in 1980 to 28% in 1990, 33.6% in 1995. In 1995, 78% were registered by both parents, often living together. In 1980 there were 940,000 single-parent families, one in eight families, with 1.5 million children; one in five families with 2.1 million children in 1992, overwhelmingly headed by mothers. Sixty per cent of the mothers were divorced or separated, 33% never married, 7% widowed. Financial security remained difficult for them. Sixty-six per cent of the mothers relied upon means-tested Income Support (IS), introduced by Heath's government, replacing

Supplementary Benefits but not more generous, and it declined in value under Thatcher.[9] They clustered in poorer districts. Much changed in the 1980s, not always in directions chosen by Thatcher.

Over-65s were a growing proportion of the population – 15% in 1984 – as average life expectancy grew and births declined.[10] Women still lived longer. In 1981 average male life expectancy at birth was 71, at 65, 78; for women, 77 and 82. Better-off men at 65 could expect to stay healthy to age 75, women to 77. The poorest of both genders had weaker health and died on average 10–15 years earlier than the better-off.[11] Inequality between rich and poor increased in the 1980s in all age groups, affecting all aspects of life. Concern revived about the 'burden' of an ageing society, again visualizing a shrinking younger workforce having to support the health, pension and care costs of a growing, dependent, older generation. Enabling women to remain active in the labour market, increasing the working population, was one possible solution. But not all older people were helpless dependants. The growing numbers of fit, comfortably off older people, male and female, made major, underestimated, contributions to society and the economy, continuing in work, paying taxes, as consumers, supporting younger relatives financially and making substantial contributions to voluntary action. Grandparents, especially grandmothers, still provided childcare for their working daughters, due to the inadequacy of publicly provided childcare,[12] while younger relatives, mainly female, provided most of the care for frail older people, often at considerable personal cost, increasingly as public services deteriorated under Thatcher.

Nevertheless, Thatcher remained convinced that 'the family' was declining from a past ideal state, undermined, she asserted, by the welfare state, 'permissiveness' and general moral deterioration. In 1982 a Cabinet Family Policy Group was appointed 'to identify characteristics of behaviour and attitude which the government might legitimately hope to see adults possess, or, conversely, avoid'.[13] A leaked paper suggested this might include 'what more could be done to encourage families, in the widest sense, to assume responsibilities taken on by the state, for example responsibility for the disabled, the elderly, unemployed 16-year-olds', overlooking the reality that such responsibilities were conventional in most families, mainly carried by women. The paper asked, 'Do present policies for supporting single parents strike the right balance between ensuring adequate child support to prevent poverty and encouraging sensible and self-reliant behaviour by adults?'[14]

Other leaked government papers described supporting one-parent families as 'subsidizing illegitimacy and immorality'. Thatcher later recalled:

> There was great pressure, which I had to fight hard to resist, to provide tax reliefs or subsidies for childcare. This would, of course, have swung the emphasis further towards discouraging women from staying at home. I believed that it was possible – as I had – to bring up a family while working, as long as one was willing to make a great effort to organize one's time properly and with some extra help. But I did not believe that it was fair to those mothers who chose to stay at home and bring up their families on the one income to give tax reliefs to those who went out to work and had two incomes.[15]

With a millionaire husband, she was better able to afford 'some extra help' than most families. Publicly funded childcare continued to deteriorate, while more mothers needed to work because male unemployment shot up. As early as 1982 total unemployment reached over three million, the highest in the twentieth century so far, partly because manufacturing and mining continued to decline and were not replaced.

Poverty rose, especially among women, while (mainly male) top salaries, especially in finance, climbed and income and wealth inequalities grew. Lone-mother and other low-income families suffered further as publicly funded support declined. Among other cuts, from 1980 local authorities were no longer required to provide school meals. In 1986 benefits were reduced for 18–25-year-olds, in 1988 withdrawn from 16–18-year-olds, along with Child Benefit from those not in full-time education or training, on the assumption that their families could support them, which the poorest often could not without help. Yet Thatcher became

> increasingly concerned . . . that . . . we could only get to the roots of crime and much else besides by concentrating on strengthening the traditional family. All the evidence – statistical and anecdotal – pointed to the breakdown of families as the starting point for a range of social ills.[16]

There was no such evidence; rather, the major cause of problems among younger, and older, people, including 'family breakdown', was poverty, which increased. Thatcher blamed Labour, the 'prophets of the permissive society ... who robbed a generation of their birth-right ... where did the hooligans, the louts and the yobs on the late-night trains learn their contempt for the security of the law-abiding citizen?'[17] Polls suggested that most British people were more positive about family life. The much-respected British Social Attitudes survey found high levels of contact and mutual support within families and changing expectations of gender roles. In 1984, 43% of respondents agreed that 'A husband's job is to earn the money; a wife's job is to look after the home and family.' By 1989, only 25% agreed.[18]

Still in 1988 the Chancellor, Nigel Lawson, claimed that the benefit system encouraged family break-up, and Thatcher referred to the 'growing problem of young girls who deliberately become pregnant in order to jump the housing queue and gain welfare payments'.[19] This accusation was beloved of the right-wing tabloid press though all research dismissed it.[20] More single mothers now had council homes, but only because this had been almost impossible before the 1977 Housing Act, discussed in the preceding chapter, obliged local authorities to house them if they were otherwise homeless. Few were teenagers. Teenage pregnancy fell slightly through the 1980s, though it was higher in the UK than elsewhere in western Europe. Any woman convinced by the rhetoric and desperate enough to become pregnant to get a council home was likely to be disappointed. As the council housing stock shrank following Thatcher's policy from 1980 of selling it off to tenants at reduced prices, without replacement, she would be allocated, at best, a substandard dwelling, sometimes a bed-and-breakfast room, with some sad outcomes, including

> Fatima Ali [who] cares for her seven-year-old child on her own. She lived in a ground floor council flat and was subjected to severe racial harassment. The flat was burgled six times, windows were broken, and excrement and rubbish were pushed through her letter box.[21]

Single-mother disadvantage was deepened by racism. The sale of council houses increased homelessness and poverty as private rents rose to meet growing demand. Shortage of affordable childcare made it as hard as ever for many single mothers to work. If they did so, they were often low-paid; if not, social security reforms reduced their incomes. Thatcher's welfare cuts increased social inequality for men and women, but more women suffered poverty, along with their children.

Thatcher became convinced that 'feckless fathers' caused the poverty of many single-mother families, contrary to the common tendency to blame the mothers. She later wrote that she 'was appalled by the way in which men fathered a child and then absconded, leaving the single mothers – and the taxpayer – to foot the bill for their irresponsibility'.[22] In the late 1980s only one lone mother in three received regular maintenance from the father. Not all non-payers were 'feckless' but were unemployed, very young and low-paid, and/or had a second family to support. Social security policy had long assumed that a father's primary responsibility was to the family with whom he lived. Thatcher vowed to make fathers responsible for all their children, partly in the improbable hope of dissuading them from forming new families they could not afford.

The outcome was the Child Support Act, 1991, drafted in a hurry with little research or consultation and rushed through parliament under pressure from Thatcher before she lost office in 1990, assisted by Treasury officials keen to cut the benefits bill.[23] It established the principle that fathers should maintain their families, with first families taking priority over others even when the father lived with the latter. Officials could initiate maintenance procedures even if claimants refused contact with the father, often due to domestic violence, which could lead to benefit reduction of up to 40%, despite evidence that one in six divorced and one in ten single or separated women gave domestic violence as the cause of separation. This was amended in parliament to allow that 'risk to her or any child living with her suffering harm or undue distress' must be considered. The Act was implemented in 1993, after Thatcher left office. It proved costly and inefficient, leaving many single mothers and their children in greater poverty and distress, as described in chapter 9.

In a rare piece of good news for some one-parent families, the Family Law Reform Act, 1987, at last removed the historical distinction between 'legitimate' and 'illegitimate' children, eliminating the words from legal language. Unmarried fathers gained rights to custody, after court scrutiny for fear of advantaging violent fathers. Children of unmarried parents gained rights to inheritance from both parents, though the Lords drew the line at their inheriting peerages. The Law Commission recommended these changes partly to bring UK law into line with EC Conventions.[24]

Campaigns for Gender Equality

Gender equality progressed very slowly under Thatcher and Major. Through the 1980s and 1990s, the WLM and other campaigning groups declined in an unresponsive political environment, though other movements remained active, including the recently formed associations of Black and Asian women. The EOC remained under firm female leadership, still active and effective. In 1989 it appointed its first Black Chief Executive, Valerie Amos, who built stronger links with BAME women's organizations. It also formed closer relations with trade unions and gained support from the EC, which was becoming an important source of pressure for equality in the UK, providing examples of greater equality in other European countries. Thatcher's waning enthusiasm for relations with Europe was not enhanced when in 1983 she was forced by a decision of the European Court of Human Rights to revise the Equal Pay Act to replace equal pay for 'like work' with 'work of comparable value'. It followed a successful case brought by women cooks at a Merseyside shipbuilding firm, aided by the EOC, arguing that their work was comparable with that of male painters, joiners and engineers employed by the company and should be paid equally. Another European court ruling in 1983 judged unlawful Britain's exemption from the EC Equal Treatment Directive of people employed in private households and businesses with fewer than five employees. In consequence, the Sex Discrimination Act, 1986, outlawed discrimination in collective bargaining agreements and extended anti-discrimination law to benefit women who were disproportionately employed in households or small businesses.

Since its foundation in 1975, the EOC had queried the gendered nature of the tax system, following pressure from the Married Women's Association and other organizations. The incomes of married couples were still aggregated for tax purposes even if both were earning. Husbands (only) received marriage allowances, hence more net pay per pound earned than wives, undermining the principle of equal pay. After long discussion and pressure from the EC, in 1989 a 'married couple's allowance' was introduced in Britain which either partner might claim, or they could opt for separate assessment. This later became automatic, and husbands and wives were treated as separate individuals for tax purposes. The change also enabled better-off couples to place unearned income, e.g., from investments, in the name of the lower earner, normally the wife, reducing their total tax liability.

The EC was committed to gender equality following pressure from women across member nations since its foundation. Another example came in 1990 when the European Court of Human Rights upheld a British man's contention that the lower UK pension age for women, 60, discriminated against men. In response, in the State Pension Act, 1995, Major's government announced the gradual rise of the female pension age to 65 from 2010 to 2020, but it failed to warn women directly and many failed to notice the change. It received little publicity. There was no evident protest at the time and, as we will see in chapter 10, women were shocked when the change came, and they had to work five years longer than expected or retire without a pension. Women's organizations continued, like the rest of society, to marginalize older people, female and male, and overlooked real inequalities they suffered.

Feminist activists engaged increasingly in formal politics, local and national, as potentially more effective than extra-parliamentary campaigns for challenging a hostile government. In Scotland nationalism revived in opposition especially to welfare cuts and privatization and the erosion of local government under Thatcher. Scottish feminists campaigned for gender equality in local government employment, for consultation with women about housing, education, childcare and leisure services, and for government support for women's organizations. They became active in the growing movement for devolution, or, ideally, full independence, determined to be fully represented in any elected Scottish government.[25] More slowly, similar movements emerged in Wales where the 1970s women's movement was weaker.[26]

An outstanding example of women's activism was the women's peace camp at Greenham Common, Berkshire, from 1981 to 1991. It was a response to Thatcher buying expensive Trident nuclear missiles from the United States and allowing the NATO-led placing of US cruise missiles on a US base at Greenham. It was a move in the Cold War which revived the UK anti-nuclear movement. Women formed a large, women-only, protest camp outside the base, holding widely publicized demonstrations against the missiles, while suffering miserable conditions, evictions and police violence. They gave up only when the missiles were removed in 1991. It was the largest, longest women's demonstration then known.

Education

Girls had long shown greater intellectual ability than their exam results and employment patterns suggested.[27] This became very evident through the 1980s. As shown in table 8.1 in both England and Scotland boys were more likely than girls to leave school without qualifications.

As their opportunities for work and further education grew, girls had greater incentives to match ability with performance at school and increasingly outperformed boys. The shift was widely interpreted as a 'problem of underperformance' by boys, as the previous lesser performance of girls had never been. Children from some minority ethnic backgrounds also performed better than 'white' children, on average, with differences among and within minority groups: girls of Black Caribbean origin outperformed boys, children of Pakistani and Bangladeshi origin included some of the best and worst performers, while those of Indian and Chinese origin on average outperformed all others.[28] There was a certain narrowing of class differences, though poverty was still seriously disadvantageous.[29] Comprehensive education had generally improved outcomes,[30] though independent schools, with smaller classes and greater funding, continued to outperform most state schools in exams and university entrance, benefitting the better-off.

Despite cuts to state education funding, as to all public services under Thatcher, more young people stayed longer at school, fewer in England

Table 8.1. Percentage of school leavers without qualifications

England		
Year	Boys	Girls
1980–1	15	10
1989–90	11	8
1995–6	11	8
Scotland		
Year	Boys	Girls
1980–1	31	26
1988–9	16	10
1996–7	7	5

Source: Based on data from A.H. Halsey and Josephine Webb, *Twentieth-Century British Social Trends* (Basingstoke: Macmillan, 2000), pp. 195–212.

than in Wales and Scotland. The introduction by Labour of GCSEs (the General Certificate of Secondary Education) as the school-leaving exam normal in comprehensives in place of GCEs available only in grammar schools, enabled more people to gain qualifications, while higher education expanded and the job market contracted, especially for the less qualified. The proportions of 18–21-year-olds in higher education rose from 12.7% to 20.3% from 1977–8 to 1990–1, despite cuts to university funding.[31] The proportion of female students increased from 28% to 38% from 1970 to 1980 and was above 50% by the mid-1990s, though courses remained gender-segregated, with women still concentrated in the arts and social sciences. The higher social classes and products of independent schools were over-represented among male and female students, while ethnic minority groups were under-represented.

Inequality at Work

Throughout the 1980s and 1990s, improved female performance in education had only a limited effect upon their employment opportunities, which continued to progress only very gradually. In his second administration, following the election in April 1992, Major made an unprecedented increase to the number of female Cabinet Ministers – to two: Gillian Shepherd at Employment for one year, April 1992–May 1993, before moving to Education until 1997, and Virginia Bottomley at Health, for three years from 1992 to 1995, then at National Heritage. He supported Shepherd's proposal to establish a Sex Equality branch at the Department of Employment and she appointed an investigation into the difficulties of working women.

There was growing pressure about these issues from the EC, which was developing structures for promoting gender equality, while other European states, including France and Germany, created dedicated Ministries for Women. But Britain continued to lag behind and women's problems at work were exacerbated by continuing labour market deregulation, reducing central government control of working conditions, causing deterioration in pay and conditions for many workers and few obvious improvements. Trade unions were much weakened under Thatcher – 'the enemy within' as she called them – and unable to prevent such problems. A slowly expanding class of high-earning, career-oriented female graduates emerged alongside growing, much larger, numbers of women in low-paid, low-skilled employment, further symptoms of increasing income and wealth inequality.

At the high-paid end, some employers seemed to embrace the anti-discrimination and equal opportunities agenda promoted by the preceding Labour government, aiming to attract female staff, especially when qualified males were in short supply in expanding areas of the economy, including banking. They were spurred on in 1983 when the EOC investigated alleged discrimination against women by Barclays Bank, which prompted large companies to introduce 'equal opportunities' policies. In the 1980s NatWest Bank devised a 'retainer' scheme which allowed employees on maternity leave to take two-week refresher courses each year while bringing up their families at home, enabling their reinstatement when they were ready to return. Women made up almost two-thirds of NatWest's workforce in 1996, though only 25% of its managerial staff. In 1981 Thames Television established a Women's Committee and an equal opportunities advisor, following a review of women's limited career progression in the organization. In 1982, oil company BP sponsored a network for women in senior posts which held regular seminars and organized training sessions tailored to their needs. Some technology firms used modern technology to enable women with small children to work from home. International Computers Ltd (ICL) led the way and by the late 1980s employed about 300 home-based staff, mostly female, though on average their pay was lower than that of on-site staff and they often had fewer employee benefits or rights.[32] Many were mothers of small children and believed their prospects for career advancement were poor, but the homeworking conditions were preferable to unemployment and the only work available fitting their needs.

Despite signs of progress women still made only limited gains, including in high-end jobs, with little support from Thatcher's governments. In 1989 the influential Hansard Society established a Commission to investigate their experiences, led by Elspeth Howe, former deputy chair of the EOC and wife of soon-to-resign Conservative Minister Geoffrey Howe. The Hansard Society for Parliamentary Democracy, its full name, was an independent organization founded in 1944, dedicated to research, its website states, on 'parliaments, political engagement and democratic innovation'.[33] It was active and influential on social issues. In 1990 the

Commission published a report, *Women on Top*, which predicted that 80% of entrants to the labour market over the next five years would be women, mostly older returners with 'major family responsibilities', while the number of school-leavers, male and female, was declining due to falling births. To recruit and retain talented staff, employers were urged to introduce women-friendly policies, including mentoring programmes, improved maternity packages and flexible working schemes. The report was followed by an employer-led campaign, Opportunity 2000, whose 61 founder members pledged to adopt best practice and set targets for promoting women to senior posts. John Major's government backed it and, led by Gillian Shepherd, hosted a series of conferences aimed at women returners, opened 'opportunity shops' across the country to provide information about training and established a working group chaired by Gillian Shepherd to bring 'fresh ideas on women's issues to government'.[34]

But gender equality at senior levels of employment continued to advance very slowly. This was demonstrated in another Hansard Society report in 1996, also titled *Women at the Top*, following up the report of 1990, prepared by Susan McRae, a Professor of Social Sciences and member of the 1990 Commission. It found that since 1990 increasing numbers of women had entered the workforce; mothers with young children had become a 'fixed feature'. There had been some improvement in women's presence in public roles: the first woman Speaker had been appointed in the House of Commons – Labour MP Betty Boothroyd – from 1992 to 2000. From 1994 women were ordained in the Church of England (34 in the first year), four former men's colleges at Oxford and Cambridge were headed by women. But it was becoming even harder for women to be elected to parliament – a smaller proportion of those standing were elected in the 1980s, partly, it was believed, because of Conservative election successes; more women stood for Labour. Baronesses made up just 7% of the House of Lords, about 13% of the most active members.

McRae reported that more employers were trying to accommodate a diverse, changing workforce. In 1984 the civil service had issued a Programme for Action for Women in the Civil Service. The number of women in the senior ranks doubled from 1984 to 1995, but still totalled only 10, not helped by the government's severe cuts to the service as to other areas of public sector employment. This made it less appealing to talented men. Fewer women than men left the civil service following the cuts and their chances of promotion slowly improved, though least at the highest levels. The proportion of women rose from 2% of Permanent Secretaries (one) in 1984 to 6% (two) in 1994, Undersecretaries from 5 to 10%, Principals from 10 to 19%. In 1995 women were more than two in five recruits to the prestigious fast-stream entrance programme to the senior civil service.[35] Action varied across departments. Some, but not all, introduced 'family-friendly' policies, improved their promotion systems and introduced equal opportunity awareness training for all managers. Part-time working expanded, marginally.

McRae reported that in 1991, 23% of all public appointments were held by women. John Major introduced a goal of 50% by 1996; 30% was reached by 1994. Women filled 35% of higher management posts at the BBC by 1996, when only 7% of university professors were female while universities expanded. The Lord Chancellor tried to encourage more women to come forward for appointment to the judiciary, but flexible working was difficult for judges and the numbers hardly increased. Women called to the Bar rose from 37% in 1987 to 46% in 1995, among practising barristers from 14 to 22%. In the same period the proportion of qualified women solicitors rose from 45 to 53% of the total, those in practice from 19 to 29%.

In the business sector, in 1990 women represented one in 1,000 boardroom executive directors, one in 15 senior managers. Opportunity 2000 then pushed for improvement and the Hansard Society urged the CBI and the Institute of Directors to ensure their members were aware of good practice in the best firms. A total of 293 businesses participated in Opportunity 2000 by 1995, covering over 25% of the workforce in both the public and private sectors. It encouraged member organizations to improve women's opportunities and tried to influence wider attitudes. There was little sign of government action but some gradual change. In 1989, 80% of firms had no women on their boards of directors, by 1995 only 50%. The proportion of female senior executives in the CBI top 100 firms rose from 7% in 1989 to 18% in 1995, but they earned substantially less than male colleagues. More women were appointed to lower levels of management.

McRae attributed inequalities to the dominance of men at the top of corporate Britain and unchanging, traditional attitudes to women:

'Unthinking or overtly sexist attitudes continue to bar women's way . . . Men recruit in their own image.' She feared that improved maternity benefits and breaks might hinder rather than help women aiming for the top. She concluded that since 1990 there had been good progress in some areas of employment, much less in others, that it was unrealistic to expect much more in just six years but 'There is yet, however, no room for relaxation.'[36]

Opportunities for working mothers remained especially limited. Mothers who returned immediately from maternity leave to full-time work had the best chance of maintaining their previous position and securing further promotion, but few found this easy, and more than half returned to part-time working.[37] Few employers provided generous maternity leave packages or help with childcare. In 1979 just 10% of working mothers received more than the very basic statutory minimum maternity pay, by 1990, 14%, mostly from public sector employers under pressure from unions, which remained relatively strong in the public sector. Fewer than 4% of mothers reported any assistance from employers with childcare costs or provision of workplace nurseries. They had still to provide for themselves, the better-paid employing carers at home, now increasingly low-paid immigrant workers from poorer countries attracted to Britain by growing demand for services they provided at low cost.[38] Nor did employers assist fathers to help. Most men now took some time off work immediately after the birth of a child, most attended the birth and slightly increased their contribution to housework, but very few employers offered paid paternity leave which was established in most of the EU (as the EC became in 1991).

Much higher-level work became more time-consuming and pressured for women and men due to employers' use of new technology to encroach upon employees' time outside working hours, increasing the difficulties for working mothers to organize their time. The term 'work–life balance' came into common use, signalling the need to respond to these new pressures. They caused more professional women to postpone or reject pregnancy, contributing to the birth-rate decline. Childlessness doubled, highest among women with university degrees and professional qualifications.[39] Some women in high-level jobs decided in their thirties that they wanted children and gave up work for full-time domesticity, or less demanding part-time work. Others established home-based businesses. Some commentators attributed these changes to women's personal choices, to their preference for maternity and home life, rather than as moves to which they felt driven by work conditions that were capable of change. Women who successfully combined maternity with high-flying careers, few as they were, might be represented in the media as arrogant, self-congratulatory and patronizing rather than as models women could follow.[40] Hostility to working mothers had not gone away.

There were gradual improvements through the 1990s in women's employment and educational opportunities, partly due to EU influence, but gender equality remained distant. In 1991, 67.6% of working-age women were employed, 70.3% in 2001,[41] many still in low-paid, often part-time, work. Major's government resisted the EOC's calls for stronger legislation on equal pay and sex discrimination, insisting that regulation hampered the free market. From 1990 employers could offset against tax the cost of workplace nurseries, the number of which increased, while local authority nursery places declined further following central government cuts to local funding.[42] The Conservative manifesto for the 1992 general election promised to 'encourage the development of childcare arrangements in the voluntary and independent sectors', and some funding was provided for pre-school and after-school care, in contrast to Thatcher's opposition to subsidizing childcare, though it was not substantial or sufficient to meet needs. In 1993 Major declared that he wanted 'over time to move to universal nursery education', but John Patten, Education Secretary, opposed this and nothing happened. A childcare allowance of up to £28 per week was introduced, to help single parents and other low-income mothers work full-time, but affordable care remained hard to find.[43]

The EU recommended accessible, affordable childcare services and flexible leave arrangements to help parents, including fathers, fulfil their family and work obligations, and extending employment rights to part-time workers, who were still overwhelmingly female. In 1994, responding reluctantly to an EU directive, the government ruled that fourteen weeks' maternity leave should be available immediately a woman took a job, rather than after two years, and extended to part-timers. After two years in the same employment, it was extended to 28 weeks. Michael Portillo, Employment Secretary from 1994 to 1995, refused to introduce paternity leave. Despite gradual improvements, Britain continued to have the worst provision for working parents in the EU and trailed in most areas of gender equality.

One hint of progress was that women were admitted to combat roles in all the armed services, though not yet in the front line, partly due to a shortage of male recruits and later than several other countries, including the United States. The women's and men's services were amalgamated. From 1990 women in the Royal Navy were at last allowed to go to sea with men, despite the trepidation of some sailors' wives; not until 2014 could they serve in the intimacy of submarines. Only in 2016 were army women admitted to front-line combat; opponents still questioned their physical capability.[44] But still in the 2020s there were concerns about sexual harassment on board naval vessels, servicewomen experienced rape by male colleagues, more abuse than support when they reported it and minimal help from the system of martial law. Few women were promoted to senior positions in any of the services.

'Rolling Back the State'

Thatcher was less restrained in her second term, from 1983 to 1987. Local authorities faced greater controls. Like the unions, many of them were perceived as socialist enemies of government principles, none more so than the Greater London Council (GLC), the largest council in the country, headed from 1981 by Labour's Ken Livingstone. In 1986 it was wound up, with the other seven metropolitan counties, all Labour-controlled. Thatcher especially opposed Livingstone's use of GLC income to regenerate the London economy, reduce transport costs and aid radical groups, including feminist and anti-racist campaigners in the increasingly culturally diverse capital. Among other excessively radical acts, Livingstone, along with other Labour-controlled authorities, funded women's refuges and rape crisis centres. He did not help to save the GLC by posting London's rising unemployment figures on large signs outside County Hall, across the river from parliament, with defiant political slogans. Many GLC powers were taken over by central government, some, including housing and education, by the London boroughs, others by new semi-independent 'agencies', including the London Regional Transport Authority. All local transport was deregulated by the Transport

Act, 1985, enabling private companies for the first time to run bus and other public transport services.

Thatcher's welfare cuts – 'rolling back the state', as she put it – especially hit mothers working in lower-skilled occupations as public services were extensively privatized, including thousands of school dinner-ladies, hospital cleaners, home helps, carers for older and disabled people in residential homes or in the community who were 'outsourced' to private employment.[45] Women from ethnic minority communities were over-represented in such work. Private contractors were not obliged to preserve their pay and work conditions in the public sector and both deteriorated. Wages councils were much restricted in 1986 and abolished in 1993, having survived since 1909 when they were established as trade boards, setting adequate if rarely generous pay mainly for low-paid women. These women now lacked protection. Trade unions tried to help, but they declined in numbers and power when Thatcher introduced controls over these 'dangerous' institutions. Some women felt forced to take up sex work as an adequately paid alternative to the employment available to them.[46]

If they became unemployed, women, even more than men, suffered from a deteriorating benefit system. From 1984 unemployed wives with husbands who were earning became ineligible for places on job creation schemes, on the grounds that they did not need to support themselves. Then, as increasing numbers of men became unemployed, it was argued, as in the inter-war years, that married women should not work because they would take work opportunities from unemployed men, though men were unlikely to be appointed to the employment open to most married women.[47] Restrictive benefit policies contributed to growing poverty through the 1980s.

Wives of unemployed men took work if they could, to support the family, sometimes working at home in conditions hardly better than at the beginning of the century.[48] Thatcher made no attempt to reduce male unemployment by assisting the development of new industries to replace those in decline. She believed the economy would thrive best from expansion of services and of the financial sector. The overwhelmingly male, higher-level employees in finance certainly gained. Salaries rose to exceptional levels. The average income of directors of Morgan Grenfell investment bank increased from £45,000 in 1979 to £225,000 in 1986 and other banking salaries and bonuses boomed, contributing to growing national inequality.[49]

Thatcher's Child Support Act, 1990, was implemented by the Child Support Agency (CSA) from 1993. The regulations, like the legislation, were drafted in a hurry and administered by inexperienced officials. The CSA took over the courts' powers to assess, collect and enforce maintenance payments to all single parents receiving benefits at the time (527,000) and new claimants, on the assumption that many were claiming benefits from the state because 'feckless fathers' failed to pay due maintenance. Income Support (IS) was reduced by the full amount of the maintenance payments due, whether or not they were paid. A large backlog quickly developed, mainly because most cases were more complex than anticipated.

The system was intended to cut total benefit costs but, remarkably, it was not foreseen that prioritizing fathers' responsibility for first families disadvantaged many second families who then needed benefits, also that many fathers were not evading maintenance but were unable to afford it. Fathers who believed they were doing their best for both families were infuriated and some fathers, not always the most deserving, staged dramatic, much-publicized protests in prominent London spaces. Most single mothers struggled with poverty and childcare rather than protesting. The Inland Revenue was expected to pursue fathers who failed to pay maintenance, but grew tired of hounding them, sometimes fruitlessly, for small sums, and the CSA added this to the tasks for which it was unprepared. It was ordered to cut £530 million from the benefits bill in the first year but undershot by £112 million, while arranging maintenance in fewer than one-third of eligible applications. It was a widely criticized fiasco, worsening the conditions of many women and children. The chief executive officer (CEO) resigned after a year. The system was modified in the Child Support Act, 1995, but little improved.[50] Thatcher's reforms went too far even for many in her party, and she was forced reluctantly to relinquish office in 1990 as her policies made her increasingly unpopular with voters, especially women, and with her Conservative colleagues.

As if they did not suffer enough from the CSA disaster and other changes, a distinctive feature of Major's time in office was an unprecedented series of public attacks on single mothers. He revealed that his sister and mother-in-law had raised children alone, to convey his understanding of single mothers, but he and Ministers pilloried them to justify cutting benefits. Like Thatcher, they blamed state welfare for encouraging partnership breakdown and unmarried motherhood. At the party conference in October 1992, Peter Lilley, Secretary of State for Social Security, intoned a widely publicized pastiche of Gilbert and Sullivan, announcing he 'had a little list' of:

> Benefit offenders who I'll soon be rooting out . . .
> Young ladies who get pregnant just to jump the housing list.
> And dads who won't support the kids of ladies they have kissed.
> And I haven't even mentioned all those sponging socialists . . .

He later argued in the *News of the World*, without evidence, that the rise in violent crime was due to growing numbers of fatherless families.

Then John Redwood, Secretary of State for Wales, visited a council estate in Cardiff which, he claimed, was 50% populated by one-parent families, including many young, never-married mothers. In fact, only 17% of the 3,500 families were headed by single mothers, 60% of them over 24, most previously married or in long-term relationships. Redwood later proposed withholding benefits from single mothers until the father moved back, to provide 'the normal love and support that fathers have offered down the ages', presumably abandoning any second families. He complained of a worrying trend 'for young women to have babies with no apparent intention of even trying marriage or a stable relationship with the father', also offering no evidence. The vice-chair of Cardiff social services committee, a social worker, commented that the main problem for the families on the council estate was poverty, in an area of high unemployment. Most mothers were loving and supportive and wanted to work if they could. A senior police officer commented: 'as the police had exclusion orders for violence against half the men involved, the last thing they wanted was to see women and children forced to allow the fathers to return'.[51]

But Redwood's pronouncements were enthusiastically received by sections of the press. *Daily Mail* columnist Keith Waterhouse attacked the:

> Single Parent State . . . the single mum can rake in over £100 a week in state benefits . . . she can jump the housing queue and raise her family in one of

those lovely tower blocks . . . Then there is the Unmarried Mothers' Union – the single parents' militant wing where having a baby is not so much a happy event as a political statement. You cradle the little mite in your boiler suit and carry a placard demanding crèche facilities at the bingo hall.[52]

An outpouring of stereotypes unrecognizable in real life, reinforcing popular prejudice against single mothers.

Single mothers did not receive priority for increasingly scarce council housing. Department of the Environment researchers discovered that over 40% of unmarried mothers under 20 lived with their parents. The liberal *Independent* pointed out how many single-parent families were placed in bed-and-breakfast accommodation by local authorities, while the *Guardian* commented that it was indeed desirable to cut the number of teenage single pregnancies, so it was unfortunate that one family-planning clinic in every four had closed following government cuts. Government representatives sounded uncomfortable. A Department of Social Security (DSS) source stated that Redwood's comments did not represent government policy. Lilley stated that single mothers would continue to receive benefits, adding, 'we can give money, but we cannot give love and commitment'.[53] But amid media denigration of 'scroungers' on benefits, the 1996 budget announced the freezing of One Parent Benefit and its abolition for new claimants. As the 1997 election approached, John Redwood proposed that, to uphold 'family values', single mothers should give up their children for adoption.

Single mothers faced the most sustained public attack from the government and the media of the twentieth century, but denigration was not universal, and cultural attitudes continued to shift. Fifty-three per cent of poll respondents believed women capable of bringing up children alone. Never before had so many children been born outside marriage or so many unmarried couples openly lived together, facing little evident disapproval from family, friends and neighbours. Cutting benefits did not get more mothers into work, given the other difficulties they faced; it made families poorer. Many mothers desired to work but were hampered by lack of childcare and shortage of adequately paid jobs. Some benefitted in 1996 when legal aid became available for divorce proceedings. In the Lords, Baroness Patricia Hollis (Labour) gained an amendment to the divorce legislation allowing partners, normally wives, to claim 50% of the other's pension rights as part of the divorce settlement.

'Rolling back the state' was intended to reduce public spending and taxation. But spending on social security benefits alone rose from £15.9 billion, 8.8% of GDP, in 1978–9, to £92.2 billion, 10.8% of GDP, in 1996–7.[54] This was partly due to inflation, more to maladministration, cuts to services, the growing shortage of affordable housing, and unemployment and poor working conditions and pay creating the need for benefits. The resulting increase in private rents following increased demand forced the government in 1982–3 to introduce the costly, means-tested Housing Benefit for the growing numbers of people unable to afford rent. Housing costs were a growing cause of poverty, which rose, especially among women and children, from 8% of all children in the UK in 1979 to 28% in 1992.[55] Poor children lived in poor families, most with single mothers.

Transgender Activism

Previously ignored equality issues concerning transgender people commanded increasing attention. They demanded legal recognition of their acquired gender and the right to NHS treatment for gender reassignment. They received more support from the EU and European institutions than from the Thatcher or Major administrations. The campaign was led by Press for Change, founded in 1992. A founder member, Stephen Whittle, a transgender law lecturer, had in 1990 founded the Female to Male support group. He and his long-term partner – wife when it became possible in 2005 – achieved change and inspired others through successful legal action. In the early 1990s they established their legal right to artificial insemination, then, through the European Court of Human Rights, their children's right to have Whittle recognized as their father, assisted by EU equality initiatives. In 1994 a British transsexual woman successfully appealed to the European Court of Justice against an employment tribunal's rejection of her sex discrimination case against her employer on the grounds that she was not female. In 1999, under the next Labour government, gender reassignment was incorporated in the sex discrimination regulations, but trans people still faced conflicts over which toilets to use and being placed in male or female hospital wards or prison cells.

Male-to-female transsexuals were forbidden to draw their pension at the female age of 60.[56]

Gay Rights

The fight for gay equality continued, made more urgent by the emergence of AIDS/HIV. By 1983 three British men were known to have died of the disease. Most people affected were gay. What the media described as a 'gay plague' deepened homophobia, attributing it to what *The Times* described as 'promiscuous male homosexuality', 'glorified . . . with the advent of "gay liberation"'.[57] It was agonizing for gay people who experienced intensified popular and media vilification, the sickness and death of close friends, and their inability to visit gay partners in hospital or inherit jointly held property because they were not legally related. This stimulated campaigns for formal partnership rights. The number of deaths from AIDS among gay and bisexual men rose to 1,000 a year by the early 1990s. The gay community established self-help and support groups, including the Terence Higgins Trust, founded in 1982 in memory of the first Briton known to have died of the disease.

In 1986 it became clear that heterosexuals were being infected, creating panic in the public and the media and arousing Thatcher's first response to the epidemic, which she now thought must be taken seriously. An unprecedented health education campaign was launched with press, radio and TV advertising and leaflets dropped to 23 million homes warning 'Don't Die of Ignorance', recommending ways to avoid potential transmission by practising safe sex and avoiding donating blood, as gay organizations had been advising since 1983. Blood transfusions were spreading the epidemic extensively. Thatcher wound down the campaign when no major heterosexual AIDS epidemic emerged, though it continued to spread among heterosexuals while declining among homosexuals.

The Labour Party was divided on gay rights, but several Labour-controlled London boroughs and the Inner London Education Authority (ILEA) began promoting positive images of gay men and lesbians as part of sex education teaching, intended to diminish homophobia. These were highly publicized and much caricatured in the press, intensifying Thatcher's hostility to the 'socialist' GLC, which was responsible for the ILEA, contributing to its closure in 1986. Manchester City Council, with other left-wing councils outside London, did everything it could to protect gay and lesbian communities against homophobia. By the late 1990s Manchester 'was emerging as Britain's cutting-edge queer capital'.[58]

Responding with horror to such developments, Thatcher made 'sexual propaganda in schools' a significant issue in the 1987 election, and the Conservative manifesto made clear her determination to 'clamp down' upon it. This was followed, after the election, by the passage of Section 28 of the 1987 Local Government Act, which made it illegal for local authorities to 'intentionally promote homosexuality' or 'promote the teaching in any maintained school of the acceptability of homosexuality as a pretended family relationship'. It aroused immediate protest. In February 1988, the night before the Bill became law, three women abseiled into the House of Lords, then invaded the BBC newsroom, protesting against its passage. An estimated 15,000 people demonstrated in Manchester. A poll in the *Sunday Telegraph* found that 60% of respondents did not believe homosexuality should be considered an acceptable lifestyle, while 34% believed that it should.

Section 28 was never firmly enforced, but it made many local authorities cautious about their handling of homosexuality and lesbianism, including banning books on the issues from schools and libraries. Campaigning against it revived gay and lesbian activism. It spurred the foundation in 1989 of Stonewall, which engaged with government on issues including Section 28, the age of consent, rights of gay and lesbian partners to adopt children and formal recognition of partnerships. In 1990 Peter Tatchell, who had experienced severe prejudice as a Labour parliamentary candidate and long remained a campaigner for homosexual rights, with others formed Outrage! for more militant protest, following the homophobic murder of actor Michael Boothe. Tatchell and his colleagues revived the term 'queer' to describe themselves, believing 'gay' had become too mainstream.

Thatcher blocked government funding for research into sexual behaviour and the effects of health education campaigns, which had developed to help combat the spread of AIDS.[59] John Major refused to overturn Section 28, but he expressed sympathy for homosexuals, writing later that 'I [did not] see homosexuality as a social evil. Many people are gay, and I saw no reason to cast them into outer darkness for that reason.'[60] He was willing to review the homosexual age of consent, which remained at 21 and was an increasing cause of protest. Religious leaders opposed reform. Then Conservative MP Edwina Currie (who was having a sexual relationship with Major at this time, it was later revealed) introduced a clause into the 1994 Criminal Justice Bill to equalize the age of consent at 16. Crowds gathered in Parliament Square to await the outcome, then erupted in protest when they heard that MPs had voted to reduce the age to 18, but not to equalize it. However, the Act made male rape an offence for the first time, decriminalized anal sex between men and women and partially extended the 1967 Act to the armed forces.

This followed a series of court cases brought by former service personnel against the Ministry of Defence (MoD) following their dismissal under the total ban on homosexuals in the services. Judges felt they had no alternative but to uphold the ban, though some urged the MoD to review it. The 1994 Act modified but did not remove it. An appeal to the European Court of Human Rights was likely when, in October 1995, a parliamentary review was announced. Service leaders defended the ban. Nicolas Soames, Armed Services Minister, insisted it should remain, 'not based on any moral judgement but on the impracticality of homosexual behaviour, which is clearly not compatible with service life'.[61] MPs in committee heard the experiences of service people discharged under the ban. A lesbian former Wren described how she was afraid to report rape by a male colleague for fear that her sexuality would be revealed. She was discharged when it became known. The ban remained but was lifted in 2000 following a ruling in the European Court of Justice.[62] Again, Europe came to the rescue of campaigners for gender equalities.

Conclusion

Advance towards gender equality was slight under Thatcher and only slightly less so under Major. Thatcher was outspokenly opposed; Major expressed some support but was timid about action. Indeed for many, especially poorer women and gay men at the peak of AIDS, inequality increased. Such gains as there were owed much to European courts and EU practices, while equality in the UK remained far behind that in much of western Europe. Improvement was most evident for those on high incomes. For others it was held back by growing inequalities of income and wealth as the rich got richer while poverty and unemployment grew. Both men and women suffered but, still, women and children were at greater risk of poverty. There were more single mothers on low incomes, and it remained hard for any woman to gain and sustain a high-income job due to continuing barriers to access and shortage of affordable childcare. Many pensioners, especially women, suffered from the declining real value of the state pension and other benefits, and from rising rents. But there were some signs of hope for the future: girls began to outperform boys in education and some employers made positive moves to improve women's employment opportunities, mainly when they experienced shortage of male labour.

NINE

Things Can Only Get Better? New Labour, 1997–2010

From 1997, government was in the hands of 'New Labour', as the party leader Tony Blair, labelled it, signalling a change of direction from what he saw as the failures of the 'Old Labour' past. Labour's theme song in the election campaign was 'Things Can Only Get Better' by the pop band D:Ream, who later regretted it being used for political purposes. Voters clearly agreed with the theme and gave Labour a substantial majority. One immediate sign of progress was the composition of the House of Commons. A remarkable (for Britain) 120 women MPs were elected, 102 for Labour, to a Commons of 659 MPs. This followed Labour adopting a policy of all-women shortlists (AWS) of candidates for selection in half of all seats judged winnable on a 6% swing, and half of all vacant Labour-held constituencies, following a long campaign by women in the party. Also, from 1990, 40% of all party offices and delegations were required to be female. These changes were promoted by John Smith, who led the party from 1992 until his sudden death in 1994 aged 55, and adopted by the party conference in 1993. And an unprecedented nine Black and Asian MPs were elected in 1997, all for Labour, two of them female, Diane Abbott and mixed-race Oona King. There were movements at this time in other parties and outside parliamentary parties for gender and ethnic equality in parliament, but they had little success and it remained distant from representing the demographic structure of the country, which still had a female majority. But the Labour results represented progress. Blair's first Cabinet included five (white) women (among 23), more than ever before.

The greater representation of women was not universally welcomed, including in the Labour Party. Before the election, too late to influence most candidate selections, disappointed Labour men made a successful court appeal against AWS under sex discrimination legislation. The leadership did not challenge it – Blair was not strongly committed to AWS – and shifted to 50/50 male/female shortlists. At the next election in 2001 Labour had six fewer female MPs (95, 23% of the parliamentary party) while the number of Conservative women MPs increased to 14, the Liberal Democrats to five. The Sexual Discrimination (Election Candidates) Act, 2002, freed all parties to take positive action to increase female representation. Labour revived AWS until 2022 when it was warned of the danger of further legal action. There was little obvious response from other parties, though the numbers of women MPs gradually increased. In 2003 Baroness Valerie Amos (a life peeress since 1997) became the first Black woman to become a Cabinet Minister, as Secretary of State for International Development. She went on to have a distinguished career of 'firsts', including as the first Black woman to lead a British university at the London University School of Oriental and African Studies (SOAS) in 2015, then in 2020 the first female Master (*sic*) of University College Oxford and first Black head of an Oxford College. Also in 2002 Paul Boateng became the first Black Cabinet Minister as Chief Secretary to the Treasury and also went on to a distinguished international career.

The 2005 election returned 128 women (98 Labour, 17 Conservative, 10 Liberal Democrats, one each for the Ulster Unionist Party (UUP) and Sinn Fein), a record 20% of MPs. They still reported discrimination in parliament, but successfully pushed certain issues up the agenda, including the right to request flexible working to assist mainly women combining employment with other, especially caring, responsibilities. Under John Smith, Labour had promised a Ministry for Women to conduct gender audits of government legislation, responding to the commitment to 'gender mainstreaming' promoted by the EU since the 1980s. Gender equality would be integrated within all policies and programmes. Blair was less enthusiastic about gender equality and no Ministry emerged. But a junior minister, Joan Ruddock, was appointed Undersecretary for Women in the Department of Social Security, where a Women and Equality Unit was established. A Women's Unit was appointed in the Cabinet Office in 1997, to pursue gender mainstreaming. It conducted useful research, but its remit was ill-defined and its influence limited.[1] However, it quickly launched a national consultation exercise, 'Listening to Women', to discover the policies women wanted prioritized: childcare, improved parental leave and flexible working came top. Action followed on all of these in the next five years, as we will see. These innovations marked progress, though less than John Smith had wanted.

Constitutional Reform

New Labour made other important contributions to gender equality, including the Human Rights Act (HRA), 1998. This embedded in UK law the European Convention on Human Rights, established after the Second World War. It led, among other things, to the establishment in 2007 of the Equality and Human Rights Commission (EHRC) to protect and promote all equality issues. This merged the EOC, the Commission for Racial Equality (CRE) and the Disability Rights Commission and took responsibility to protect and promote equalities for gay, transgender and older people, still in 2025 commissioning research on and making public a growing range of equality issues.[2] In Northern Ireland a statutory Human Rights Commission was established in 1998 with similar responsibilities.

Immediately on taking power, Labour implemented a manifesto promise by appointing a Select Committee on Modernization of the House of Commons, chaired by the Leader of the House, Ann Taylor until 2001, then Robin Cook from 2001 to 2003. Over several years its recommendations led to changes to parliamentary hours, weeks and years of sitting to make parliamentary life more compatible with family responsibilities. Combining work for a constituency distant from London and that in Westminster with family needs could be dauntingly difficult. Established hours of parliamentary sitting were 2.30–10 pm Monday to Thursday, though debates might continue well past 10 pm, plus Wednesday mornings. From January 1999, Thursday sitting was changed to 11.30 am–7 pm, to ease travel to spend Friday in the constituency, as MPs normally did. From 2003, the 11.30 am–7 pm sittings were extended to Tuesdays and Wednesdays, and Thursday sessions ended at 6 pm. The changes made parliamentary work more compatible with family life and responsibilities.

Another New Labour constitutional reform initiated by Scotsman John Smith was devolution of powers to Scotland and Wales (more to Scotland than to Wales), where nationalism had been growing for some decades. It followed referendum votes in favour of devolution in both countries in 1997. It did not go as far as the full independence nationalists desired, but both countries gained independent elected assemblies and a range of devolved powers. The first elections were held in May 1999 under the additional-member PR system. This was partly due to the intense involvement of women activists in the negotiations for the devolved constitutions. They were determined to gain fair female representation, which international experience showed was promoted by PR.[3] In both countries Labour and the nationalist parties, and in Scotland the Liberal Democrats, committed to equal numbers of male and female candidates. In Wales, 41.7% of representatives elected to the first Assembly were female, in Scotland 37.2%, both far ahead of Westminster's 18.2%. Only 13.6% of Scottish MPs at Westminster were female, elected under the first-past-the-post system normal in UK general elections. The second devolved election, in 2002, returned 51.7% female representatives in Wales. It was the first elected assembly in the world to achieve gender equality, even a female majority, remarkably since no women were elected to parliament for Welsh constituencies from 1970 to 1984; before 1997 only four women had been elected in the country's history.[4]

In both countries, elected women pressed with some success for equality measures and progressive social policies. In 1999 both established Equality Units committed to gender mainstreaming. The Scottish government had greater devolved powers than the Welsh and in 1999 established a standing Equal Opportunities Committee. Female members of the Scottish Parliament (MSPs) pressed successfully for improved childcare, support for carers of older and disabled people and stronger measures to prevent domestic violence.[5] The Welsh government also improved childcare and support for carers and increased pressure on employers to provide equal pay. By 2016, in Scotland the three major parties (SNP, Labour and Conservative) had female leaders, as did nationalist Plaid Cymru in Wales. In 2001 the Fawcett Society surveyed women's experience of candidate selection in British political parties in the light of Westminster's poor performance by international standards. They concluded that 'British political parties are institutionally sexist', especially against women from ethnic minorities, and they were 'culturally masculine'. They advocated positive measures for change, including PR for Westminster elections.[6]

The Greater London Authority (GLA) was re-established and re-named, reviving the GLC abolished by Thatcher in 1986, also following a supportive referendum. The first election for its mayor and 25 Assembly members was held in 2000 under the single transferable vote PR system. Of the elected Assembly members, 44% were female. The mayor was male Ken Livingstone, returned to his pre-1986 post, as an Independent, opposed by the New Labour leadership, as by Thatcher, for his Old Labour radicalism.

Equal Opportunities at Work?

Blair had a distant relationship with trade unions and disappointed them by not restoring the rights they had lost under the Conservatives as fully as they hoped. But he promised and delivered an exceptional new framework of workers' rights and sought to persuade business, with whom he worked hard to build good relations, that a more secure workforce satisfied with its pay and conditions would benefit, not disadvantage, production. He introduced the first minimum wage in UK history in 1999, much later than most high-income countries. It was set at a cautiously low level: £3.60 per hour for workers aged 22+, £3 for those aged 18–22, who were assumed to have fewer expenses. Expected to benefit were 1.9 million workers, male and female. Business leaders forecast catastrophic effects on their competitiveness, which proved unfounded.

The minimum wage was established in the EU and Blair implemented other EU improvements to employee rights, especially benefitting women: equal rights for part-time and full-time workers, including holiday and sickness pay; for all workers, increased protection against, and compensation for, unfair dismissal; universal paid maternity leave extended from 14 to 26 weeks; paternity leave after one year's service, but for only two weeks; women had the right to return to their previous job, or a suitable equivalent, after maternity leave and could not be dismissed for any reason connected with pregnancy and maternity, as was still all too common; parents could request flexible working hours to match their childcare responsibilities, though employers could refuse; 'reasonable' unpaid leave following deaths or accidents among close family or friends became a right; all workers gained four weeks annual paid leave, excluding public holidays; night-working was restricted to eight hours; minimum rest periods were established; discrimination at work on grounds of gender, age, race, disability, sexual orientation, union membership or part-time working was prohibited; processes for trade union recognition in the workplace were established and strengthened.[7] Employees who felt that their rights had been transgressed could appeal to an employment tribunal.

Blair and the Chancellor Gordon Brown (Prime Minister 2007–10), who led the way on most of the government's social and economic policies, shared 'Old' Labour's commitment to full employment and entered government with a programme of 'Employment Opportunities for All', a 'New Deal' to increase employment at all ages, assisted by revival of economic growth. It included a New Deal for Lone Parents which provided free childcare while they were seeking work or taking training. Just 45% of single parents (overwhelmingly mothers) were in work in 1997, 57% by 2008; the number of children under 16 in workless families fell from 2.4 million in 1997 to 1.7 million in 2008. There were concerns that many single mothers felt forced into work while their children were young due to the inadequacy of benefits. In 2009 the rules were eased to require single mothers to take employment only if it matched school hours and they had adequate childcare, and benefits improved.[8]

But poverty among women still grew as the numbers of single mothers continued to rise. In 2006 there were 1.8 million single-parent families, most headed by mothers, caring for almost three million children. Forty-two per cent of children in poverty were in single-parent households, and only 3% of single mothers were teenagers. Twelve per cent were from ethnic minority groups, with major differences particularly between households of Black Caribbean origin where single parenthood was widespread and Muslims for whom it was unacceptable.[9] Inflation, including of housing costs, continued to deepen the relative poverty of single mothers and contributed to shorter career breaks for most working mothers. Labour gave greater support to the homeless than did its predecessors, including funding hostel accommodation, but did little to remedy the shortage of affordable housing for those on low incomes.

By 2000 most mothers of children under five were employed, often part-time. Childcare provision improved but not universally and mothers still needed help from grandparents and others. Demand for childcare grew from 2001 when the birth rate unexpectedly reversed its long decline and rose from the exceptionally low level of 1.63 births to each set of parents to 1.94 in 2010. This was still not replacement rate but it was closer to it than since the early 1970s. This was partly due to births to immigrant women, most of whom were young, but more to higher fertility among native-born women in their later thirties and forties. More women delayed childbirth until they were established in a career with a good salary and/or found a stable partner and felt they could afford the costs of a family, then had more than one child.[10] Parents did not necessarily marry; still about one-third of babies were born to unmarried parents, often living together. By 2010 the number of marriages in the UK had fallen to an all-time low of 280,000.[11]

Girls in all ethnic and socio-economic groups now outperformed boys at all levels of education. By the mid-1990s more than half the university intake was female, though courses remained heavily gender-divided, with still few women studying sciences and engineering.[12] And still, despite outperforming them in education, women, young and old, married and unmarried, had more limited career opportunities than men. A series of studies of gender inequality at work during the New Labour years provided detailed information, indicating and reinforcing awareness of the problem and its causes. An EOC investigation of the professions reported that in July 1999, 35% of practising solicitors in England and Wales were female, up from 21% in 1989, but fewer than 25% of female solicitors were partners in a firm, compared with more than 50% of males. In October 2000, 26% of independent barristers in England and Wales were female, up from 18% in 1990. Women accounted for 18% of those called to the Bar in 1990, 46% in 1999–2000, but only 8% were Queen's Counsels (QCs) in October 2000. In early 2001, 7% of High Court judges were female (8 out of 99) up from 1% in 1989. In 2005, 10 high court judges out of 107 were female; 67 circuit judges among 626, up from 45 women and 528 men in 2001; 85 district judges were female among 433, compared with 67 and 352 in 2001. There was one female judge from an ethnic minority background above circuit level. Among 1,078 QCs in 2005, 87 were female, including Tony Blair's wife Cherie, mother of three, from 1994.[13]

Women made up 34% of hospital medical staff in England in September 1999, up from 26% in 1989, but still in 1999 men accounted for 79% of consultants and 95% of consultant surgeons. Of GPs in England, 34% were women, up from 25% in 1989. The EOC believed the change was mainly due to more part-time work and job-sharing in the sector. In 1999, 41% of female GPs worked half- or three-quarters-time or were in a job-share while 93.5% of men were full-time. In higher-education posts in 1998–9, full-time women were still over-represented in lower grades, under-represented in higher ones: 90% of professors and 78% of senior lecturers and researchers were male. Disciplines were still highly segregated, especially engineering and technology, in which 88% of full-time academic staff and 97% of professors were male. Women accounted for 84% of full-time teachers in state-funded nursery and primary schools in England in 1999; 47% of full-time teachers in secondary schools were male; seven out of ten secondary school heads were male.[14] Also in 1999 women made up only 2% of registered engineers, 5,728, a 12-fold increase from 478 in 1984 when the Women into Science and Engineering (WISE) initiative was launched to draw in more women. At the end of 2000 the Institute of Chartered Accountants in England and Wales had 22,000 female members, 19% of the total, up from 9,000 and 10% in 1989.[15] The EOC found similar patterns in Scotland and Wales.[16]

It also reported that in 2001 women's representation in senior management had doubled among executives since the mid-1990s, tripled among company directors and grown overall, but they still accounted for less than 25% of executives, only one in ten company directors. Of all managers in Britain, 30% were women, but unevenly spread across sectors. Women were well represented among personnel staff and there were more in management in the public than the private sector. Two-thirds of managers in health and social work services were women. An analysis of FTSE 100 companies showed that 57% had at least one female director in October 2001, but only one chief executive was female. In April 2001, 22% of senior civil servants were women and 50% of all civil servants. Just 1% of chief executives were women in local authorities in England and Wales, increasing to 12% in 2001, 29% of directors/chief officers in social services, and just 7% in finance. In the police there were no female chief constables in 1990 in England and Wales, three in March 2001 and 13 Assistant Chief Constables, up from one in 1990. Patterns in Scotland were similar.

Even where women broke through the glass ceiling into management, they were generally paid less than men. The EOC reported that in spring 2001 women full-time managers or senior officials received on average £12.23 per hour, men £16.03, a wider pay gap than in any other major occupational group, women averaging £34,789 per annum in 2001, men £40,289. Pay was highly diverse across occupations. The gender pay gap in the professions (9%) was narrower than in employment as a whole (18%). It remained especially stark in business, particularly in finance, where women still reported much discrimination. Personnel and industrial relations officers in these sectors, who were predominantly female, earned less than half the hourly pay of underwriters, brokers and investment analysts who were mostly male.[17] Employers were urged by the EOC to carry out regular pay reviews in collaboration with trade unions or staff representatives and to work to reduce inequalities.[18]

A study by the Cabinet Office Women's Unit in 2000, *Women's Incomes Over the Lifetime: The Mother Gap*, showed that having and caring for children affected women's incomes compared with men's over their lifetimes into old age. It estimated that a 'mid-skilled' (with GCSE qualifications) mother of two, probably a clerical worker, earned £381,000 less than a man with equivalent qualifications over her lifetime; a 'low-skilled' mother, with no qualifications, perhaps a shopworker, £482,000 less; a 'high-skilled' mother, with a degree or above, £161,000 less. At all skill levels earnings foregone rose with the number of children. The 'mother gap' had narrowed since 1980: the 'cost of motherhood' had dropped from 55% to 26% of potential earnings for the 'mid-skilled'. The reasons given for the narrowing gaps were, firstly, that the number of women returning to work within nine months of giving birth rose from 24% in 1979 to 67% in 1996. Also, the availability of more family-friendly work, including more part-time work, the increased importance of the woman's earnings for family income following inflation, including of housing costs, and women delaying their first birth: the younger their age, the greater the loss. In 1981 the average age at first birth was 25.3, in 1993, 28. In 1980, 28% of mothers of children under five were in paid work, in 1999, 53%; in full-time work 6% in 1979, 19% in 1999. In all, 41.7% of mothers were employed full-time. A high-skilled mother of two was likely to be in continuous employment, with one year part-time; a low-skilled mother of two to be out of work for nine years, with 28 years part-time. The higher a woman's earning power before childbirth, the less she then lost. Mothers also lost out on pensions. The mid-skilled woman paid an average £2,000 less in contributions and received £7,000 less in pension than a comparable man. The study did not take account of childcare costs.[19]

The Women and Equality Unit also reported on the gender pay gap in 2001. They found that women working full-time on average earned 82% of the average pay of full-time men, those working part-time 61%. Women's full-time earnings had improved since the 1970s, at varying rates across occupations, while part-time earnings relative to men's fell from the late 1970s to the late 1980s, and from 1993 to 2000. They concluded that the main reason for the pay gaps was that women were concentrated in low-paid occupations mainly due to discrimination, which was pervasive in the labour market.[20]

In 2002 the EOC studied gender inequality in public sector posts. They were concerned that from April 2001 public authorities had a duty to promote racial equality but not gender equality. They sought evidence from public sector bodies across England, Wales and Scotland that such a duty was needed. Authorities in devolved Scotland and Wales, in Northern Ireland and the GLA since its re-establishment, had introduced a duty to promote gender equality, along with some other local authorities. The EOC concluded that the New Labour government's agenda to modernize and improve public services took insufficient account of gender equality and recommended placing it at the heart of policy making, adequately funded and monitored, as John Smith had promised.

The EOC identified as the main barrier to progress the gulf between official statements and practice at all levels. Since 1998, 'Guidelines for Equal Treatment' and gender mainstreaming had been issued to all government departments, but they found little evidence that they were effectively implemented. Government performance targets increasingly drove local spending priorities, but the targets for 2001–4 made little reference to gender equality. In 2002 the Audit Commission (an independent public corporation founded in 1983) judged that 'Although the majority of councils have some kind of equality policy, it is rarely translated into strategy and even more rarely into action plans with challenging targets.' The problem lay not only with public sector posts but with the large number still contracted out to private providers. There were no firm rules ensuring that private employers treated women fairly. The EOC recommended urgent government action to ensure that public authorities received detailed guidance concerning their own practices and those of their contractors, including regular auditing to reduce the gender pay gap and job segregation and to improve the situation of part-timers.[21]

In 2000 a study for the Fawcett Society and the Hansard Society of the barriers to women entering 'top jobs' in the public and private sectors followed up the Hansard Society's 1990 study, reinforcing the findings of the other surveys. The Fawcett Society described itself, then and now, as 'the UK's leading charity campaigning for gender equality and women's rights'.[22] It was the direct descendant of Millicent Garrett Fawcett's NUWSS. The study was led by Karen Ross, who summarized her findings in an article for the *Times Higher Education Supplement* in December 2000: 'some progress has been achieved' but

> The attitudinal barrier (the 'clubby culture' as it is sometimes called) to women entering the very top decision-making levels remains firmly fixed ... This review makes plain the continued failure to select from the increasingly visible pool of experienced and talented women with the right seniority to these top jobs – in the private or public sectors or indeed in the political parties.

She described the gradual progress in some areas of management discussed above and urged, like others, that 'what is needed now is a determined joint effort to ensure that the last – hugely resistant – layer of the glass ceiling is actually removed'.

She noted recent real improvements at lower levels (only) of some civil service departments, including a childcare voucher scheme for Cabinet Office staff with children of school age, and a 'Mothers in Management' scheme, whereby senior women acted as mentors to women in junior grades. In 2000, for the first time, equal numbers of men and women had been recruited to the Fast Stream system of entry leading to higher-level posts. But although the civil service had had a programme since 1984 to encourage more women into the service, in 2000 the number of female permanent secretaries had still only risen from one to three out of 16. Ross believed this confirmed that 'the yawning chasm that divides the rhetoric of equality and the reality of women's life experience and career trajectories can be explained principally by a deep lack of will'. Further evidence of this was that Tony Blair's 'Modernizing Government' White Paper of 1999 had included a clear commitment to equality across the whole public sector for all under-represented groups, including women, 'A significant step change' from the approach of previous governments – but it had been ignored by those responsible for implementation.[23]

Ross recommended attracting more women to stand for parliament by reducing the long-hours culture and reorganizing parliamentary procedures to make them more compatible with women's needs, later implemented under this government, as we have seen. The devolved Scottish parliament, with its larger female membership, had already introduced a 'normal working week' and the Westminster parliament should do likewise: 'the anomaly of no creche but a rifle range' should be remedied. A commitment by the Lord Chancellor in 1999 to create 'an open, effective and accessible system, where everyone who is eligible for appointment or who wants appointment shall have a fair chance to secure appointment' at all levels of the justice system, had familiar disappointing outcomes. In 1999 seven women applied to be High Court judges, but none was appointed. She found similar patterns in the police, higher education, the media and the NHS, despite New Labour targeting it with a framework of planned progress to equality. Women fared no better in the corporate sector. She concluded that, overall, 'the position of women related to men continues to be extremely poor' and it could only be remedied, not by more legislation, but by 'specific acts of will, positive action strategies and a strong steer from government and other policy makers. We can achieve equality between women and men, but we have to *want* to.'[24]

Yet more evidence of gender inequality at work emerged when in 1998 the independent, government-funded Economic and Social Research Council (ESRC) launched a Future of Work Programme. It commissioned a report by Robert Taylor, a journalist and specialist in industrial relations, published in 2001, *Diversity in Britain's Labour Market*. Based on interviews with many workers in a wide range of occupations, Taylor argued that the current government's programme of modernizing the labour market was aimed at the 'creation of employment opportunities for all' and had produced a more diverse workforce, including more workers over age 50 and more women. He believed that gender inequalities in the workplace had increased in the 1990s, but 'meeting the specific needs of women in paid work is the focus for a good deal of the present government's public policy attention'. Some 72% of working-age women were economically active in 2001, 43% working part-time, whereas only 8% of men were part-timers. Women still predominated in administrative and secretarial work, personal services, sales and customer services.

Efforts to promote gender equality had helped graduate women secure promotion but not the large number in more routine work. Increasing numbers of women, and men, were dissatisfied with their pay, prospects, employment benefits, use of their abilities at work and lengthening hours of work due to the development and spread of modern technology and increased managerial control. Conservative cuts to public services had increased pressure on remaining staff in universities, schools, the health service and social services. Dissatisfaction was greatest among women with the lowest educational qualifications in lower-level jobs, rare at high levels. Women in lower-paid work with dependent children were finding it most difficult to balance work and family responsibilities. It was harder for them than for better-paid women to fund childcare and help with housework. Too little was changing for the better.

Taylor concluded that much ongoing debate about working women focused on the 'glass ceiling' and senior posts but it was necessary to give much higher priority to the needs of the larger numbers of women at lower levels, who were most vulnerable to discrimination and exploitation at work, unlikely to be in a trade union 'and without a voice in their place of work'. He pointed out that Britain was still a long way from a publicly funded national childcare programme comparable with many European countries, so could not expect women on low incomes with dependent children to be active in the labour market 'without having to endure an unfair burden'. He believed it was becoming more difficult for most women to fulfil their potential contribution to the labour market due to childcare difficulties.[25] Professional women who took several years out of work to bring up children could find only low-paid clerical work when they returned, especially to work in business or finance.

Journalist Polly Toynbee supported Taylor's findings about low-paid women when she set out in 2002 to investigate their experiences by participating in them. She found it impossible to get a routine job at a school, hospital or municipal centre, including as a dinner lady, cleaner or nursery assistant, in which she would not be employed by a private contractor. These companies exploited mothers by keeping the length of shifts below the threshold at which they qualified for employment protection and state benefits and offered minimal training or opportunities for promotion. Every worker she met complained about the pay, 'but because of children no-one here had any choice but to take it'.[26] Even

Table 9.1. Percentage of women in senior posts

Role	2003	Year 2007–8	2011
Directors of top FTSE 100 companies	8.3	11	12.56
Editors of national newspapers	9.1	13.6	9.5
Local authority chief executives	13.1	19.5	22.8
Senior officers in the armed services	0.6	0.9	1.0
Senior police officers	7.5	11.9	16.8
Senior judges	6.8	9.6	12.9
Civil service top management	22.9	26.6	29.2
Secondary-school heads	30.1	34.1	35.5

Source: Based on data from Equality and Human Rights Commission, *Sex and Power: Who Runs Britain, 2011* (London: EHRC, 2011).

under the system of tax credits introduced by New Labour to supplement low pay, a working mother on the minimum wage struggled to pay for childcare.[27]

The EHRC and the EOC both reported continuing gradual improvements in women's opportunities, but that gender equality remained distant (see table 9.1).

The EOC reported that in 2007–8 only 6% of all managers were employed part-time, the lowest of any occupation. Women in full-time management were less likely to have dependent children than full-time men. The EOC urged employers to open non-traditional opportunities to women through staff development and improved recruitment practices and provide more opportunities for part-time and flexible working, though they admitted this might be difficult in some areas of management. They noted the increasing levels of stress in the workplace and suggested that more part-time work, job-sharing, working from home and lessening the long-hours culture might be considered to reduce the stress of heavy management responsibilities which especially disadvantaged employees with family commitments and discouraged applications for such posts. The average gender pay gap was 27.5% in 1997, 16.4% in 2010, with variations across occupations. Women remained concentrated in low-paid, low-status work.

That so many surveys showed the extent and continuity of gender inequality at all levels of work, and the lack of urgency to find remedies at senior levels in politics and in all occupations, despite clear recommendations by the researchers, indicates how deeply inequality was embedded in the culture at the beginning of the twenty-first century and the extent of prejudice and resistance to change. New Labour demonstrated some commitment to improvement but no determined effort to achieve it. There was at best gradual progress before the international financial crisis of 2007–10 disrupted the economy.

Criminal Justice

Nor was there significant improvement in the treatment of women by the criminal justice system. The Fawcett Society became concerned to discover how far the dominance of men among judges and senior lawyers influenced the treatment of women in court. They appointed a commission of legal experts to investigate, with a female majority and chair. In 2003 it described the gender inequality in the legal profession we have seen and reported that since 1991 the female prison population had risen from 1,577 to over 4,000. They interviewed women with prison experience. Most had suffered domestic violence or sexual assault.

Domestic violence made up 25% of known violent crimes. Under New Labour there were efforts to establish its extent and to seek remedies. In 1999 a Cabinet Office document, *Living without Fear*, reported that one woman in four would experience domestic violence at some point in her life and two women each week were killed by violent partners. A Home Office study found that 5% of women had been raped since age 16 but many rapes were not reported and only 5.8% of those reported led to conviction. Domestic violence was also under-reported, so actual rates were hard to ascertain. The Home Office calculated that, on average, women were assaulted 35 times before reporting. It appointed a National Victims Advisory Panel to advise on remedies. In 2003 the government published a consultation paper on domestic violence as a precursor to legislation and the Sexual Offences Act, 2003, tightened the law, including making rape within marriage a criminal offence for the first time.

The Fawcett Commission found that women, especially Black women and lesbians who particularly feared discrimination, were still reluctant to report crimes because they were indeed deterred by a criminal justice system that was so overwhelmingly white, male and middle class. Victims of domestic violence feared retaliation against them or their children, and rape victims still feared blame for being drunk or wearing 'provocative' clothing, realistically expecting humiliation in court over their lifestyle. The Commission found that police now had more positive policies to support victims but still tended to underestimate the effects of domestic violence. Efforts to train police to be more sympathetic and supportive of rape victims had led to a large increase in cases brought by victims, but not all the 43 police forces in England and Wales were supportive and handling of cases varied. Some women still complained of being treated with disbelief and disrespect, that they felt like they were the defendants on trial, and only half of all rape cases reported to the police progressed to the courts. Even then, they did not always take priority and could take a year to get to court, with the victims not knowing when to expect proceedings.

There were signs of improvement. Some magistrates' courts now specialized in domestic violence cases. The government announced funding for a 24-hour national helpline for victims of domestic violence, backed up by a database of local refuges and support services, due to start at the end of 2003. The Commission discussed with the Home Office the possibility of funding a national rape crisis helpline, without response by the time of the report. Fawcett concluded that government support was progressing faster for victims of domestic violence than of rape, that good practice existed concerning both types of crime, but was unevenly distributed and should be extended to every area of the UK. Every victim of both crimes should have a specialist police officer allocated from the first complaint.[28] The voluntary rape crisis centres and helplines established since the 1980s were short of funding by the 2000s and received little help from the government.

Income Inequality and Poverty

As all these examples suggest, women still experienced discrimination and inequality at all ages and in most areas of life. On average, they still outlived men, with the shortest gender gap among the poorest. The continuing increase in single motherhood and high housing costs perpetuated women's poverty, but the Blair government sought to reduce it, including by helping single mothers to find work, as we have seen. Blair focused upon improving opportunities at the bottom of the income scale, reducing the income gap between the bottom and the middle, not the growing gap between the middle and the top. He made clear that he did not wish to hold back ambition or financial success, which would offend business leaders, and he himself became very wealthy after his retirement as Prime Minister in 2007. Redistribution and poverty reduction owed most to Gordon Brown, who continued to be active in helping the poor long after his defeat in the 2010 election.

In March 1999, in a lecture to commemorate William Beveridge, Blair unexpectedly announced: 'Our historic aim [is] that ours is the first generation to end child poverty forever . . . it is a twenty-year mission, but I believe it can be done.'[29] He promised to end child poverty by 2020. There was no sign of a strategy to fulfil the pledge, though Brown – as surprised as anyone by the announcement – was working on it. In September 1999 the Department of Social Security issued the first of a series of annual audits of poverty and exclusion, *Opportunity for All*, much influenced by Brown. It promised an 'integrated and radical policy response' to childhood deprivation, worklessness, health inequalities, crime, poor areas, poor housing, pensioner poverty, ill-health, and isolation and discrimination on grounds of age, ethnicity, gender or disability. A list of policies followed, including a comprehensive 'Sure Start' programme for children under 4 in deprived areas; more generous maternity leave; substantial increases in health and education funding, especially favouring poorer areas; and targets for employment, crime, education, health and housing in the most disadvantaged areas, with another ambitious aim that 'within 10–20 years, no-one should be seriously disadvantaged by where they live'. The government had already, in 1998, launched a National Childcare Strategy with a Green Paper, *Meeting the Childcare Challenge*, intended to reverse the decline in public services for children under 5 and meet growing parental demand for high-quality, affordable day-care.

It also announced Educational Maintenance Allowances (EMAs) to help young men and women from low-income households stay in education from ages 16 to 18; improved benefits for disabled adults, pensioners and children; and action to reduce inequalities in income between ethnic groups, including grants to local authorities to improve and equalize educational attainment. As we will see, all were implemented and helped to reduce poverty and inequality to varying degrees. By 2010 about 1.1 million children had been removed from poverty, not meeting Blair's

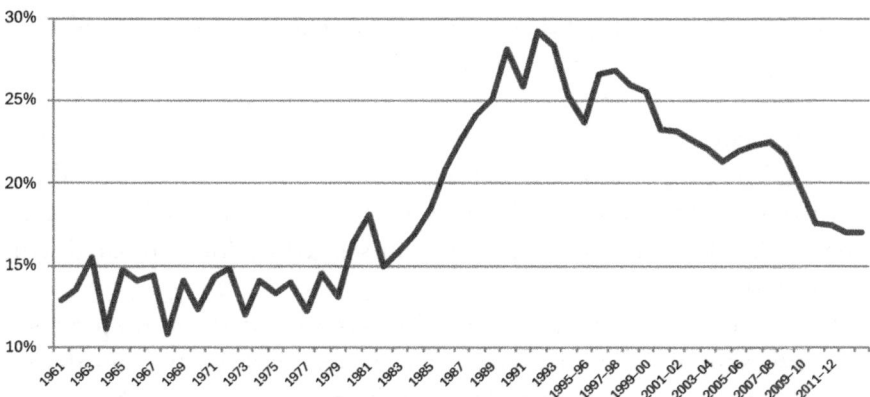

Figure 9.1 Relative child poverty rates since 1961 (GB)

Note: Poverty line is 60% of median income. Years up to and including 1992 are calendar years; thereafter financial years. Incomes are measured before deduction of housing costs and equivalised using the modified OECD equivalence scale.

Source: Jonathan Cribb, Robert Joyce and David Phillips, *Living Standards, Poverty and Inequality in the UK: 2012* (IFS, 2012), https://ifs.org.uk/publications/living-standards-poverty-and-inequality-uk-2012. Used with permission.

target of halving child poverty since 2000, but a substantial improvement, as shown in figure 9.1. Long-term poverty fell, from 12% of the UK population and approximately 16.5% of all children in 1998, to 8% and 10%, respectively, in 2003, though following the financial crisis it had returned by 2010 to 2000 levels.[30]

Declining poverty was partly due to economic growth resulting from Labour's successful management of the economy and rising employment. Brown also introduced in 1999 the Working Families Tax Credit (WFTC), a means-tested supplement to low earnings paid through the tax system, and Child Benefit was increased. The minimum wage, along with the employment New Deals and the increased length and generosity of maternity pay, increased family incomes and reduced poverty among parents and children.[31] In 2003, WFTC was extended to low-wage households without children and renamed Working Tax Credit (WTC), while a new Child Tax Credit (CTC) amalgamated means-tested IS and tax credits for children, particularly benefitting low-income families and significantly reducing child poverty. Take-up of WFTC was initially low, as ever with means-tested measures, but as it was extended, take-up increased. Support for the youngest children improved, including publicly funded childcare. In 1997 there were 5.5 pre-schoolers for every full-time nursery or childminder place; by 2003 there were four, by 2008 3.4, with places provided by the private, voluntary and state sectors, facilitated by increased government funding and vouchers and tax credits granted to parents. The proportion of under-2s receiving publicly funded childcare rose from 25% to almost 40% by 2008. By 2002, 93% of 3- and 4-year-olds from social classes IV and V received nursery education compared with 17% in 1997.

In 500 of the most disadvantaged districts Sure Start centres provided parenting support, childcare, play and learning opportunities, health care and advice and support for children with 'special needs', as the various forms of childhood disability were now known. Outcomes were positive and Sure Start was popular with parents. There were 1,000 centres by 2006, when it came under local authority control and centres spread through England and Wales, beyond deprived areas.[32] They benefitted children and enabled more mothers to work. In 2003 Labour introduced two weeks' paternity leave after birth or adoption of a child, but it was so brief and low-paid that few fathers took it up, often preferring to take better-paid holiday leave for childcare purposes. Public support for childcare improved but it remained inferior to many other countries and still did not meet the needs of all mothers who worked or wished to work.

The Ageing Society

In 1997, 20% of pensioners were poor by the official measure (income below 60% of median income), 14% in 2005–8. This decline also owed much to measures introduced by Brown. Annual winter fuel payments of £100 to everyone over 60 began in 1997, raised by 2008 to £250, £400 from age 80, to protect older peoples' health. Everyone aged 75 and over received a free BBC licence and all pensioners were eligible for free eye tests and an increased income tax allowance. From 1999 the means-tested supplement to pensions for those with low incomes received an above-inflation rise with future increases linked to the more generous measure of earnings rather than the current measure of prices. In 2003 it was renamed Pension Credit (PC).

Older peoples' benefits, including pensions, rose to the highest level ever, though still only just above the official poverty line. More women than men benefitted because they made up the majority of pensioners and more of them were poor. But still in 2024 up to one-third of eligible people did not apply for means-tested benefits, including PC, because they were unaware of their rights, did not know how to apply or resisted the stigma. In 2008 Brown introduced free travel for all over-60s on local public transport throughout England. It was already available in Scotland, Wales and some English towns and cities, including Greater London. Universal free travel and winter fuel allowances were criticized for benefitting rich as well as poor pensioners but means-testing was costly and inefficient while universal benefits reached all of the poorest.[33] Pensioners, like the rest of the population, gained from the government's increased funding of the NHS, which significantly improved services and patient satisfaction.

Pensioner poverty mattered especially because their numbers grew as life expectancy continued to rise, though unequally: in 2010 men born in wealthy Kensington and Chelsea, London, lived on average to 88 years; in poorer, mixed-race Tottenham just to 71, with comparable inequalities for women.[34] It was lowest in poorer parts of Glasgow: 70 for males, 77 for females. Of the UK population, 16% were aged 65 or over, the highest proportion ever. Some, mostly men and their partners, were wealthy, benefitting from high pay while working, good private pensions and the unprecedented rise in the value of homes bought before prices boomed from the 1980s. Some commentators constructed from this minority good fortune a narrative of generational conflict, with a wholly wealthy 'baby-boomer' generation, born between around 1945 and the 1960s, living in luxury while younger people suffered from rising housing costs and funding through taxes the health care and pensions of their selfish elders.[35] This overlooked continuing pensioner poverty, especially among women, and the considerable financial and personal support provided by older people who could afford it for their children and grandchildren. Thirty-one per cent of grandparents helped their grandchildren buy a home. They also paid university costs and left substantial legacies. In reality, inequalities within the older and younger generations were at least as great as those between generations.[36]

As more people remained fit and capable of work to later ages and population ageing continued, Labour abolished fixed retirement ages, implemented after it left office in 2011. Employers could then insist on retirement only by workers demonstrably unable to work efficiently. But gender discrimination in retirement continued, still experienced by women at earlier ages than men, including in high-profile occupations. In 2011 Miriam O'Reilly successfully brought a much-publicized case for age discrimination against the BBC when she was sacked as presenter of a TV show, aged 53, on grounds of her ageing appearance, while her visibly older, male co-presenter continued. She then campaigned on behalf of other victims.[37]

Contrary to caricatures of 'baby-boomers' as selfish, dependent burdens, they contributed significantly to society and the economy. Annual Home Office surveys from 2001 showed that 65–74-year-olds were the largest age group regularly engaged in voluntary action, volunteering regularly with NGOs or helping sick and frail family, friends and neighbours.[38] The surveys did not distinguish volunteers by gender; they certainly included men and women. Also, despite improvements to publicly funded childcare, as more mothers worked, by 2010 one in three working mothers relied on grandparents (mostly but not entirely female) for childcare, some giving up their own employment to help their daughters work.

Gay and Transgender Rights

In 1997 Chris Smith became Minister for National Heritage and the first openly gay Cabinet Minister. Angela Eagle, soon to be a junior minister, became Labour's second backbencher, following Maureen Colquhoun in 1978, to come out as lesbian, exciting the media less than in the 1970s. In the election, the 'out' gay Labour candidate, Ben Bradshaw, fought Exeter against the Director of the Conservative Family Campaign, Adrian Rodgers, who warned of the danger to children of electing a gay MP. A sign of change was that, in contrast to Peter Tatchell's defeat in Bermondsey, south London, in 1982, following attacks on his sexuality in a seriously homophobic campaign, Bradshaw won with a swing of 12%.

Also in 1997 the Equality Network was founded in Scotland to fight for lesbian, gay, bisexual and transgender rights, and foreign partners of lesbians and gay men were granted immigration rights to the UK on the same terms as straight couples. Labour promised free votes on equalizing the age of consent at 16 and repealing Section 28, established by Thatcher (discussed in chapter 8). Then the European Commission on Human Rights (succeeded in 1998 by the European Court of Human Rights, ECtHR) accepted the plea of a British man that the unequal age breached the Convention on Human Rights. Some tabloids, echoed in parliament, again warned of teenagers being seduced by predatory gay men and that change would encourage homosexuality. Labour MP Ann Kean introduced an amendment to the Crime and Disorder Bill, 1998, equalizing the ages, which passed the Commons but was defeated in the Lords. It was reintroduced in the government's Sexual Offences (Amendment) Act, 1998, using the Parliament Act to over-rule the Lords. It was adopted in Scotland, and in Northern Ireland, where equality existed but at age 17. Public opinion continued to shift. In 1994 NOP found only 13% of respondents supporting equality, by 1999 66%.[39]

In 1999 Channel 4 broadcast the first high-profile TV drama about gay life, *Queer as Folk*. From the first scene, featuring a 30-year-old man seducing a 15-year-old schoolboy, it tested public attitudes and those of the Broadcasting Standards Commission. It survived and was popular. Sensationalized sex became more common on TV.[40] Individual and local attitudes were still highly diverse and, less positively, in 1999 a nail bomb exploded in a well-known gay pub in Soho, central London, the Admiral Duncan, killing three people. The prejudices expressed over the age of consent recurred in debates about repeal of Section 28 and gay adoption. The Scottish parliament easily repealed Section 28 in 2000, despite vigorous opposition from religious groups and the tabloids. At Westminster, the Lords were again opposed but it was forced through in 2003.[41] It was repealed also in Northern Ireland. The legislation also introduced equal rights for same-sex couples to adopt children. This caused protest from the Anglican and Roman Catholic churches, arguing that it was contrary to the Human Rights Act – which had been invoked to justify the measure – because requiring their adoption organizations to assist gay and lesbian couples infringed their members' right to practise their faith. Faith-based adoption agencies were granted a 21-month exemption.[42] When this expired, in January 2009, many of them observed the law. It was introduced in Northern Ireland in 2013.

In 2003 Employment Equality (Sexual Orientation) Regulations made workplace discrimination against lesbians and gays illegal.[43] The Sexual Offences Act, 2004, abolished the crimes of buggery and gross indecency between men, and the Civil Partnership Act granted registered same-sex couples the same rights and responsibilities as married, heterosexual couples.[44] Some unmarried heterosexual couples complained that they had no such rights, but nothing changed for them while gay couples celebrated real progress. In 2005 the first gay civil partnerships were registered. The 2006 Equality Act outlawed discrimination on grounds of sexuality in provision of goods and services. Some boarding-house keepers argued in court, unsuccessfully, that the requirement to let shared rooms to gay couples contravened their religious beliefs. In 2008 incitement to homophobic hatred became an offence, for which Stonewall had long campaigned. Polls indicated high levels of public support for the reforms, from 68% for civil partnership to 93% for protection of gay people from discrimination and harassment at work.[45] This liberalizing legislation was adopted, with variations, throughout the UK. In general, in the early twenty-first century gay and lesbian people felt more accepted and able to be more visible, much assisted by this run of New Labour reforms. Gay and lesbian bars ceased to be hidden underground and became more public, visible and available to all. Regional Pride events proliferated, reaching 119 by 2021.[46]

Trans campaigners continued to lobby politicians and make effective use of the courts. In 1999 Sex Discrimination (Gender Reassignment) Regulations established that employment rights gained in European courts applied to those intending to undergo gender reassignment as well as those who had completed or were undergoing it, following (tardily) a decision by the European Court of Justice in 1994 concerning a British transsexual woman. Also in 1999 the Court of Appeal held that the NHS could not refuse gender reassignment treatment to those requesting it, on the grounds that gender dysphoria (the feeling of being trapped in a body of the wrong sex) was an illness under the terms of the NHS legislation. But trans people continued to face prejudice and conflicts over which hospital wards or prisons they were assigned to, over which public and workplace toilets they used and over pension rights.

In 2002 the ECHR ruled that the inability of UK citizens who changed gender to change their sex as recorded on their birth certificate was a breach of their rights under the European Convention on Human Rights, including their right to marry and receive respect for their private lives. This led to the introduction of the Gender Recognition Act, 2004, in England and Wales, followed by similar legislation in Scotland, which had devolved rights in this field whereas Wales did not, and in Northern Ireland in 2005. It gave people the legal right to live in their acquired gender, enabling transgender people to obtain a Gender Recognition Certificate if they provided medical evidence of diagnosis of gender dysphoria, had lived in their acquired gender for at least two years and made a statutory declaration that they intended to do so for the remainder of their lives. Successful applicants gained all the rights of their lived gender, including to pensions and other benefits, and the right to marry and to protection under anti-discrimination and equality legislation. In 2005 the first certificates were awarded and the first transsexual marriages celebrated, but trans people still experienced discrimination, including from some gay and lesbian groups.[47]

The Conservatives officially opposed most reforms concerning gay and transgender equalities, though members were divided and there were hints of change.[48] In 2002 Theresa May, the first female Chairman (*sic*) of the party, from 2016 its second female leader and Premier, berated the party at its annual conference for appearing as a 'nasty party' especially on these topics. In the same year, Alan Duncan was the first Tory MP to come out as gay and, as a respected MP, was widely supported, including by Iain Duncan Smith, then leader, a committed Catholic. In 2015 a review by the Brussels-based International Lesbian, Gay, Bisexual, Trans and Intersex Association, founded in 1996 and recognized by the UN, gave the UK the highest score in Europe for 86% progress towards 'respect of human rights and full equality for LGBT'. Scotland was awarded 92%.[49]

Conclusion

Under New Labour there was visible, if incomplete, progress on most aspects of gender inequalities, more on gay and transgender than male/female rights. Nevertheless, in 2002 Tessa Jowell, Minister for Culture, Media and Sport, described it as 'the most feminist government in history', expressing some truth, though the government did not have strong competition.[50] Its achievements probably owed something to the unprecedented number of female Labour MPs, though European courts and other institutions again played an important part. It expressed its desire to increase the female workforce and did more to improve publicly provided, affordable childcare than any peacetime government of the twentieth century, but the support it gave women workers, especially mothers, and their career opportunities was limited, as demonstrated in an exceptional number of expert surveys.[51]

Blair resigned as Prime Minister in 2007, and was succeeded by Brown. He was soon overtaken by the international financial crisis. He did much to mitigate its effects in Britain and elsewhere but received little credit for it from the Conservatives, who, preparing for an unavoidable election in 2010, unjustly blamed Labour's 'overspending' for a crisis originating in the US which was certainly not Labour's fault. Conservatives led the next government, but did not win over enough voters to form a majority government and had to agree a coalition government with the Liberal Democrats.

TEN

Austerity, 2010–2024

The Coalition lasted until 2015, led by the Conservatives. Five successive Conservative governments were then in power until 2024 when Labour won a substantial majority in the July election. The government formed in 2010 expressed no explicit commitment to gender equality, though the Prime Minister, David Cameron, unexpectedly introduced same-sex marriage in England, Wales and Scotland in 2013. It did not reach Northern Ireland until 2020.

In 2010 the government immediately introduced a programme of cuts to welfare and taxes, labelled 'Austerity', initiated by Chancellor George Osborne supported by Cameron. They justified it by continuing to blame Labour 'overspending' for damaging the economy. They revived and extended Thatcherite policies with reduced and privatized state services and benefits, deregulation of the labour market and lower taxes. They reversed many of New Labour's reforms and established lower pay, greater insecurity and increasing poverty for many workers and their families and further disadvantages for female workers. Most Sure Start centres were closed. Cuts to local authority budgets caused closure or privatization of other services, including social care for older and disabled people and childcare, and disadvantageous 'outsourcing' of staff. Childcare became even scarcer and more expensive than in any comparable country, severely impacting mothers in the labour market and preventing many from working. In devolved Scotland it was still provided by local authorities, cheaper, and with better-trained staff. The EMA was quickly abolished. There were fewer cuts to Labour's benefits for pensioners, who were believed to disproportionately vote Tory.

Under successive Conservative governments, but owing little to them, there was a slight narrowing of gender inequalities, including under another female Prime Minister, Theresa May, from 2016 to 2019 and a very brief, 48-day, financially disastrous, term under Liz Truss in 2022. It probably owed most to the continuing gradual increase in the representation of women in parliament. In 2010, 143 women were elected to a House of Commons of 650 members (22%), the highest proportion so far, up from 128 (20%) in 2005. In 2010, 49 were Conservatives, 81 Labour. In the 2015 election the total rose to 191 (29%), in 2017 to 208 (32%), and in 2019 to 220 (34%), all mostly Labour. They worked to make parliament more receptive to women, still much needed. Following the 2015 election a new cross-party Select Committee of the House of Commons, the Women and Equalities Committee, was established to scrutinize government policy and administration concerning all inequalities, including of gender, gay, lesbian and transgender rights. As we will see, it published several reports but had limited impact.

In 2010 four women were appointed to the Cabinet, four others at various points to 2014, some for short periods. A succession of female Ministers held the title Minister for Women and Equalities (the title chosen by Cameron), but all as a secondary role to a more senior ministerial position. First was Theresa May as Home Secretary, who passed the secondary role to Maria Miller, less senior as Minister for Culture, Media and Sport, in 2012 until in 2014 it passed to Nicky Morgan, Minister for Education. None made an obvious contribution to furthering gender equality. Women's groups, including those representing ethnic minorities, continued to campaign for the government to provide adequate, affordable childcare, close the gender pay gap, introduce flexible working when needed, raise benefits and much else, with little effect.

Poverty and Inequality

Again, lone-parent families headed by mothers were hardest hit by welfare cuts. From 2010 to 2013–14, poverty among women rose significantly faster than among men, especially among single mothers, mainly due to low pay, cuts to benefits and services and further increase in the costs of housing and other essentials. Homelessness grew again. Surveys by respected independent organizations showed that national poverty rose from 2011–12, after falling through the 2000s. The Joseph Rowntree Foundation (JRF) found 20% of the UK population in poverty in 2015–16, 60% in households including a full-time worker so low-paid that she or he could not support the family.[1] The CPAG estimated that 30% of children in the UK (4.1 million) were in poverty in 2016–17,

67% in households with at least one full-time worker.[2] The Institute for Fiscal Studies (IFS) supported this estimate and stressed regional variations: in 2016–17, 24% of children in Scotland were in poverty, 37% in London, the difference driven mainly by housing costs.[3] As ever, London contained some of the richest and poorest people in the UK. In 2020, the IFS reported that 49% of children in lone-parent families in Britain were in poverty, 25% in two-parent families. All these findings were derived from official government surveys of reported household incomes and employed the internationally accepted measure of relative poverty in high-income countries: incomes below 60% of the national median. Poverty was still rising in 2024.[4]

In 2013 the Conservatives launched Universal Credit (UC), a means-tested benefit system replacing with a single payment the six main existing means-tested benefits, Income Support, Jobseeker's Allowance, Employment and Support Allowance, Housing Benefit, Child Tax Credit and Working Tax Credit. Consequently, it was less flexible concerning the variety of difficulties that could drive people into need. Previously, if a claimant's rent rose, only Housing Benefit would be adjusted; now all benefit income was halted for adjustment, sometimes for as long as five weeks, driving claimants further into poverty and debt. The main objective was to force anyone judged capable into work – any work – a return to ancient Poor Law principles assuming that claimants were poor because they were too idle to work. In reality, most claimants were in work, but low-paid in the deteriorating labour market. UC increased poverty as much as it relieved it, due partly to slow, incompetent administration.

It further increased child and family poverty when Osborne banned payment of UC, Child Benefit or tax credits for the third and any subsequent child born after 6 April 2017, regardless of the family's circumstances at the time of birth. It was based on the assumption that families on benefits were carelessly having children at the taxpayers' expense. A spokesperson for the Department of Work and Pensions (DWP) explained that 'families on benefits are asked to make the same financial decisions as families supporting themselves solely through work'. No account was taken of the fact that the children might have been born before the family needed benefits. One survey by academic experts described it as 'the worst social security policy ever'.[5] The Children's Commissioners for Wales and Northern Ireland called unsuccessfully for it to be scrapped; this was outside their devolved powers. Scottish powers over social security spending were partially extended in 2016 and it abolished the two-child limit and established a new weekly payment of £10 for each child up to age 16 in families on UC, raising it to £25 in November 2022. In England surveys showed how much the change increased child poverty. In August 2024 the Resolution Foundation reported that this was now highest, at 48%, in Birmingham and Manchester, still very severe elsewhere, including parts of London.[6] Lone-mother families continued to be especially vulnerable. The Labour government elected in July 2024 immediately faced strong pressure to remove the cap. It did not, but established a task force to 'develop an ambitious child poverty strategy to tackle the crisis', aiming to end child poverty by the end of the current parliament in 2029.[7]

In 2014 Cameron's government announced a rise in the pension age for men and women to 67 in 2026–8, in line with New Labour proposals, discussed in chapter 9, both influenced by the steady rise in average life expectancy and expectation of healthy life for all social groups over many decades. But from 2011 another sign of growing poverty and inequality was that both averages declined, especially among poorer women. From 2011 to 2018 average life expectancy for women in the most deprived areas fell, for the first time in decades, by several months to just above age 78. In the least deprived areas, it rose by several months to 86. By 2023 average life expectancy in the most deprived areas was 73.5 years for men, 78.3 for women, in the least deprived 83.2 and 86.3.[8] The decline took place across Europe but was greatest in England.[9] The number of births also fell again, by 12.2% in England and Wales from 2012 to 2016, continuing thereafter and increasing the proportion of older people in the population.

Older women were further disadvantaged by the rise in their state pension age from 60 to 65, to match that of men, from 2010 to 2020, as announced in 1995, but previous governments had failed to warn them, and they were unprepared, as described in chapter 8. Many discovered only at the last minute that they needed to work five years longer than expected if they had insufficient savings, no high-income husband or no good occupational pension enabling them to retire comfortably at 60. They formed Women Against State Pension Inequality (WASPI) in protest. They were not opposed to equal pension ages but to the lack of adequate warning of their introduction.[10] But in 2020 the government announced that it would not compensate women disadvantaged by the change. In 2024 the Labour government came under immediate pressure from WASPI to provide compensation, but it also refused, arousing much anger.[11] It later announced that it was reconsidering.

As we have seen, women had long suffered from pension inequality due to low pay and working lives interrupted by caring responsibilities which reduced their contributions and pensions. This especially affected occupational pensions which were fixed in relation to salary and contributions, both influenced by years of work and the discrimination women experienced in the labour market. In 2022 the average annual occupational pension received by women was £11,581, by men £16,034, with large variations among both.[12] More people, more women than men, now worked past the state pension age because they enjoyed their work or their pension income was low. But growing numbers could not work even to pension age due to sickness, disability or caring responsibilities. A study by the Fabian Society found poverty increasing from 2010 among people aged 60–64, from 13.6% of women and about 18% of men in 2009–10 to 25.4% of women and 23.6% of men in 2021–2. The state pension has never provided a sufficient income for adequate survival. In 2024 the DWP surveyed 'deprivation' among people over 66 in the UK, asking whether they had access to substantial meals, heating, electricity and a home in a good state, among other essentials. Almost a million were found to be suffering deprivation in 2022–3, more than one-third higher than in 2019.[13]

The decline of public services accelerated when substantial numbers of staff who had migrated to Britain from EU countries, particularly to work in the health and care services, fled after Britain voted in 2016 to leave the EU and finally left in 2020. They were concerned about the effects on their rights. This caused further decline in residential and community care for older and disabled people and for children in need, shifting still greater responsibility for care onto family members, mostly female. Many gave up work or reduced their hours; more than 25% reported cutting back on eating, heating and leisure and suffering mental health problems due to the stress of unsupported caring and resulting low incomes.[14] The state Carers Allowance, introduced by Labour in 1976 and raised by New Labour, was cut in real terms to become the lowest state benefit and quite inadequate. The 2021 census showed that 10.4%

of women in the UK and 7.6% of men provided unpaid social care, most among women aged 55–59 (19.9%).[15]

Health Inequalities

Women received poorer treatment than men in a declining NHS. Maternal deaths in pregnancy and childbirth and infant deaths rose after 2010, especially in the most deprived areas and among ethnic minorities, largely due to inadequate funding of the NHS and staff shortages. By 2017, 9.6 women were dying within six weeks of childbirth for every 100,000 births. The World Health Organization (WHO) reported that the death rates were higher than in comparable countries. Following a review in 2017 of one NHS Trust whose maternity services aroused serious concerns, the UK government committed to halve by 2025 the 2010 rate of stillbirths, neonatal and maternal deaths and brain injuries to babies during and after birth in England and Wales. It invested a further £127 million in the NHS workforce and introduced plans to investigate and improve all maternity services, without evident success since severe problems continued to be found. In May 2024 a research study reported major concerns, including disparities in maternal health across ethnic groups, Black women having especially poor outcomes. They experienced poorer care during labour and expressed concern at professional responses to their complaints which they believed demonstrated implicit or explicit racism and negative perceptions of religious and cultural practices.[16]

Also in 2024, a report by the Fawcett Society, *The Gender Health Gap*, found 'sexism and misogyny' widespread in the health system, creating relatively poor health outcomes for women of all ages. Compared with men, they experienced more late and incorrect diagnoses, which exacerbated symptoms, and outright dismissal of their requests for care. Fawcett found that 60% of women in the UK believed their health issues were not taken seriously, 57% had a negative experience with a health care professional, and 42% had heard derogatory comments in the workplace about a female colleague's health. The report estimated that the UK was losing 150 million working days each year due to women's poor health and lack of suitable support.[17]

There was increasing public concern about the effects of the menopause on women's health, work and everyday life. Such effects were not new, but they were increasingly widely discussed following research and campaigns by women. They were perhaps more evident now that a high proportion of middle-aged women were employed. In 2022 Fawcett published a report, *Menopause and the Workplace*, focusing especially upon women employed in financial services. It revealed that eight in ten said their employer had not trained staff on the issue or put in place a menopause absence policy. Only four in ten received a timely offer of beneficial hormone replacement therapy (HRT) from their GP. Some 77% experienced one or more symptoms they described as 'very difficult' due to menopause: 69% suffered anxiety or depression, 84% sleeping problems, 73% 'brain fog'. Working-class women suffered more severe symptoms, with 44% of women saying their ability to work was affected, 10% – roughly 333,000 – of employed women left work due to symptoms, 12% worked reduced hours, 14% went part-time, and 8% did not apply for promotion. Disabled women were especially affected; 22% left their jobs. But only 30% of women who took time off gave the menopause as the reason on their sick note, for fear of prejudice. Only 55% spoke to their GP about their need for leave, and 67% of those who did so believed that health care professionals were well informed about menopause, but 30% experienced delays in diagnosis. Fawcett called on the government to require employers to produce menopause action plans and make flexible work a default. They also called for the government to implement a public information campaign about menopause, invite every woman to speak to her GP about it at an appropriate age and ensure that GPs received mandatory training on its effects and treatment.[18] In 2021 the DWP published guidelines for employers on support for employees undergoing menopause, but by 2024 they were still not mandatory.[19]

In England in 2022 the Women and Equalities Select Committee recommended that the government make the menopause a protected characteristic in the workplace. The government commissioned an independent review. In 2023 it appointed a Menopause Employment Champion to support women in need and provided free period products to schools and further education colleges, following reports that poverty put them out of the reach of many people. In 2021 it had abolished the VAT on period products (the so-called 'tampon tax') and established a Period Poverty Taskforce to tackle the issue, but this was paused due to the Covid pandemic and not reinstated by 2024. In 2021 the Scottish government placed a duty on local authority education departments to provide period products free of charge to those in need in schools and all public buildings, including libraries. In 2023 the Welsh government's 'Period Proud Wales Action Plan' aimed to eradicate period poverty and promote period dignity across Wales. The results were not clear by early 2025.

Inequalities at Work

In addition to the effects of menopause, women continued to experience other significant gender inequalities at work while they still outperformed males in education. In 2021–2, 71.9% of girls were assessed as having attained 'a good level of development' at school compared with only 58.7% of boys. More boys than girls were identified as having special educational needs and more were excluded from school. In higher education, the number of female undergraduates continued to increase but specialisms remained highly gender-segregated. Most PhD students were female for the first time in 2020–1.[20]

Partly due to more women having higher educational qualifications, the gender employment gap narrowed slightly from 2010–11 to 2019–20, when 57% of adult women and 65.8% of men were employed. Highly educated women benefitted most. Those whose qualifications were GCSE or lower experienced a larger gender gap in opportunities and pay due to the demands and cost of childcare, employer bias and the effects of austerity and increasing poverty. Gender inequalities in employment were even more extensively researched than before, especially by women's organizations, revealing an increasingly complex situation as more women worked in a growing range of occupations.

Pay inequalities remained a major problem and preoccupation of women workers, campaigners and researchers. There were some improvements. Employer returns under equal-pay legislation showed that in 2010–11 average median male hourly earnings were 19.8% above those of women, 17.4% above in 2019, 15.5% in 2020, with great variations around the averages. The changed average was mainly due to the narrowing gap at the top end with less improvement at lower levels. In 2019 the Westminster government published 'Gender Equality at Every Stage, a Roadmap for Change', apparently aiming to address barriers to women entering or returning to the labour market and occupational segregation, and to close the gender pay gap, but it had little obvious effect, not assisted by the Covid pandemic breaking out soon after.[21] In 2022 the government committed to a pay transparency pilot to address pay inequality, but by the time of the 2024 election, there had been no action.

The Fawcett Society had long been concerned about unequal pay. Each year it reported on Equal Pay Day, the internationally recognized day on which the median earnings of women workers in each nation, when added to their earnings for the whole preceding year, equalled annual total male median earnings. On Equal Pay Day 2023 (22 November), Fawcett reported that, on average in Great Britain, women earned £574 per month less than men, £6,888 per annum. At this rate the gap would not close before 2051. It argued that making flexible work available in high-quality, high-paid jobs was essential to close the gap more quickly, because women took lower-paid, lower-quality work – often part-time, insecure work on zero-hours contracts, below the level of their skills and abilities – because they could not otherwise combine caring responsibilities with paid work. This disadvantaged the economy as well as the women by wasting their skills. Forty per cent of women not currently employed said that access to flexible working would enable them to work, and 77% said they were more likely to apply for work that advertised flexible opportunities.

Fawcett concluded that the gender pay gap must close if the economy was to thrive. To achieve this the government must insist that employers introduce flexible working, for men and women, enabling men to take a fair share of childcare and domestic responsibilities and giving women access to work they were qualified and eager to do.[22] By the time of the election in July 2024, there was no government response, but, as we will see, the incoming Labour government soon committed to requiring employers to provide flexible working as a default, as part of a much-needed wider reform of the labour market.

In November 2023 Fawcett published another detailed report on the multiple influences sustaining the pay gap.[23] It pointed out that the gap had narrowed significantly in the 1970s and 1980s, then slowed until the mean gap for full-time workers narrowed again from 20.7% in 1997 to 10.7% in 2023. The IFS concluded in 2021 that the narrowing gap over the previous 25 years was mainly due to women's improved educational attainments. The minimum wage also made a significant difference.[24] The report observed that these changes were unlikely to advance further, so further reforms were needed, especially improvements to parental leave, to early childhood education and care and an end to gender segregation in employment. Occupations perceived as 'female', including early childhood education and care, adult social care, teaching, administrative or secretarial work, were generally lower-paid, despite the importance of teaching and caring work to the economy, and women, especially mothers, continued to be under-represented in higher-status, higher-paid work. Pay tended to fall as more women moved into any sector, due above all to discrimination. Motherhood had a negative effect on women's earnings and career progression over the life course in most European countries, known as the 'motherhood penalty'. In Britain it accounted for a 45% reduction in women's long-term income. Fawcett's research established that in the UK a woman with two children took home 26% less pay on average than a woman without children. The gap for Black or other minority ethnic mothers was wider. In contrast, fathers with two children were paid on average 22% more than childless men for reasons that were unclear.

Fawcett explained the 'motherhood penalty' partly on the obvious grounds that mothers did more unpaid caring and domestic work than other women and men. Also, mothers were generally less free than others to choose their working and caring patterns but were tied to gendered norms, policies and restrictions that led to lower pay. The existing system of parental leave encouraged fathers to take very little time off after childbirth – they still received just two weeks leave at low pay. Polling by Fawcett found that 41% of fathers and 36% of mothers felt they did not have enough parental leave. Their choices were also restricted by the high cost of early childhood care and education. And some women left work involuntarily due to discrimination; each year 54,000 women were dismissed, illegally, due to pregnancy. The British Social Attitudes Survey showed that in 2022 only 9% of the population still believed that a man's main job was to earn money, a woman's to look after the home. Men now made a somewhat bigger contribution to housework but, internationally, it was still overwhelmingly carried out by women.[25]

In 2019 the IFS found that the gender pay gap was greater for older women. In 2023 the mean hourly pay gap was 3.6% for women aged

26–29, 14.5% for those aged 50–59. The average mean gap for all ages was 10.7%. The main reason was probably motherhood, whose effects increased over time, together with the effects of other gender inequalities in the workplace, including pay discrimination, lack of promotion opportunities for women and discrimination against older women. The Fawcett Society found that the pay gap for women aged 22–39 had not narrowed from 2018 to 2023. For those aged 18–21, a recent dip in inequality had been followed by a rise. According to the Office for National Statistics (ONS), for women over 40 there had been a very slight narrowing over time, but the pace had slowed recently.

The 2023 Fawcett Report described the considerable variation in the pay gap across occupations and regions. It was greatest in the creative arts, entertainment and leisure pursuits – including libraries, museums and sports – with a 28.2% average. Finance and insurance had a large average gap for full-time workers at 22.5% in 2023, and the largest median gap of all occupations, suggesting a big gap across all levels of pay and seniority. London and south-east England consistently had the highest gender gap in hourly pay for full-time workers, Scotland and Northern Ireland the lowest.[26] The pay gap of course led to a pensions gap. A TUC report in 2023, 'The Gender Pensions Gap', indicated that this averaged 37.9% in 2019–20, much higher than the pay gap. The average pension gap in most OECD countries was 25.6% in 2015, when it was 40.5% in the UK.[27]

From 2017 employers with more than 250 employees were legally required to publish their gender pay gap. Research for the Centre for Economic Performance at the LSE found that reporting led to a narrower gap. The Fawcett Society suggested there was a strong case for lowering the threshold to 100 employees and for mandatory reporting also of ethnicity and disability pay gaps. They also called for mandatory action plans for employers to address the gaps and for the EHRC to gain powers to fine organizations failing to close them within a given time. Female workers should have a legally enforceable right to know what a male colleague was paid for equal work, so that they could challenge unequal pay. The studies of pay inequalities made clear that gender inequality pervaded all levels and sectors of the labour market, especially lower levels, and that successive governments from 2010 had done little to reduce it.

In early 2023 the Westminster government announced a pilot designed to increase the small number of women in science, technology, engineering and mathematics (STEM-based) employment, where they represented just 27% of the workforce in 2019–20.[28] In October 2023 the Fawcett Society published a survey, *Diversifying the Tech Sector*, reporting that just 19% of tech employees were female and even fewer were disabled or from minority ethnic communities in a sector vital to the economy but experiencing difficulties in recruiting enough people with suitable skills. One in five men working in technology believed that women were naturally less suited to working in the sector. Of women with STEM qualifications working outside the sector, 43% believed there was more sexist behaviour in tech than in any other sector, and 72% of women in tech roles had experienced at least one form of sexism at work, including being paid less than male colleagues for the same work, sexist 'banter' (22%) and questioning of their skills and abilities whatever their qualifications (20%). Three in four workers from an ethnic minority background had experienced racism at work, one in three Black women had been assumed by colleagues not to hold a tech role. The report commented that all of this 'rings alarm bells for a sector that prides itself on being "future-facing"'.

The survey called for action to ensure that job advertisements used gender-neutral language, and that businesses set targets to improve the representation of women and other under-represented groups and offer returner training in tech skills. There should be more funding for teaching technical expertise in the education system and measures to counter gender stereotypes in schools since inequalities began early in women's lives. Tech businesses should normalize and expand flexible and part-time work and parental leave to attract more women. They should promote an inclusive culture, challenging misogyny and racism; create transparent mechanisms for reporting grievances and harassment; and support employees experiencing workplace discrimination, while providing equitable training, pay and progression and ensuring pay transparency and clear promotion criteria. The report called on the government to require all businesses to publish gender and ethnicity pay data.[29]

The Westminster government committed to reforming redundancy laws to prevent continuing discrimination against women in pregnancy or on returning from maternity leave, and to ensure their increased protection against sexual harassment in the workplace. This was arousing unprecedented protest from women around the world, notably the #MeToo movement, sparked by women in the Hollywood film industry protesting against harassment by a male producer. It stimulated the foundation of another international movement, #TimesUp, dedicated to raising funds to help victims of sexual harassment. With much celebrity support it did so successfully, including in the UK until it was wound up in 2021.

At Westminster, Private Members' Bills led to legislation in 2023 to increase protection against redundancy following pregnancy or family leave, and to the Employment Relations (Flexible Working) Act, 2023, which gave workers the right to request flexible working from day one of a new job. They could make up to two requests each year and employers were required not to refuse without good reason. The law included no measures against sexual harassment of women and gay men at work or elsewhere. In 2024 Fawcett launched a project designed to tackle sexual harassment in the workplace. It produced an 'employer toolkit', a free resource to enable employers to 'create an environment where sexual harassment does not happen'. It aimed to help them change the workplace culture, introduce a sexual harassment policy, train employees, make it safe and easy to report harassment and respond appropriately. It developed an Anti-Sexual Harassment training programme that could be downloaded. Most of these recommendations were included in Labour's Employment Rights Bill in late 2024.

Women workers continued to be concentrated in public social services at all levels, holding 77% of posts in health and social care in 2022, 70% in education, only 16% in construction services, though this was progress.[30] Conservative governments supported in principle the FTSE Women Leaders Annual Review, established in 2011 to advise leading businesses on how to increase the representation of women at senior levels. By 2023, 350 higher-level companies met the target of 40% female board members, but the Review reported that there were still too few top female executives.[31] The government established the Woman-led High Growth Enterprise Taskforce in the Cabinet Office in 2022 to investigate the number of such businesses led by women across Britain. It reported in March 2024 that only 18% of 'high growth enterprises' had at least one woman among its leaders.[32] Management consultancy McKinsey reported that companies in the top 25% for gender diversity in their executive teams were 25% more likely to have above average profitability than those in the bottom 25%.[33] There were signs, including from the FTSE review, that business was gradually becoming more open to gender equality at higher levels, while it declined at lower levels. There were fears that some businesses were abandoning diversity policies, encouraged by the Conservative government's representing them as 'woke red tape'.[34] Women were also increasingly present, though still minorities, at higher levels of the professions: in 2022 they were 30% of High Court judges, 38% of Civil Service Permanent Secretaries and 40% of secondary-school heads.[35]

Following devolution, employment policies differed across Scotland, Wales and England, with more signs of positive action for equality in Scotland and Wales than in England. In Scotland the Workplace Equality Fund opened in 2018 and offered employers financial support to improve equality-related outcomes for all disadvantaged groups. In 2019 the Scottish government published *A Fairer Scotland for Women: Gender Pay Gap Action Plan* aiming to narrow the pay gap and address labour market inequalities. In 2020 a Woman Returners Programme was launched to help women return to work after a career break. The outcomes of these measures remained uncertain in 2025.[36] In Wales the government published in 2019 a 'Prosperity for All Economic Action Plan' committed to increasing female representation in traditionally male-dominated sectors. It was followed in 2022 by 'Stronger, Fairer, Greener Wales: A Plan for Employability and Skills' to tackle economic inequality and ensure fair work opportunities for all, again with uncertain outcomes by 2025.

Both Scotland and Wales, with higher proportions of elected women in their representative assemblies, made more effort than England to increase the presence of women in official roles. The Gender Representation on Public Boards (Scotland) Act, 2018, aimed to increase women's representation to 50% of non-executive personnel on public boards. The Welsh 'Reflecting Wales in Running Wales' strategy, 2020, was designed to improve 'diversity in decision-making in public life through board-level appointments to public bodies'. Both achieved gradual change, but still in 2022 the EHRC reported that just 47% of public appointments across Great Britain were held by women, up from 44% in 2019, and only 38% of chairs of public boards were female.[37] The distribution across England, Wales and Scotland was unclear. There was no functioning Northern Ireland government from 2017 until early 2024 to consider initiatives concerning gender equality.

Fawcett's research reinforced the findings of other surveys, including showing there was not enough part-time work available to match the skills and experience of women who could, if it was provided, contribute valuably to the economy while observing their caring duties. It was most widespread in lower-level employment. Fawcett described how illegal pay discrimination persisted, with men and women unequally paid for equal work, especially Black and other minority ethnic women, who had even poorer opportunities for promotion than white women. Fawcett recommended that employers should be required to consider what flexible working options were available to them, including part-time work, job-sharing, flexible hours or remote working, since this was vital especially for ensuring that disabled people and those with caring responsibilities could manage their lives while contributing to the economy. At the same time, it was also essential to reduce pay inequality. Fawcett also recommended that the high cost of childcare and exploitation of its low-paid, predominantly female workforce must end, because it faced parents with impossible decisions around work and parenthood and increased pay and opportunity gaps. Britain needed a universal free childcare system as in comparable countries, and a strategy to improve workforce conditions.

Fawcett followed up with another report in 2023 on *Transforming Early Childhood Education and Care*.[38] They examined services in a select group of countries to identify good practice for adoption in England. They focused on England because Wales, Scotland and Northern Ireland had their own, often better, systems. They believed that high-quality early childhood education and care (ECEC) was critical to achieving progress on gender equality. Even in England they found 'a lot of strong practice'. The overall quality of education and care was high, with 96% of providers rated good or outstanding, but they reached too few children in greatest need. Economically disadvantaged children started school on average four months behind their peers in development and the gap widened over the remainder of their school lives. It could be narrowed by high-quality early-years education, as New Labour's Sure Start system had shown.

The inadequacies of the care system were more widely publicized later in 2023 when the government announced a series of improvements to access to childcare and early-years education. From April 2024 working parents of 2-year-olds would be eligible for up to 15 hours of free education and care for 38 weeks per year. From September 2024 this would be extended to eligible working parents of children aged from nine months. From September 2025 they could access up to 30 free hours per week, for 38 weeks per year for children aged from nine months to school age. To qualify, parents must work or be in education or training for at least 16 hours per week and earn above £9,518 and less than £100,000 per year. Parents on certain benefits – mainly means-tested benefits and tax credits – also qualified.[39]

The proposals were widely criticized above all because there were too few places to meet the need and likely demand. Many parents and guardians were excluded because they did not work the required hours or had inadequate incomes. The IFS noted that the poorest one-third of families would see almost no benefit from these entitlements though they had most to gain from them.[40] One reason was that some providers charged for extras, including meals and nappies. Parents could provide these items, but the organization Pregnant Then Screwed reported that 23% of parents affected said they could not afford this and so could not afford 'free' childcare.[41] Childcare was a devolved issue and in Scotland children aged 3–4 received 1,140 hours of free childcare per year on similar conditions to those in England. It was also available to 2-year-olds in the care of a local council, a relative or an appointed guardian. Improvements were promised in 2023, then delayed by a change in the leadership of the Scottish government. In Wales in 2023–4, parents and guardians of 3–4-year-olds could claim up to 30 hours free childcare per week for up to 48 weeks per year, if, as in England, they earned under £100,000 per annum, were in work or training for at least 16 hours per week or on certain benefits.

The shortage of childcare places and staff in England was expected to grow due to increased demand when the new measures were introduced. The Department for Education estimated that 85,000 more places and 40,000 extra staff would be needed by September 2025. The Women's Budget Group calculated that funding for all the free hours promised by 2025–6 would cost at least an additional £5.26 million, more if the minimum wage rose and raised staff costs. The additional hours could be expected to increase the already severe pressure on staff, causing more of them to leave if staffing and pay did not improve. Ninety-four per cent of local authorities already reported difficulty in finding qualified staff in current conditions and they were losing staff to higher-paid or more flexible work due to poor pay and poor career progression.[42] The workload was also intensifying because increasing numbers of children were diagnosed with special educational needs and disabilities (SEND). The Conservative plans included no guarantee of providing more places or better-paid and better-trained staff.[43] In the 2024 election campaign, Labour promised to implement the Tory proposals and increase childcare places. It continued these promises after winning the election but recognized they would take time to achieve.

The National Audit Office (NAO) felt 'significant' uncertainty about whether nurseries and childminders providing care in their own homes could deliver on the proposals. The Coram children's charity reported that in 2023–4, places for all pre-school ages across England, Wales and Scotland had fallen. Only 29% of councils in the whole of Great Britain had enough spaces for under-2s in 2024, down from 42% in 2023. In England and Wales councils with sufficient places for 3- and 4-year-olds had fallen from 69% in 2023 to 59% in 2024. The number of childminders also continued to fall.[44] Coram pointed out that the average annual cost of 50 hours per week full-time nursery care for a child under 2 was £15,709 in 2024 compared with £15,000 in 2023, with local variations.[45] The Fawcett Society reported that the UK had the most expensive childcare in the OECD as a percentage of women's median full-time earnings and, unlike most OECD countries, costs as a proportion of income were highest for families with the lowest incomes. Fifty-seven per cent of local authorities reported that parents of children under five said they had reduced their working hours due to shortage or high costs of childcare, including 67% of Asian parents and 75% of parents of disabled children. Fawcett found that 35% of women wished to work more hours but could not, mainly due to lack of access to flexible working and affordable childcare. This was true of 43% of women of Black and other minority communities. They concluded that 'affordable, accessible, high quality and culturally inclusive ECEC was essential, to allow married women who wished to return to work to do so and to work the hours and in the type of job they chose'.[46]

They reported that in England in 2023, 49% of ECEC places were delivered by private providers, either non-profit or (mainly) for-profit institutions. Fawcett did not share the government's conviction that profit-making providers were more efficient and less costly than public services. There were strong indications that the growing numbers of business chains involved, created through opaque financial structures, were less focused on vulnerable and disadvantaged children and their staff costs were up to 14% lower than in non-profit institutions due to low pay and understaffing, while they imposed high charges on users to maximize profits. Similar processes were evident in the adult and child social care sectors, bringing rising costs for users and high profits for providers and putting provision at risk. A significant number of providers went bankrupt around this time as fewer people could afford to use their services and fewer were willing to work for them. Fawcett feared that if the government increased controls over private providers to improve services there was a real danger that investors would leave the market and more providers would close, leaving even fewer places. Return to improved public sector provision was the most effective solution.

Comparing England with other countries, Fawcett found that nowhere had perfect ECEC, but many other countries were more willing to provide funding and to grapple with the challenges, with beneficial results. Success elsewhere followed improvements to the quality, quantity and pay of the workforce, including training to provide for cultural and linguistic diversity and for children with special needs. They concluded that England must focus more on the needs of vulnerable children. Also, many countries capped fees. Children at risk were more likely to take up ECEC when it was universal, low-cost and publicly funded. Access to good-quality childcare increased women's labour market participation, especially when it was free, as shown by the impact of Quebec's universal free system.[47]

Seeking further to improve early-years care and education to support caregivers, in May 2023 Fawcett launched another project, 'Closing the Gender Play Gap'. It aimed to end the inculcation of gender stereotypes into young children, which influenced their whole lives. Fawcett argued that stereotypes 'contribute to the mental health crises among children and young people ... to violence against women and girls ... stereotyped assumptions also significantly limit career choices and contribute to the gender pay gap ... Ultimately [they] limit children's freedom and stop them from being themselves.' The project aimed to provide advice and resources for adults, based on the findings of Fawcett's

Commission on Gender Stereotypes in Early Childhood, which in 2020 had gathered evidence from experts, politicians and relevant organizations, including Mumsnet, the National Childbirth Trust and the National Education Union. Its key findings were that 74% of parents stated that boys and girls were treated differently, 60% that this had a negative impact. Asked what work they could see their children doing when they grew up, parents expressed clearly gendered expectations: 22% could see their sons working in construction, only 3% their daughters; 66% wanted companies to advertise toys to boys and girls in the same ways; and 38% of education practitioners had negligible training or none on challenging gender stereotypes. Among those working with under-7s – nursery nurses, childminders, playworkers, primary-school teachers – more than half had heard other staff say 'boys will be boys' sympathetically when boys misbehaved, 60% 'often' or 'sometimes' saw colleagues assume that boys and girls would choose different activities. Fifty-eight per cent of mothers and 50% of fathers believed that pervasive stereotypes limited the occupations girls felt able to enter when they grew older. An audit of shops and online retailers found that children's clothes, cards and stationery were often sold with explicit gender segregation, and toys were marketed using gender-stereotyped colours and separate grouping of 'girls' and 'boys' toys, along with racial stereotyping.

The Commission called for improved representation of female characters in books, on TV and online and more support for parents to challenge stereotyping. Among other problems, it led to boys developing poorer reading skills than girls, to girls developing expectations of their body image which led to eating and mental disorders, and to expectations of the 'male breadwinner' and the 'stoic man' which led some men to suicide, others to misogyny. Challenging gender-stereotyped behaviour in early childhood reduced misogyny and violence against women and girls at later ages. Also, how parents divided domestic and paid tasks influenced children's perceptions of gender roles. The Commission believed that getting fathers more involved could change this, assisted by longer, better-paid parental leave after childbirth.

It urged the government to equalize parental leave, as in Sweden and some other countries. Awareness of gender stereotypes and the attendant dangers should be embedded in antenatal and health-visiting training and practice, and actively challenging gender and racial stereotypes made integral to teacher training and early-years practice. Ofsted should incorporate it into their inspection framework for schools. The Department of Education and the Government Equalities Office should fund evaluations of school and early-years interventions and promote the most effective practice. The Department of Culture, Media and Sport should seek voluntary agreement with manufacturers, distributors and advertisers to end stereotyping of toys and other goods, and Ofcom should audit gender and minority ethnic representation on children's TV, ending the 'princessification' of girls and the 'toxification' of boys as active and scientific, never caring or vulnerable.[48] The report expressed very clearly some sources of gender inequalities which showed little sign of declining, providing unprecedented, convincing analyses of the influences shaping continuing gender inequalities from early in life, and ways to combat them.

Unequal Representation in Parliament

Another occupation in which, as we have seen, women's representation was very gradually increasing but remained highly unequal was elected membership of the House of Commons. By 2020 the Women and Equalities Select Committee had produced fourteen reports recommending ways to attract more women to stand for parliament. These were assessed in a report in September 2023 by an All-Party Parliamentary Group (APPG) on Women in Parliament, chaired by Conservative MP Maria Miller. Like all APPGs, it was an informal group of MPs, in this case composed of women MPs and supported by the Fawcett Society.[49]

The report stated that 'all the main parties have extensive programmes to address imbalance in female representation in parliament', but the system 'still struggles to accommodate them'.[50] Even when women were elected to the Commons, their tenure was often shorter than men's due to the difficulties of combining their duties with family life. It was necessary to modernize the Commons into a workplace that 'attracts the full diversity of the UK population'.[51] An important reason to have more women MPs was that they were more likely than men to speak up for their constituents' needs and interests.[52] Many positive recommendations for change had been made but change was not happening fast enough. One recommendation that had recently been implemented was the introduction of proxy voting and extra funds for new parents to ease the tasks of combining constituency, parliamentary and family duties. The APPG thought this essential since so few mothers of young children entered parliament because 'parliamentary workloads and schedules make the life of an MP difficult to balance with other care responsibilities'.[53] It was the major barrier to women coming forward for election. It was progress that more women were being elected, that the Women and Equalities Select Committee existed and more women were being appointed to leadership roles, including as Leader of the House of Commons, but it was not enough.

A key recommendation of the report was to establish an advisory body to the Speaker of the Commons to push forward a gender-sensitive, family-friendly agenda for parliamentary reform, including reviewing sitting days and hours and voting practices. It suggested that parliament might learn from the experience of the Covid pandemic, when distance working, including online debates and voting, had been effective. The advisory body should also review the security of MPs in parliament and in their constituencies following the recent murders of Labour MP Jo Cox and Conservative MP David Amess in their constituencies. Women MPs especially also needed safeguards against extensive online abuse and 'bullying, harassment and sexual abuse' within parliament.[54] Parliament had recently set up an Independent Complaints and Grievance Scheme for this purpose. It had provoked more open discussion of abusive behaviour and abuse of power, but they continued. MPs and staff required training in the Code of Conduct mandatory for all parliamentary passholders and MPs in gender mainstreaming to enable them to scrutinize legislation with the gender sensitivity desirable in all parliamentary activities. All legislation should be informed by gender impact assessments. The report concluded that a Women's Caucus should be established in parliament to promote a women's agenda. There was cross-party support by women for change, but it needed support from those, mainly men, at higher levels. It recommended that the leaders of all political parties should commit to achieving gender equality in parliament by 2028. No commitments had been made before the 2024 election. However, after the election, in September 2024, Fawcett established parliament's first-ever Women's Caucus, gathering together 64 women MPs from four parties to work together to ensure that women were at the centre of future policy-making in order to improve women's lives.⁵⁵ Fawcett felt that it had good relations with Labour and was optimistic that it would promote gender equality.⁵⁶

The Coronavirus Pandemic

Inequalities increased especially for low-income women when the Coronavirus (Covid-19) pandemic hit Britain early in 2020. Many of them suffered unemployment following the closure of shops, restaurants and other hospitality venues which employed many women in low-paid, low-status jobs. Closure was initially temporary due to the government-mandated lockdown to limit the spread of the virus, but the resulting loss of trade and income caused some to close permanently. The government's compensatory furlough scheme, paying 80% of normal salary during temporary lay-offs due to the pandemic, was inadequate for the needs of already low-paid workers. Unprecedented school closures created especial difficulties for mothers who had either to give up work or, if possible, work from home, which was hard to combine with caring and helping with schoolwork for children whose schools were closed.

The pandemic also exposed and increased deterioration of already declining residential and community care services as sickness increased demand and reduced staff numbers, further increasing pressure mainly upon female family members to provide care. Poverty continued to rise during and after the pandemic for all these reasons, hugely increasing the numbers of families, again especially lone-mother families, needing free food from voluntary food banks. These were almost unheard of in Britain before 2010, then grew until in 2017–18 the largest voluntary supplier, the Trussell Trust, gave out 1.3 million food parcels. In the first pandemic lockdown, covering the whole UK from March to June 2020, it distributed 89% more food parcels than in the same period in 2019, almost 100% more to families with children.⁵⁷ There were hundreds of smaller local food banks and total provision and need is unknown. Parents, especially mothers, spoke of skipping meals to prevent their children starving. Malnutrition was increasingly widespread in all age groups. When schools reopened, many of them provided free breakfasts and teachers reported bringing food and clothing at their own expense to help children in obvious need. Ethnic minority families, especially those originating in Bangladesh and Pakistan, suffered especially from Covid sickness and death and from poverty, due mainly to low-paid work which they could rarely carry out at home, and living in overcrowded homes. Domestic violence, mental illness and suicide increased in all social groups due to household lockdown and financial stress.

In 2020 Fawcett began to assess the impact of the pandemic on women and families. It issued a series of briefings and was still investigating the impact in 2024, together with other feminist organizations and experts.[58] The first briefing in August 2020 was published jointly with the Women's Budget Group and researchers at Queen Mary University of London and the LSE. It examined the experiences of parents at the height of the lockdown, analysing data from 1,424 parents of under-11s in mid-April 2020 and information from the weekly diaries of 70–100 women. The dates and details of the lockdowns varied across the countries of the UK but had broad similarities. In England the first, heavily restricted, lockdown began in March 2020 and was gradually relaxed in May/June. A second more complex and localized partial lockdown ran from 5 November 2020 to February 2021.

The key findings were that mothers in couple-households were one-and-a-half times more likely than fathers to provide schoolwork supervision and care during school and nursery closures. Sixty-six per cent of single mothers said they had struggled with necessities like shopping due to lockdown controls, including being forbidden to visit shops in company with others, even their own children. Mothers were more likely than fathers to lose their jobs or to have their work interrupted due to the pandemic, while those who continued in work either at home or in the workplace found their total workload and resulting stress much increased because children were at home. Mothers working at home spent on average over 3.5 hours per day on childcare, fathers doing so averaged 2.5 hours. The Resolution Foundation found that the closure of businesses due to lockdown rules, including restaurants and many retail stores, affected 23% of women workers, 16% of men. Women were 5% more likely to lose their jobs altogether. ONS data showed that the lockdown rules about shielding and distancing from contact with others, especially firm for older and vulnerable people, reduced the capacity of relatives or others to care for them and reduced childcare by grandparents and other older relatives by 90%, further increasing pressure on parents.[59]

There was also a risk that many voluntary and private childcare providers would go out of business during or following lockdown due to reduced demand. Surveys by the Early Years Alliance in April 2020 found that 25% of providers, across all types, believed they might close within a year. In May 2020, 69% said they were running at a loss. They were not supported by the government, indeed promised support was cut. This put mothers' current and future work at risk. Some 48.3% of mothers and 39.1% of fathers living in couples said they were struggling even more than usual to balance paid work and childcare. In some households, care became more equally shared. Schools gave parents varying degrees of help with homeschooling. It was easier for better-off, better-educated parents, who could afford IT equipment and were educationally more skilled, whereas children from lower-income backgrounds and many from ethnic minorities suffered serious long-term disadvantage.

In August 2020, while the lockdown was ongoing, a Fawcett briefing recommended that mothers needed more government support because they were bearing a disproportionate childcare and domestic load. They proposed greater flexibility of the furlough scheme to cover a wider range of working arrangements, and also that the government should consider improvements to parental working rights, a rescue package for childcare providers and investment in the childcare infrastructure to create jobs beneficial to the economy and to gender equality. It was especially necessary to improve the very limited scheme of paid parental leave which only 1% of fathers took up. Evidence from Sweden indicated that increasing the duration and payment of leave for fathers led to a more even division of childcare and household tasks between parents. Concerning homeschooling, the government should give more help to low-income households, including access to technology. Families needed more financial assistance, including raising Child Benefit to £50 per child per week (more than double current rates), ending the two-child limit for Universal Credit and raising payments, while increasing the Local Housing Allowance for renters.[60] These recommendations were not taken up before the 2024 election.

Violence against Women and Girls

Violence against women and girls was another major, long-running public issue, including the dangers of walking the streets at night. It revived strongly as an issue in the early twenty-first century, in particular following much-publicized offences by two London policemen who raped and murdered women they encountered on night-time streets, and reports of offensive sexist comments by police on social media. In 2019 the new offence of 'upskirting' was created in England and Wales by the Voyeurism (Offences) Act, following a campaign by women. Upskirting is the taking of photographs under a woman's clothing without her permission, normally in public places, including on public transport and in schools. Ten men were convicted of 16 offences in 2019, some against children.[61]

In 2021 the Westminster government introduced a 'Tackling Violence against Women and Girls Strategy' for England and Wales, outlining a 'whole system approach', including support for victims, prevention of violence through education of young people and increasing public awareness, while bringing more perpetrators to justice. It had no obvious impact and violence continued. The Domestic Abuse Act, 2021, further clarified the law around domestic violence, creating a statutory definition, new police powers to tackle it and establishing the office of Domestic Abuse Commissioner. It obliged local authorities in England to provide accommodation and services for victims, but these were limited by cuts to local authority funding, and since 2010 many refuges had closed as a result. Growing delays in the court system, also following funding cuts, limited victims' capacity to seek redress. In 2019–20 an estimated 1.6 million women and 757,000 men aged 16–74 experienced domestic abuse in England and Wales, 7/100 women, 4/100 men. In Scotland by 2019–20, 20.2% of women and 11.26% of men had experienced domestic violence at some time in their lives past age 16.[62]

Rape convictions fell significantly, but not because rape declined. In 2021 an estimated 121,000 women were raped each year in England and Wales and 7,000 men. A government review concluded that victims of rape were being failed across England and Wales due to delays in the justice system, mainly due to the severe cuts to court funding causing fewer cases to be heard, often after long delays. Victims were also failed, as they had long been, by stereotyping and blame, and they received little support, with few specialist resources available to them. In consequence victims were reluctant to bring cases to court. Following protest, the Conservative government committed to addressing these issues and by 2022 there were more police referrals, more charges by the Crown Prosecution Service and more cases reached the Crown Court, but the government recognized that it was not on track to meet its target of more than doubling the numbers of adult rape cases reaching court by the end of the current parliament in 2024, as it did not.

In 2022 the UK ratified the Council of Europe Convention on preventing violence against women and domestic violence but refused to be required to grant independent residence to victims whose immigrant status depended upon an abusive partner. The Westminster government announced a commitment to reducing violence against women and girls, but a report by the NAO in January 2025 demonstrated that the resulting 'disjointed approach to tackling the epidemic of violence against women and girls has so far failed to improve outcomes'; indeed, the report showed that most forms of violence had increased.[63]

In 2021 the Law Commission of England and Wales recommended a new offence of stirring up hatred on grounds of sex or gender, which had been growing with social media. Increasing numbers of anonymous assertions were posted expressing extreme misogyny, and women in the public eye, including MPs, received persistent abuse online, including threats of rape and murder. Prominent women had always experienced prejudice but the capacity of social media to spread foul messages to vast audiences gave it new dimensions and social influence. The Fawcett Society campaigned vigorously for misogyny to be made a hate crime. The Law Commission also proposed that the government consider making sexual harassment a specific offence. It failed to respond on either issue.[64] In 2022 MPs voted by a large majority against making misogyny a hate crime in the Police, Crime, Sentencing and Courts Bill. In the 2024 election campaign Labour, the Liberal Democrats, Greens and the SNP all pledged to put this into law.

In July 2024, after the change of government, the National Police Chiefs Council released its first national analysis of the scale of violence against women and girls. It estimated that two million women were victims of male violence every year. It was 20% of all police-recorded crime, amounting to a 'national emergency'. On average a woman was killed by a man in Britain every three days. The number of recorded offences had risen by 37% in the past five years. Women's organizations campaigned vigorously against misogyny and violence against women, including with their own online posts. Following its election to government, in August 2024 Labour repeated its pledge to halve violence against women and girls in a decade, a pledge repeated by the Home Secretary, Yvette Cooper, the following month.[65] It announced its intention to punish and prevent 'extreme misogyny' conveyed online and by other means because it influenced the attitudes of boys and men and caused violence against women and girls. Following the Workers Protection Act, 2024, from 26 October 2024 employers were required to 'take reasonable steps' to prevent sexual harassment in the workplace, 'discipline or hold accountable' those found guilty of sexual harassment, including online, and establish procedures enabling victims to lodge complaints. In January 2025 Labour responded to the NAO report on the failure of the previous government's promised strategy by announcing that it was working hard on the issue and would announce a new strategy in the spring.

Also in October 2024, the mayor of London, Sadiq Khan, wrote to heads of every primary school in London urging them to counter online misogyny with classes and workshops. He stated, 'It's never too early to start educating young Londoners about the need to treat one another fairly and kindly.' He was anxious to stop violence against women and girls in London and launched a £1 million toolkit to help teachers counter dangerous online messages. Devised by the healthy-relationships charity Tender, it trains teachers how to run workshops, drama and interactive classroom sessions to teach 9–11-year-olds how to recognize and report inequality and sexism.[66]

Transgender Inequalities

There was increasing public attention throughout this period to issues concerning people who changed their sex/gender or wished to, or claimed to be 'non-binary', i.e., of both genders or neither. People undergoing these transitions were now more outspoken and reported various forms of discrimination by health services, at work and in everyday life, including in the increasingly influential social media. The Equality Act, 2010, passed under New Labour and implemented after the 2010 election, penalized discrimination, direct and indirect, against trans people as against others, including harassment and victimization. Among other transgressions, it was unlawful for an employer to refuse time off to attend appointments concerning gender reassignment. But the law was not strongly enforced and discrimination continued.

YouGov opinion polls revealed an 'overall erosion in support towards transgender rights' among the public by the early 2020s, perhaps because anti-trans sentiment was more frequently expressed in public, especially on social media. In 2020 the ECHR classified the legal procedures for recognition of gender change in 28 European countries according to barriers to access. They placed the UK Gender Recognition Act, 2004, second from the bottom, due to 'intrusive medical requirements' that did not match international human rights standards. The procedures were described by critics in the UK as costly, bureaucratic and time-consuming, taking up to two years to complete. A government consultation in England and Wales in 2018 found that a majority of over 100,000 respondents favoured removing most of the requirements for qualification for the Gender Recognition Certificate (GRC), but in 2020 the Westminster government refused to do so, despite the ECHR criticisms. In 2021 a report by the Council of Europe criticized the 'baseless and concerning' level of transphobia in Britain.

Following public consultations with similar results to those in England and Wales, the Scottish government responded differently. Proposed reforms were delayed by the Covid pandemic, but in 2023 the Scottish parliament passed the Gender Recognition Reform (Scotland) Act, amending the 2004 Act. It lowered the age at which people could change their legal gender from 18 to 16, removed the requirement for medical diagnosis of gender dysphoria and reduced from two years to six months the time required for applicants to have lived in their acquired gender. It passed easily through the Scottish parliament, but in January 2023 was vetoed by the Westminster government, as it had the right to do. A legal appeal by the Scottish government failed in the Edinburgh court and in May 2024 the new leader of the SNP and First Minister of Scotland, John Swinney, said he would not pursue the case further. The episode aroused sometimes angry debate in Scotland and elsewhere in the UK. Some feminists feared that the change would encourage violent men to pretend to transition, enabling them to attack women in woman-only environments such as single-sex toilets, changing rooms or even prisons. There was one much-publicized example at the time of a man convicted of rape in Scotland, who then claimed to have transitioned and was placed in a women's jail until a public outcry caused his removal.[67]

Professor Stephen Whittle, who transitioned as a teenager in 1975, when few people went through the process of hormone treatment then surgery which was conventional by the 2000s, reported that, at that time, 90% of people he knew, including his father, 'who was quite a Victorian man in his attitudes', accepted it. 'But from strangers or people who barely knew me, there was a lot of discrimination and prejudice. I had sexual and physical assaults on the street, and I lost job after job. None of it was easy.'[68] Such hostility was still evident in 2024, though Whittle believed it had become much easier to debate the issues sympathetically. He co-founded Press for Change in 1992 to campaign on behalf of people like himself against discrimination and for marriage and other rights, became a university professor of equalities law, married and had four children when it became legally possible under the 2004 Gender Recognition Act.

By the 2020s increasing numbers of people, including children, underwent transition, which continued to be highly contentious, arousing fierce exchanges between people who believed that biological sex was fixed for life at birth and those who did not, with opponents arguing that it was promoted by biased medical professionals, unjustified by firm evidence. Among other issues there was intense international debate – prominent in the 2024 Olympic Games in Paris – about whether men who transitioned into women should compete as women in sports, since they were believed to gain a lasting biological advantage from having undergone male puberty and its effects upon testosterone levels. In some countries and sports they were banned amid continuing controversy.

The tensions and especially concerns about the poor quality of research in the field led NHS England in 2020 to commission a report into gender identity services for children and young people by Hilary Cass, a retired consultant paediatrician. She delivered her final report in April 2024.[69] This described how the 'toxic debate' around the issue had created a 'culture of fear' among medical professionals in the field, due to abuse on social media among other onslaughts. They feared to openly discuss the treatment of children questioning their gender identity, or to undertake research in an area in desperate need of stronger evidence.[70] Cass's report was critical of the current state of treatment of children and young people seeking gender reassignment and of available research on their conditions, needs and appropriate treatment and care. She was commissioned to recommend improvements in these areas because demand from children and young people had risen rapidly over the previous five to ten years in Britain and other Western countries – from more birth-registered females than males – but in England they were waiting several years for clinical support (along with many others needing medical care at this time), which created 'considerable challenges and upheavals' to them and their families due to their condition.

Cass could find no clear explanation for the increasing numbers. She found the available evidence of poor quality, providing no reliable basis for clinical decisions or for children and families to make informed choices. There was uncertainty about the best care and treatment for individuals, including some practices in widespread use, such as the safety and efficacy of puberty blockers given to children, cross-sex hormones used to masculinize or feminize people, and psychosocial interventions to help those contemplating or undergoing transition. There was no long-term follow-up data or adequate information on outcomes. Cass pointed out that medical treatment of any kind was unlikely to be beneficial if associated mental health and/or psychosocial needs were not also addressed.

She recommended a changed approach to health care in the sector, more closely aligned with conventional NHS practice and of the same standards. Capacity to support young people should be expanded and more widely distributed, based on paediatric services and with stronger links between services. The NHS had begun this process in 2022 when, controversially, it closed the Tavistock Centre in London which specialized in gender reassignment of young people in order to develop more accessible services around England, as recommended by Cass in an earlier report. She now recommended that the services should create a separate pathway for pre-pubertal children and their families and prioritize early discussion about how parents could best support their child in a balanced, non-judgemental way. She recognized the difficulties families faced and proposed that NHS England should ensure that each regional centre had a follow-up service for 17–25-year-olds to provide continuity of care and support at a potentially vulnerable stage. This would enable longer-term clinical research data to be collected. Provision was needed for people considering de-transition, recognizing that they might not wish to re-engage with services they previously used when undergoing transition. In August 2024 the Labour government announced measures to improve regional services.

Cass proposed a programme of research evaluating the outcomes of psychosocial and physical interventions, including use of masculinizing/feminizing hormones. She recommended extreme caution about providing these hormones as early as age 16, advocating waiting until 18. Every method considered for medical treatment should be carefully discussed by a national multidisciplinary team.

It was a very thorough report based upon discussions with health care and other professionals, children and young people uncertain of their gender identity and their parents. Cass clearly took very seriously the needs of these children and young people and found the handling of their needs by health professionals too often severely inadequate. Her report received a mixed reception, not surprisingly in view of the public and private tensions and uncertainties around the subject. Some accused Cass of being too critical of existing procedures and influenced by anti-trans bias, others agreed with her criticisms and welcomed her recommendations as potentially very helpful to gender-uncertain people. Other views were mixed, including those of Stephen Whittle. He said there was 'masses' in the report that he agreed with, especially on the problems with services, 'But I also think you can see the fingerprints of transphobia on the report' and he believed that some women's groups had undue influence upon government and officials. But he agreed with many of the recommendations, stating that 'Cass has the potential for positive change, but it has to be backed up with significant funding.'[71]

Rather than funding the changes recommended by Cass, the Conservative government rather confirmed Whittle's concern about the influence of some campaigners by introducing a ban on prescribing puberty blockers. Cass had not recommended this but argued that their effects were uncertain and should be investigated. The ban imposed two years' imprisonment for prescribing the drugs. The independent non-profit legal organization the Good Law Project and the transgender advocacy group Trans-Actual instructed lawyers to challenge the ban, demanding a judicial review. But it was implemented as an emergency measure on 30 May 2024 before the sudden dissolution of parliament for the general election, without consultation with experts and with no opportunity for parliamentary scrutiny. In August 2024 it was extended by the Labour government.

In June 2024 the then government Minister for Women and Equalities, Kemi Badenoch (soon to be the fourth female and first Black female leader of the Conservative party when Rishi Sunak resigned after decisively losing the election) announced that, concerning one highly contentious issue, the Conservatives would ban men who transitioned into womanhood from single-sex female spaces, including hospital wards, women's prisons, toilets and sports events. They would make clear that same-sex spaces were defined by biological sex, i.e., the sex conferred on people at birth. This was highly contentious, but Sunak supported the change, announcing that 'The safety of women and girls is too important to allow the current confusion around definitions of sex and gender to persist.'[72] It was implemented following a highly controversial ruling in its favour by the Supreme Court in April 2025. Labour expressed no views on the subject in the election campaign, though it had previously appeared committed to transgender rights. Culture wars continued in a significant area of gender inequality.

Election 2024

Labour won a substantial majority of MPs in the election on 5 July 2024, 411, an overall majority of 174, but a disappointingly low proportion of votes, 33.7%. The turnout – 60% across the UK – was the second lowest since 1885, suggesting little voter enthusiasm for any party. The Conservative vote share was 24%. More positively, 263 women were elected, 40% of MPs, the highest-ever proportion, 190 Labour (41% of Labour MPs), 29 Conservative, 32 Liberal Democrats, and 11 others. Sir Keir Starmer, the new Prime Minister, was not known to be strongly committed to gender equality, but he appointed 12 women to a Cabinet of 23, also the largest proportion ever and the first female majority. The previous Conservative Cabinet from 2022 to 2024 included six women among 24 members. Angela Rayner, previously Deputy Leader of the party, was appointed Deputy Prime Minister and Secretary of State for

Housing, Communities and Local Government. She was a single mother who grew up in northern England in a council house, in poverty, in contrast to the former public school boys who had dominated Conservative cabinets. She attended a comprehensive school and left at the age of 16 without qualifications due to unmarried pregnancy. She later became a social worker, then a trade union official before entering parliament in 2015. She married and had two further children before becoming an MP. She supported gender and transgender equality. She resigned from all her government and party posts in September 2025 following some unfortunate errors in her tax payments.

Starmer also appointed the first female Chancellor of the Exchequer, Rachel Reeves. She grew up in London, the daughter of schoolteachers, attended a comprehensive school and Oxford University, then worked for the Bank of England and other banks before her election to parliament in 2010. She is also married with two children, like her colleagues juggling family responsibilities with constituency duties, in her case in Leeds, and parliamentary and ministerial work. Her attitudes to gender equality are uncertain; she is not known for her radical views. Shortly after the election, Starmer appointed a new Chair of the Labour Party, Ellie Reeves, younger sister of Rachel, also educated at a comprehensive and Oxford. She then worked as a barrister before being elected to parliament in 2017. She is also married with two children.

Bridget Phillipson was appointed Minister for Women and Equalities, though she became more prominent in her primary role as Secretary of State for Education. She grew up in poverty in a council house in Sunderland, with a single mother, living on benefits and free school meals. Her mother founded a charity for victims of domestic violence. Bridget attended a comprehensive school then graduated from Oxford University. She worked in local government, then for her mother's charity from 2007 to 2010, when she became an MP. She, too, is married with two children. Before the 2024 election she spoke and wrote extensively about the importance of childcare and early-years education for children and parents and the need for a comprehensive, funded system.

Anneliese Dodds was appointed her junior Minister for Women and Equalities and, primarily, Minister of State for Development. She grew up in Aberdeen in a more privileged background, attended an independent school then Oxford, where she still lived in 2024 and represented

Oxford East in parliament. She studied for a PhD at the LSE and became a university lecturer in Public Policy before being elected an MEP in 2014. She gave this up in 2017 when she was elected an MP. She has stated her support for what she believes is Labour's commitment to 'trans people and women'. She also is married with two children.

Before the election the Fawcett Society called for a Secretary of State for Women and Girls as a dedicated Cabinet-level post. However, it had long-standing relationships with both Phillipson and Dodds and believed that 'combined with the most gender-equal ministerial team ever, they have the skills and commitment to drive real change for women'.[73] When Labour completed its first 100 days in office in October 2024, Fawcett published a blog, 'Labour's First 100 Days: A New Era for Women?' It recognized that: 'They inherited a difficult picture for women: with the gender pay gap stagnant, violence against women skyrocketing and overlapping inequalities making the cost-of-living crisis even harder for women of different backgrounds, there is a lot for the new government to do.' They were 'delighted' that the Chancellor had stated her desire to close the gender pay gap; that a British government had 'finally achieved a 50% split of ministerial roles for women, with women from working-class backgrounds at the top of government'; that it had been quick to take a stand against misogyny and had introduced 'buffer zones' around abortion clinics so that women could access them without the harassment from anti-abortionists that was all too common. They concluded: 'The Labour government's first 100 days shows a commitment to advancing women's rights ... a hopeful shift towards equality.' They pledged to work with the government to ensure that it delivered on its promises.[74]

Further evidence of Labour's commitment was that, also in October 2024, Seema Malhotra was appointed Parliamentary Undersecretary of State for Equalities, including the neglected equalities of race and disability with gender. She was already Parliamentary Undersecretary for Migrants and Citizenship; neither role was in the Cabinet. Malhotra announced that the government had 'absolute commitment' to tackling racial inequality, diversity and inclusion. She shared fears that some businesses were scaling this back and reported that in 2025 the government would launch a consultation on an Equality (Race and Disability) Bill which would compel large employers to report on ethnicity and disability pay gaps, benefitting women and men within these groups.[75]

Also in October 2024 the government introduced an Employment Rights Bill designed to reduce insecurity and inequality in the workplace for men and women, including ethnic minorities and disabled people. It included strengthened provision for equal pay, for raising the minimum wage and extending rights to paternity leave, enabling fathers to increase their contribution to childcare. All workers would gain protection from unfair dismissal, and women further protection against dismissal while pregnant and for six months after their return to work from maternity leave. Employers would be required to take 'all reasonable preventative steps' against sexual harassment of their employees and to specify the steps, and workers given stronger rights to appeal against harassment. It introduces measures to ensure that outsourced workers are offered terms and conditions 'broadly equivalent' to those in comparable public sector employment, including for pay and security. Fair Pay Agreements will be required in the severely underpaid adult social care sector, and in all sectors rights to flexible working will be strengthened and employers required to explain the grounds on which any request is refused. The legislation is planned to be implemented in 2026, allowing employers time to make necessary adjustments. It covers many, but not all, of the most severe inequalities in the labour market. We await the outcome.

Conclusion

Under Conservative governments from 2010 to 2024 there was little progress towards male/female, gay and transgender equalities, even under two female Prime Ministers and despite substantial evidence of continuing inequalities. Slight progress in pay equality and employment opportunities mainly benefitted women qualified for high-level posts, part of the wider growth in inequality between rich and poor. Poorer people experienced increasing inequalities as poverty and income and wealth inequality reached levels not seen for over a century. When governments introduced measures to increase equality, including by reducing violence against women and girls, they were often not enforced effectively. 'Austerity' cuts to funding of services, including the law courts and police forces, contributed to increased violence against women and girls, and cuts to childcare and social care for adults and children to greater stress and poverty among women by restricting their employment options and increasing their caring responsibilities. The Covid pandemic further increased inequalities, including of age and race within gender groups. In 2024 the UK remained behind most other high-income countries on most measures of equality between men and women, ranking better on LGBT rights.

In 2025 we still await the new Labour government's contribution to promoting gender equality, given the party's stronger, if imperfect, record of progress compared with the Conservatives, and the exceptional representation of women in its ranks in parliament, including women in influential Cabinet positions who have experienced many of the disadvantages of women's unequal experiences, while achieving successful lives, and are committed to equality. They might potentially draw upon this experience and their knowledge of the lives of less fortunate women to influence government policies, of which there were some promising indications in the government's first months.

Conclusion

Why, after over a century of protest, does profound gender inequality persist in Britain in 2025? Will it ever end? If so, how? In 1900 there were gender inequalities in almost every area of life. Some have since been eliminated or diminished, mostly following women's campaigns. Equal voting rights were achieved in 1928 following active, persistent campaigns, and women used their votes to gain more equalities through pressure on politicians who needed their votes, though the outcomes were often incomplete compromises and campaigns continued. Women still have not achieved equal representation in the English parliament, though the number of female MPs has gradually increased, and equality has grown closer in the early twenty-first century. Equality has been achieved in the devolved Welsh parliament, the Senedd, and is close in Scotland, where women became 45% of MSPs following the 2021 election. This has resulted from the devolution of powers to both nations in 1997 and successful women's campaigns for election to their national assemblies by proportional representation, which generally improves women's opportunities for election more effectively than the English first-past-the-post voting system.

In just one area – education – have females achieved not only equality with males but superiority. Women campaigned from the nineteenth century for equal access to schools and universities, achieving almost complete success only by the 1970s. Once they had equal access, they quickly and persistently outperformed males at all levels, as the cultural assumption that the only career women should expect was motherhood declined, and their opportunities potentially expanded. They were motivated to develop previously hidden talents, demonstrating real gender differences in abilities. But cultural bias and stereotyping continue to limit female participation in the sciences, engineering and technology and confine most of them to the humanities and social sciences. And clear evidence of women's skills and talents has not had equal impact upon their opportunities in employment, where their abilities continue to be disparaged, perhaps increasingly as their success in education further stokes male fears of competition.

We have strong evidence of these experiences from women's own accounts and the growth since the 1950s of surveys, mainly by women, especially of their treatment in the labour market. These reveal repeatedly that the main obstacle to their gaining equal opportunities in employment, including equal pay, despite ongoing campaigns, has been the prejudice and discrimination of men in positions of power expressed in their repeated, unproven, assertions of women's lesser abilities in every type of occupation, except in the few, generally at lower levels, judged especially suited to their capabilities. Surveys have also demonstrated the unwillingness of men with relevant powers to assist equal access of women to all types and levels of work, including by improving childcare facilities and flexibility in the workplace. This was not represented as being universal among men; some have always supported and promoted equality at work and elsewhere, and it has gradually and incompletely advanced. Politicians, once women had the vote, could not risk substantially alienating them with obviously exclusionary measures, though they generally proceeded cautiously with attempts to advance equality. Male Labour politicians have been somewhat more responsive to women's campaigns than Conservatives throughout the period. Many, but not all, women in both major and smaller parties have been supportive.

Employment was not the only area of gender inequality. Among others, sexual and physical violence was experienced more severely by women than by men persistently through the period. But while we have extensive evidence of women's experiences of, attitudes to and protest against gender inequalities of many kinds, as described in this book, it is much harder to find explanations of the persistence of male discrimination against women. Is prejudice at work motivated just by fear of women's competition for promotion and higher pay, perhaps deepened by female educational achievements? Or, as some research has suggested, also the result of conditioning of boys and girls in early life into stereotypical conceptions of their different abilities and life prospects which have been pervasive in the culture? Some men have protested on the rare occasions when they believed they were exposed to unequal opportunities with women, such as the successful court appeal by Labour men in 1997 against measures to improve women's opportunities to stand as parliamentary candidates, a challenge upheld by a male-dominated justice system. Also, the successful male protest to a European court against the lower state pension age for women in Britain.

We learn more about how men have felt about gender inequalities when, like women but much less frequently, they protested as victims of persistent and serious inequalities, mainly as homosexuals, later as transexuals, two dimensions of inequality due to gender identity which entered public discourse and protest only in the later twentieth century, having been previously silenced as matters of criminality and shame. 'Straight' men experienced gender inequality much more rarely. Protest achieved some progress for homosexuals, though equality remains incomplete, and homophobia still rages. Lesbians and transgender men and women shared this more gradual public acknowledgement of their existence and needs, and they have also experienced gradual shifts towards equality, most gradually in the case of transexuals.

This book must sometimes read like a volume of women's history because women experienced more gender inequalities than men and they are more fully documented. Many more sources tell us about female than male experiences and attitudes, also more about some inequalities than others. It is particularly difficult to trace the history of one persistent and severely damaging source of conflict between women and men: sexual and physical violence. We cannot assess the extent to which rape, domestic violence, sexual harassment in the street, at work, everywhere, have increased or diminished since around 1900 because, until the relatively recent past, they were regarded as shameful and rarely publicly discussed or measured. But they were certainly major problems in the early twentieth century and remain extremely severe in the early twenty-first, showing no sign of decline despite legal changes and protest and publicity around them, currently at a high level internationally. There is also greater evidence than in the past of extreme misogyny among a minority of men, especially expressed on social media. Its growth enables messages to MPs and other prominent women threatening rape or even death, while providing easy access to vast audiences, including to promote baseless assertions of women's determination to displace all men from positions of power and to express generalized contempt for their abilities. Such attitudes may be long-established but the growth of social media has made them more evident and given them a wider reach, including to influence young men and boys. They have perhaps been intensified by signs of women gaining some equalities, deepening fears among some men. Misogyny has reached such a level that shortly after the 2024 election, the Labour government opened an investigation into making it a hate crime for the first time.

In certain respects, especially in the labour market, over time gender inequalities have narrowed for better-off women while growing for poorer women, especially the growing numbers of single mothers, and especially since 2010 as the gap between rich and poor grew even wider than before in all respects. The intersection of gender inequalities with inequalities of race, class and age are major and have not diminished over time, with women from minority ethnic communities still severely disadvantaged, and older and disabled women disadvantaged compared with younger people.

I hope that this book provides the most comprehensive study so far of gender inequalities in Britain and of how cultural, economic, social, legal and political inequalities have intersected through the recent past, though it is surely incomplete in a complex and shifting field. It is not a story of glorious progress since 1900 against gender, or any other, inequality, despite the length and intensity of women's campaigns. They still cannot triumphantly proclaim equality with men, though they can celebrate real if uneven gains. It is rather a tale of steady, slow, incomplete progress from the 1900s to the 1980s, followed by stasis and some decline beginning under the UK's first, unsympathetic, female Prime Minister, Margaret Thatcher. A brief, partial revival of progress under New Labour from 1997 was followed by a return to profound social and economic, including gender, divisions under Conservative governments from 2010 to 2024. The EC/EU, which Britain joined in 1973, provided a valuable model of measures to promote gender equality, implemented more effectively in most EU countries than in the UK, while European courts assisted appeals against UK inequalities. Pressures from Europe assisted moves to equality in the UK until this ceased following 'Brexit' in 2020. Perhaps the EU's role in promoting gender equality helped motivate some supporters of Brexit.

By 2024 the UK matched or was in advance of much of Europe concerning homosexual rights but lagged far behind most developed countries on equal rights for women, including in career opportunities, pay and working conditions, childcare provision, pensions and other benefits. Are there prospects for change? In 2025 there are signs of the new Labour government responding to women's, and men's, protests. It has promised increased funding and provision for childcare and announced that: 'Tackling violence against women and girls is a top priority for this government.' It has established a review to recommend a strategy to make misogyny a criminal offence, as the previous Conservative government refused to do. As we have seen, Labour's comprehensive Employment Rights Bill includes measures to increase work security and pay for women and men, and work flexibility and other measures to assist mothers to combine employment and childcare. If fully implemented these measures could substantially reduce gender inequalities.

The Fawcett Society, the most persistent campaigner for women's rights in recent decades, and politically independent, is hopeful. It has blogged that it 'celebrated' publication of the Employment Rights Bill: 'After years of feminist campaigning today marks a significant step forward towards women's workplace equality in Britain ... It contains sensible new protections for women workers which Fawcett has been campaigning for over a number of years. This could help to increase women's equality at work and contribute to inclusive growth for workers and business alike.'[1] The Bill appeared all the more necessary at the end of October 2024, when the annual Gender Pay Gap data for 2024 was published. It stated that Equal Pay Day would be 20 November 2024, two days earlier than in 2023 because the gender pay gap had grown from 10.4% in 2023 to 11.3%, the first decline after 'years of slow progress' towards filling the gap.[2] Despite over a century of campaigns, gender inequalities remain severe.

Notes

Introduction
1 Joan Wallach Scott, *Gender and the Politics of History* (New York: Columbia University Press, 1988), p. 10.
2 Ibid., pp. 40–1.
3 Ibid., p. 2.
4 Pat Thane, *The Rise and Fall of the British Welfare State: From Poverty in 1900 to Poverty in 2023* (London: Bloomsbury, 2024).

Chapter 1: Women Fighting for a Political Voice, 1900–1918
1 For surveys of nineteenth-century women's protest, see Kathryn Gleadle, *British Women in the Nineteenth Century* (London: Palgrave, 2001); Barbara Caine, *English Feminism 1780–1980* (Oxford: Oxford University Press, 1997); Jane Rendall (ed.), *Equal or Different: Women's Politics, 1800–1914* (Oxford: Blackwell, 1987); Krista Cowman, *Women in British Politics, 1689–1979* (London: Palgrave, 2010).
2 Stephen Cretney, *Family Law in the Twentieth Century: A History* (Oxford: Oxford University Press, 2003), pp. 161–95; O.R. McGregor, *Divorce in England: A Centenary Study* (London: Heinemann, 1957).
3 Laura King, *Family Men: Fatherhood and Masculinity in Britain, 1914–1960* (Oxford: Oxford University Press, 2015), pp. 1–8.
4 Pat Thane, 'The British imperial state and the construction of national identities', in Billie Melman (ed.), *Borderlines: Genders and Identities in War and Peace* (London: Routledge, 1998), pp. 29–46.
5 Jeffrey Weeks, *Sex, Politics and Society: The Regulation of Sexuality Since 1800*, 2nd edn (London: Longman, 1989), pp. 216–19.
6 Pat Thane, '"Well-bred and conventional ladies": the National Council of Women of Great Britain and Northern Ireland'. *Women's History Review*, 32:2 (2023), pp. 172–89; Norman and Jeanne Mackenzie (eds) *The Diary of Beatrice Webb* (London: Virago, 1982), p. 233.
7 Patricia Hollis, *Ladies Elect: Women in English Local Government, 1865–1914* (Oxford: Clarendon Press, 1987).
8 Cretney, *Family Law*, p. 632.
9 Cowman, *Women in British Politics*; Pat Thane, 'Women and political participation in England, 1918–1970', in Esther Breitenbach and Pat Thane (eds), *Women and Political Participation in Britain and Ireland in the Twentieth Century* (London: Bloomsbury, 2010), pp. 11–12.
10 Frank Prochaska, *Women and Philanthropy in Nineteenth Century England* (Oxford: Oxford University Press, 1980).

11 Emmeline Pankhurst, *My Own Story* (1914, reprinted London: Virago, 1979).
12 Jill Liddington and Jill Norris, *One Hand Tied Behind Us: The Rise of the Women's Suffrage Movement* (London: Virago, 1978).
13 Lesley A. Hall, *Sex, Gender and Social Change in Britain Since 1880* (London: Macmillan, 2000), p. 85.
14 Jad Adams, *Women and the Vote: A World History* (Oxford: Oxford University Press, 2014), p. 204.
15 Jill Liddington, *Vanishing for the Vote: Suffrage, Citizenship and the Battle for the Census* (Manchester: Manchester University Press, 2014).
16 Sandra Stanley Holton, *Feminism and Democracy: Women's Suffrage and Reform Politics in Britain, 1900–1918* (Cambridge: Cambridge University Press, 1986).
17 Geoffrey Searle, *The Quest for National Efficiency* (Oxford: Blackwell, 1971).
18 B.R. Mitchell and P. Deane, *Abstract of British Historical Statistics* (Cambridge: Cambridge University Press, 1962), p. 37.
19 Margaret Llewellyn Davies, 'Introduction', in Margaret Llewellyn Davies (ed.), *Maternity: Letters from Working Women* (London: G. Bell, 1915, reprinted London: Virago, 1978), pp. 1–17.
20 Christine Collette, *For Labour and For Women: The Women's Labour League, 1906–1918* (Manchester: Manchester University Press, 1989).
21 Deborah Dwork, *War Is Good for Babies and Other Young Children: A History of the Infant and Child Welfare Movement in England, 1898–1918* (London: Tavistock, 1987).
22 Clare Debenham, *Birth Control and the Rights of Women* (London: I.B. Tauris, 2014).
23 E.P. Hennock, *The Origin of the Welfare State in England and Germany, 1850–1914* (Cambridge: Cambridge University Press, 2007), pp. 293–304, 227–42.
24 Pat Thane, *Old Age in English History: Past Experiences, Present Issues* (Oxford: Oxford University Press, 2000), pp. 216–35.
25 Maud Pember Reeves, *Round About a Pound a Week* (London: Virago 1979).
26 Louise A. Jackson, *Women Police: Gender, Welfare and Surveillance in the Twentieth Century* (Manchester: Manchester University Press, 2006); Thane, 'Well-bred and conventional ladies', pp. 172–89.
27 Hall, *Sex, Gender and Social Change*, pp. 68–70; Weeks, *Sex, Politics and Society*, pp. 104, 215.
28 Christabel Pankhurst, *The Great Scourge and How to End It* (London: E. Pankhurst, 1913).
29 Anne Logan, *Feminism and Criminal Justice: A Historical Perspective* (London: Palgrave Macmillan, 2008), pp. 140–2.
30 Michael Anderson, 'The social implications of Demographic change', in F.M.L. Thompson (ed.), *The Cambridge Social History of Britain, 1750–1950*, Vol. 2 (Cambridge: Cambridge University Press, 1991), pp. 29–32.
31 McGregor, *Divorce in England*; Cretney, *Family Law*, pp. 161–249.
32 Eleanor Gordon, 'Irregular marriage: myth and reality', *Journal of Social History*, 47:2 (2013), pp. 507–25.
33 Jane Lewis, *The End of Marriage? Individualism and Intimate Relations* (Cheltenham: Edward Elgar, 2001), p. 34.
34 Hall, *Sex, Gender and Social Change*, p. 72.

35 Christabel Pankhurst, *Unshackled: The Story of How We Won the Vote* (London: Hutchinson, 1959), p. 288.
36 Jackson, *Women Police*; Thane, 'Well-bred and conventional ladies', pp. 172–89.
37 Holton, *Feminism and Democracy*, p. 130.
38 J.M. Winter, *The Great War and the British People* (London: Macmillan, 1985).
39 Sylvia Pankhurst, *The Home Front* (London: Hutchinson, 1932, reprinted London: The Cresset Library, 1987), p. 19.
40 Pat Thane and Tanya Evans, *Sinners? Scroungers? Saints? Unmarried Motherhood in Twentieth-Century England* (Oxford: Oxford University Press, 2012), pp. 11–13.
41 Winter, *Great War*, p. 236.
42 Susan Pedersen, *Eleanor Rathbone and the Politics of Conscience* (New Haven, CT: Yale University Press, 2004), pp. 151–3.
43 S. Damer, 'State, class and housing: Glasgow 1875–1919', in J. Melling (ed.), *Housing, Social Policy and the State* (London: Croom Helm, 1980), p. 93.
44 J. Melling, 'Clydeside housing and the evolution of state rent control', in Melling (ed.), *Housing*; J. Melling, *Rent Strikes: People's Struggle for Housing in West Scotland, 1890–1916* (Edinburgh: Polygon, 1983); D. Englander, *Landlord and Tenant* (Oxford: Oxford University Press, 1983), chs 10–12.
45 Vera Brittain, *Testament of Youth: An Autobiographical Study of the Years 1900–1925* (London: Gollancz 1933).
46 Carol Dyhouse, 'Women students and the London medical schools, 1914–1939: the anatomy of a masculine culture', in *Students: A Gendered History* (London: Routledge, 2006), pp. 137–55.
47 Deborah Thom, *Nice Girls and Rude Girls: Women Workers and the First World War* (London: I.B. Tauris, 1998/2000).
48 Peter Clarke, *Hope and Glory: Britain 1900–1990* (London: Penguin Books, 1996), p. 94.
49 Alastair J. Reid, *United We Stand: A History of Britain's Trade Unions* (London: Allen Lane, 2004).
50 Gail Braybon, *Women Workers in the First World War* (London: Routledge, 1989).
51 Report of the War Cabinet Committee on Women in Industry. Parliamentary Papers, 1919 xiii Cmd 135.
52 Winter, *Great War*, p. 498.
53 Pat Thane, *Foundations of the Welfare State*, 2nd edn (London: Pearson Longman, 1996), p. 127.
54 Winter, *Great War*, p. 141.
55 Ibid., p. 148.
56 Weeks, *Sex, Politics and Society*, p. 188.
57 Hall, *Sex, Gender and Social Change*, p. 95.
58 Chaired by the Speaker of the House of Commons.
59 Holton, *Feminism and Democracy*, pp. 146–8.
60 Ibid.
61 Mari Takayanagi, '"One of the most revolutionary proposals that has ever been put before the House": the passage of the Parliament (Qualification of Women) Act, 1918', in Lucy Bland and Richard Carr (eds), *Labour and British Radicalism in the First World War* (Manchester: Manchester University Press, 2018), pp. 56–72.

Chapter 2: What Difference Did the Vote Make? 1918–1939

1 Thane, 'Women and political participation in England', pp. 14–15; Martin Pugh, *Women and the Women's Movement in Britain*, 2nd edn (London: Macmillan, 2000), pp. 125–53; David Jarvis, '"Behind every great party": women and conservatism in twentieth-century Britain', in Amanda Vickery (ed.), *Women, Privilege and Power: British Politics, 1750 to the Present* (Stanford: Stanford University Press, 2001), pp. 289–316.
2 Cheryl Law, *Suffrage and Power: The Women's Movement, 1918–28* (London: I.B. Tauris, 1987).
3 J. Lovenduski, P. Norris and C. Burgess, 'The Party and women', in A. Seldon and S. Ball (eds), *Conservative Century: The Conservative Party Since 1900* (Oxford: Oxford University Press, 1994), pp. 611–36.
4 Thane, 'Women and political participation in England', pp. 11–28.
5 Susan Kingsley Kent, 'Gender reconstruction after the First World War', in H.L. Smith (ed.), *British Feminism in the Twentieth Century* (Cheltenham: Edward Elgar, 1990), pp. 66–83; H.L. Smith 'The effect of the war on the status of women', in H.L. Smith (ed.), *War and Social Change* (Manchester: Manchester University Press, 1986), pp. 208–29; Smith, 'British feminism in the 1920s', in Smith (ed.), *British Feminism*, pp. 47–65; M. Pugh, 'Domesticity and the decline of feminism, 1930–1952', in Smith (ed.), *British Feminism*, pp. 144–64.
6 David Thackeray, 'From prudent housewife to empire shopper: party appeals to the female voter, 1918–28', in Julie V. Gottlieb and Richard Toye (eds), *The Aftermath of Suffrage: Women, Gender and Politics in Britain, 1918–1945* (London: Palgrave Macmillan, 2013), pp. 37–53; Thane, 'Women and political participation in England', pp. 12–28; Cowman, *Women in British Politics*.
7 Hollis, *Ladies Elect*; Lori Newman, '"Providing an opportunity to exercise their energies": the role of the Labour Women's Sections in shaping political identities, south Wales, 1918–39', pp. 29–44; Thane, 'Women and political participation in England', pp. 11–28; Esther Breitenbach, 'Scottish women's organizations and the exercise of citizenship, c.1900–c.1970', pp. 63–78, all in Breitenbach and Thane, *Women and Citizenship*.
8 Pugh, *Women and the Women's Movement*, p. 57.
9 Michael Savage, *The Dynamics of Working-Class Politics: The Labour Movement in Preston, 1880–1940* (Cambridge: Cambridge University Press, 1987).
10 Caitriona Beaumont, *Housewives and Citizens: Domesticity and the Women's Movement in England, 1928–1964* (Manchester: Manchester University Press, 2013), pp. 40–67.
11 In 'What difference did the vote make?' in Vickery (ed.), *Women, Privilege and Power*, p. 268, I mistakenly state that they merged in 1924. This happened only in Glasgow.
12 On extensive women's activism in Scotland, see Breitenbach, 'Scottish women's organizations'.
13 Maggie Andrews, *The Acceptable Face of Feminism: The Women's Institute as a Social Movement* (London: Lawrence and Wishart, 1997); On WIs in Scotland, see Breitenbach, 'Scottish women's organizations'.
14 Thane, 'What difference did the vote make?', pp. 267–73.
15 I am grateful to the late Sue Innes for this information.

16 Law, *Suffrage*, pp. 232–8.
17 Takayanagi, 'Parliament and women, c. 1900–1945', PhD thesis, King's College London, 2012.
18 Law, *Suffrage*, pp. 82–4; Helen Glew, *Gender, Rhetoric and Regulation: Women's Work in the Civil Service and the London County Council, 1900–1955* (Manchester: Manchester University Press, 2016).
19 Judith Bourne, *Helena Normanton and the Opening of the Bar to Women* (London: Waterside Press, 2016).
20 Logan, *Feminism and Criminal Justice*.
21 Ibid., pp. 87–8.
22 Ibid., pp. 110–11.
23 Glew, *Gender, Rhetoric and Regulation*, pp. 100–21.
24 Kate Murphy, *Behind the Wireless: A History of Early Women at the BBC* (London: Palgrave Macmillan, 2016), pp. 83–114, 242.
25 Jackson, *Women Police*, p. 21.
26 Law, *Suffrage*, p. 104.
27 Selina Todd, *Young Women, Work and Family 1918–1950* (Oxford: Oxford University Press, 2005), pp. 20–32.
28 Glew, *Gender, Rhetoric and Regulation*, pp. 136–7.
29 Pat Thane, 'Women of the British Labour Party and feminism,1906–45', in Smith (ed.), *British Feminism*, pp. 124–43.
30 Pedersen, *Eleanor Rathbone*.
31 Thane, *Old Age*, pp. 284–6.
32 Ibid., p. 332.
33 Hall, *Sex, Gender and Social Change*, p. 97.
34 Weeks, *Sex, Politics and Society*, pp. 183–4.
35 Ibid., pp. 112–14.
36 Ibid., p. 215; Hall, *Sex, Gender and Social Change*, pp. 122–3.
37 Deborah Cohen, *Family Secrets: Living with Shame from the Victorians to the Present Day* (London: Penguin Viking, 2013), pp. 181–211; Adrian Bingham, *Family Newspapers: Sex, Private Life and the British Popular Press, 1918–78* (Oxford: Oxford University Press, 2009).
38 Weeks, *Sex, Politics and Society*, p. 212.
39 Roger Davidson, '"This pernicious delusion": law, medicine and child sexual abuse in early-twentieth-century Scotland', *Journal of the History of Sexuality*, 10:1 (2001), 62–77. Breitenbach, 'Scottish women's organizations', pp. 69–70.
40 Cretney, *Family Law*, pp. 196–318.
41 Thane and Evans, *Sinners?*, pp. 29–53.
42 Jenny Keating, *A Child for Keeps: The History of Adoption in England, 1918–45* (London: Palgrave, 2009).
43 Thane and Evans, *Sinners?*, p. 24.
44 R. Mortimore and A. Blick (eds), *Butler's British Political Facts* (London: Palgrave Macmillan, 2018), p. 467.
45 King, *Family Men*, pp. 195–8; Adrian Bingham, *Gender, Modernity and the Popular Press* (Oxford: Oxford University Press, 2004), pp. 216–43.
46 Bingham, *Gender, Modernity*, p. 79.

47 Law, *Suffrage*, p. 202.
48 Adrian Bingham, 'Enfranchisement, feminism and the modern woman: debates in the British popular press, 1918–1939', in Gottlieb and Toye (eds), *The Aftermath of Suffrage*, p. 96.
49 Bingham, *Gender, Modernity*, p. 136; Adrian Bingham, '"Stop the flapper vote folly": Lord Rothermere, the *Daily Mail* and the equalization of the franchise, 1927–28', *Twentieth Century British History*, 13:1 (2002), 17–37.
50 Angela V. John, *Turning the Tide: The Life of Lady Rhondda* (Cardigan: Parthian, 2013).
51 Law, *Suffrage*, pp. 208–18.
52 Thane, *Foundations*, pp. 178–82.
53 Paul Johnson, *Saving and Spending: The Working-class Economy in Britain 1870–1939* (Oxford: Oxford University Press, 1985).
54 Margery Spring Rice, *Working-class Wives: Their Health and Social Conditions* (London: Penguin, 1939, reprinted London: Virago, 1981).
55 Ibid., p. 86.
56 Debenham, *Birth Control*.
57 Ibid., pp. 159–61; Beaumont, *Housewives and Citizens*, pp. 81–7.
58 Simon Szreter and Kate Fisher, *Sex before the Sexual Revolution: Intimate Life in England, 1918–1963* (Cambridge: Cambridge University Press, 2010); Hera Cook, *The Long Sexual Revolution: Englishwomen, Sex and Contraception, 1800–1975* (Oxford: Oxford University Press, 2004).
59 Mass Observation, *Britain and her Birth-Rate* (John Murray, 1945).
60 Pat Thane, 'The debate on the declining birth-rate in Britain: the "menace" of an ageing population, 1920s–1950s', *Continuity and Change*, 5:2 (1999), 283–305.
61 I. Loudon, *Death in Childbirth: An International Study of Maternal Care and Maternal Mortality* (Oxford: Oxford University Press, 1994), pp. 240–6.
62 Barbara Brookes, *Abortion in England, 1900–1967* (London: Routledge, 1988), p. 43.
63 Ibid., p. 17.
64 Ibid., p. 51.
65 Glew, *Gender, Rhetoric and Regulation*, pp. 122–45, 178–215.
66 Thane, 'What difference did the vote make?', pp. 253–88.
67 Cretney, *Family Law*, p. 236.
68 David Coleman, 'Population and the family', in A.H. Halsey and J. Webb (eds), *Twentieth-Century British Social Trends* (London: Macmillan, 2000), p. 62.

Chapter 3: Gender in Wartime, 1939–1945

1 H.L. Smith, 'The effect of the war on the status of women', in Smith (ed.), *War and Social Change*, p. 213.
2 Julie V. Gottleib, *'Guilty Women', Foreign Policy and Appeasement in Inter-war Britain* (London: Palgrave Macmillan, 2015).
3 Lucy Noakes, 'War and peace', in Ina Zweiniger-Bargielowska (ed.), *Women in Twentieth-Century Britain* (London: Pearson Education, 2001), p. 310.
4 Ibid., p. 314.
5 Ibid., p. 307.

6. Lucy Noakes, *War and the British: Gender and National Identity, 1939–1990* (London: I.B. Tauris, 1997).
7. Pat Thane, 'Girton graduates: earning and learning, 1920s–1950s', *Women's History Review*, 13:3 (2004), 347–86.
8. James Hinton, *Women, Social Leadership, and the Second World War: Continuities of Class* (Oxford: Oxford University Press, 2002), pp. 20–2.
9. R.M. Titmuss, *Problems of Social Policy* (London: HMSO and Longmans, Green and Co., 1950); John Welshman, *Churchill's Children: The Evacuation Experience in Wartime Britain* (Oxford: Oxford University Press, 2010).
10. Titmuss, *Problems of Social Policy*, pp. 142–82; Maggie Andrews, *Women and Evacuation in the Second World War: Femininity, Domesticity and Motherhood* (London: Bloomsbury Academic, 2019).
11. Penny Summerfield, 'The "levelling of class"', in Smith (ed.), *War and Social Change*, pp. 196–8.
12. Anne Hardy, *Health and Social Medicine in Britain since 1860* (London: Palgrave, 2002), p. 124.
13. Phoebe Hall, Hilary Land, Roy Parker and Adrian Webb, *Change, Choice and Conflict in Social Policy* (London: Heinemann, 1975), p. 155.
14. Carol Dyhouse, *Students: A Gendered History* (London: Routledge, 2006), pp. 77–8.
15. Brian Abel-Smith, *The Hospitals, 1800–1948* (London: Heinemann 1964), pp. 424–40.
16. Hardy, *Health and Social Medicine in Britain*, pp. 110–38.
17. Abel-Smith, *The Hospitals*, pp. 424–71.
18. J.M. Winter, 'The demographic consequences of the war', in Smith (ed.), *War and Social Change*, pp. 154–6.
19. Ibid., pp. 168–70.
20. Sheena Evans, *Bloomsbury, Belsen, Oxford: Janet Vaughan, Medical Pioneer* (Chester: University of Chester Press, 2024).
21. H.L. Smith, 'The effect of the war on the status of women', in Smith (ed.), *War and Social Change*, pp. 210–11.
22. Penny Summerfield, *Women Workers and the Second World War: Production and Patriarchy in Conflict*, 2nd edn (London: Routledge, 2012), ch. 5; Richard Croucher, *Engineers at War* (London: Merlin, 1982), p. 29.
23. Beaumont, *Housewives and Citizens*, p. 145.
24. Sheila Ferguson and Hilde Fitzgerald, *Studies in the Social Services* (London: HMSO and Longmans, Green and Co., 1954), p. 178, n. 1.
25. Summerfield, *Women Workers*, p. 120.
26. Ibid., pp. 190–1.
27. Helen McCarthy, *Double Lives: A History of Working Motherhood* (London: Bloomsbury, 2020), pp. 178–82.
28. Thane and Evans, *Sinners?*, pp. 58–64.
29. Beaumont, *Women and Domesticity*, pp. 146–53.
30. Croucher, *Engineers at War*, p. 29.
31. Summerfield, *Women Workers*, p. 200; Summerfield, 'The "levelling of class"', pp. 187–8.
32. Ibid., pp. 136–7.
33. Beaumont, *Housewives and Citizens*, pp. 138–41.
34. Ibid., p. 171.

35 Ibid., pp. 173–4.
36 Glew, *Gender, Rhetoric and Regulation*, p. 137.
37 Sir William Beveridge, *Social Insurance and Allied Services*, Cmd 6404 (HMSO, 1942), para. 8.
38 Kathleen Kiernan, Hilary Land and Jane Lewis, *Lone Motherhood in Twentieth-Century Britain* (Oxford: Oxford University Press, 1999), pp. 179–80.
39 Beveridge, Cmd. 6404, para. 107.
40 Thane, 'The women of the British Labour Party and feminism, 1918–1945', in Smith (ed.), *British Feminism*; Pedersen, *Eleanor Rathbone*.
41 Mitchell and Deane, *Abstract of British Historical Statistics*, table 16, p. 46; B.R. Mitchell and H.G. Jones, *Second Abstract of British Historical Statistics* (Cambridge: Cambridge University Press, 1971), table 14, p. 30.
42 Mitchell and Deane, *Abstract of British Historical Statistics*, table 10, pp. 30–3; Mitchell and Jones, *Second Abstract of British Historical Statistics*, table 8, pp. 21–2.
43 Thane, 'The debate on the declining birth-rate'; Eva M. Hubback, *The Population of Britain* (London: Penguin, 1957).
44 Virginia Wimperis, *The Unmarried Mother and Her Child* (London: George Allen and Unwin, 1960), Appendix table 2a.
45 Ferguson and Fitzgerald, *Social Services*, p. 103.
46 Ibid., pp. 93–4.
47 *Registrar General's Statistical Review of England and Wales for the Six Years 1940–1945*, Text, Vol. 11, Civil, p. 144.
48 Sonya Rose, *Which People's War? National Identity and Citizenship in Wartime Britain, 1938–45* (Oxford: Oxford University Press, 2002), p. 74.
49 G. Braybon and P. Summerfield, *Out of the Cage: Women's Experiences in Two World Wars* (London: Pandora, 1987), pp. 206–7.
50 Ibid., p. 95.
51 Ibid.
52 Thane and Evans, *Sinners?*, pp. 54–81.
53 Ibid., pp. 76–8; Ferguson and Fitzgerald, *Social Services*, pp. 131–2; Lucy Bland, *Britain's Brown Babies: The Stories of Children Born to Black GIs and White Women in the Second World War* (Manchester: Manchester University Press, 2019).
54 Ferguson and Fitgerald, *Social Services*, p. 104.
55 Thane and Evans, *Sinners?*, pp. 79–81.
56 Bernard Crick, *George Orwell: A Life* (London: Secker and Warburg, 1980), pp. 463–4.
57 Helen Jones (ed.), *Duty and Citizenship: The Correspondence and Papers of Violet Markham, 1896–1953* (London: The Historians' Press, 1994).
58 Helen Jones, 'Markham, Violet Rosa (1872–1959)', *Oxford Dictionary of National Biography* (ODNB) (2004), www.oxforddnb.com.
59 *Report of the Committee on Amenities and Welfare, Conditions in the Three Women's Services*, 1942, Cmd 6384, pp. 31, 50.

Chapter 4: Making the 'Welfare State', 1945–1951

1 Monica Charlot, 'Women and elections in Britain', in H.R. Penniman (ed.), *Britain at the Polls, 1979: A Study of the General Election* (Washington, DC: American Enterprise Institute for Public Policy Research, 1981), p. 244.

2 Jose Harris, *William Beveridge: A Biography*, 2nd edn (Oxford: Oxford University Press, 1997), pp. 451–2.
3 Thane, *Old Age*, pp. 369–71.
4 Pat Thane, 'Labour and welfare', in Duncan Tanner, Pat Thane and Nick Tiratsoo (eds), *Labour's First Century* (Cambridge: Cambridge University Press, 2000), pp. 80 ff.
5 Pat Thane, 'Towards equal opportunities? Women in Britain since 1945', in Terry Gourvish and Alan O'Day (eds), *Britain Since 1945* (London: Macmillan, 1991), pp. 191–5.
6 John Bowlby, *Maternal Care and Mental Health*, 2nd edn (Geneva: World Health Organization, 1952); John Bowlby, *Child Care and the Growth of Love* (London: Penguin, 1953).
7 Denise Riley, *War in the Nursery: Theories of the Child and the Mother* (London: Virago, 1983).
8 Ibid., p. 209.
9 McCarthy, *Double Lives*, p. 197.
10 Ibid., p. 204.
11 Ibid.
12 Helen McCarthy, *Women of the World: The Rise of the Female Diplomat* (London: Bloomsbury, 2014), p. 238.
13 McCarthy, *Double Lives*, p. 205.
14 Ibid.
15 Ibid., pp. 202–3.
16 Ibid., p. 201.
17 Veronica Beechey and Tessa Perkins, *A Matter of Hours: Women, Part-time Work and the Labour Market* (Minneapolis, MN: University of Minnesota Press, 1987), p. 16.
18 Helen Glew, 'A new phase of activism: women's occupational organizations and married women's paid work after the Second World War in Britain', *Women's History Review*, 34:4 (2025), 545–63.
19 Linda McDowell, *Working Lives: Gender, Migration and Employment in Britain, 1945–2007* (Oxford: Wiley-Blackwell, 2013); Colin Holmes, 'Immigration', in Gourvish and O'Day (eds), *Britain Since 1945*, pp. 209–18; Mike Phillips and Trevor Phillips, *Windrush: The Irresistible Rise of Multicultural Britain* (London: HarperCollins, 1998).
20 *Report of the Royal Commission on Equal Pay* (London: HMSO, 1946), p. 43.
21 Ibid., p. 163.
22 Thane, 'The British imperial state', pp. 29–46.
23 Sharon Thompson, *Quiet Revolutionaries: The Married Women's Association and Family Law* (Oxford: Hart/Bloomsbury, 2022).
24 Lewis, *The End of Marriage?*, p. 30.
25 Kiernan et al., *Lone Motherhood*, pp. 60 ff.
26 Ibid., p. 35.
27 Wimperis, *The Unmarried Mother*, table 4.
28 Ibid., pp. 124–6.
29 Thane and Evans, *Sinners?*, p. 106; NCUMC Annual Report 1949, p. 13.
30 James Hinton, 'Women and the Labour vote, 1945–50', *Labour History Review*, 57:3 (1992), 59–66.
31 Ibid.

Chapter 5: 'Never Had It So Good'? 1951–1964

1. John, *Turning the Tide*, pp. 468–71.
2. Joyce Freeguard, 'It's time for women of the 1950s to stand up and be counted', D.Phil thesis, University of Sussex (2004), pp. 175–83.
3. Eustace Chesser, *The Sexual, Marital and Family Relationships of the English Woman* (London: Hutchinson's Medical, 1956).
4. Glew, 'A new phase of activism'.
5. Glew, *Gender, Rhetoric and Regulation*, pp. 157–67.
6. Ibid., pp. 165–6.
7. McCarthy, *Double Lives*, p. 249.
8. Ibid., pp. 250–2.
9. King, *Family Men*, p. 78.
10. Margaret Wynn, *Fatherless Families* (London: Michael Joseph, 1964), p. 18.
11. Ferdynand Zweig, *The Worker in an Affluent Society: Family, Life and Industry* (Glencoe, IL: Free Press of Glencoe, 1961).
12. Venetia Murray, 'The children of mothers who work', *Picture Post*, 7 January 1956, p. 7; McCarthy, *Double Lives*, p. 248.
13. Viola Klein, *Working Wives: The Survey of Facts and Opinions Concerning the Gainful Employment of Married Women in Britain* (London: Institute of Personnel Management, 1960); Viola Klein, *Britain's Married Women Workers* (London: Routledge and Kegan Paul, 1965).
14. Zweig, *The Worker in an Affluent Society*; McCarthy, *Double Lives*, p. 236.
15. Audrey Hunt, *A Survey of Women's Employment* (London: HMSO, 1968).
16. King, *Family Men*.
17. McCarthy, *Double Lives*, p. 243.
18. 'Survey of the employment of women scientists and engineers', *Ministry of Labour Gazette*, September 1960, pp. 356–7.
19. Nancy Seear, Veronica Roberts and John Brock, *A Career for Women in Industry* (Edinburgh: Oliver and Boyd, 1964).
20. Ibid.
21. Hunt, *Survey of Women's Employment*.
22. Department of Education, White Paper, *Technical Education*, Cmd. 973, 1956.
23. Ministry of Education, *The Crowther Report. 15 to 18: A Report of the Central Advisory Council for Education (England)* (London: HMSO, 1959), https://education-uk.org/documents/crowther/crowther1959-1.html.
24. Judith Hubback, *From Dawn to Dusk: Autobiography of Judith Hubback* (Wilmette, IL: Chiron Publications, 2003).
25. Judith Hubback, *Wives Who Went to College* (London: Heinemann, 1957).
26. McCarthy, *Double Lives*, p. 262.
27. Ibid., pp. 263–4.
28. Ibid., p. 266.
29. Pearl Jephcott, Nancy Seear and John H. Smith, *Married Women Working* (London: Allen and Unwin, 1962); McCarthy, *Double Lives*, pp. 227–9.
30. Margot Jefferys and Patricia Elliott, *Women in Medicine: The Results of an Inquiry Conducted by the Medical Practitioners Union in 1962–3* (London: Medical Practitioners Union, 1966).

31 Freeguard, 'It's time for women', pp. 72–3.
32 McCarthy, *Double Lives*, pp. 276–8.
33 Political and Economic Planning, *Women in Top Jobs: Interim Report* (London: PEP, 1967).
34 Ibid., p. 233.
35 Lynn Abrams, *Feminist Lives: Women, Feelings and the Self in Post-war Britain* (Oxford: Oxford University Press, 2023), pp. 187–9.
36 Hannah Gavron, *The Captive Wife* (London: Pelican, 1968).
37 Helen Coffey, 'Hannah Gavron, the pioneering 1960s feminist you've never heard of', *The Independent*, 31 July 2024.
38 McCarthy, *Double Lives*, p. 237.
39 Ibid., p. 239.
40 Andrew Thorpe, *History of the British Labour Party*, 4th edn (London: Palgrave Macmillan, 2014), p. 141.
41 Coleman, 'Population and family', p. 62.
42 *Report of the Royal Commission on Marriage and Divorce, 1951–5* (London: HMSO, 1955) Cmd. 9678, para. 45; Cretney, *Family Law*, p. 335.
43 Logan, *Feminism and Criminal Justice*.
44 Selina Todd, *Tastes of Honey: The Making of Shelagh Delaney and a Cultural Revolution* (London: Vintage, 2021).
45 Stephen Brooke, 'Slumming in swinging London: class, gender and the post-war city in Nell Dunn's *Up the Junction*', *Cultural and Social History*, 9 (2012), 429–44; Stephen Brooke, *Sexual Politics: Sexuality, Family Planning and the British Left from the 1880s to the Present Day* (Oxford: Oxford University Press, 2011), pp. 156–8.
46 Peter K. Steinberg (ed.), *The Collected Prose of Sylvia Plath* (London: Faber, 2024).
47 Weeks, *Sex, Politics and Society*, pp. 238–40.
48 Adrian Bingham, 'The "K-Bomb": social surveys, the popular press and British sexual culture in the 1940s and 1950s', *Journal of British Studies*, 50:1 (2011), 156–79.
49 Weeks, *Sex, Politics and Society*, p. 240.
50 Ibid., p. 239.
51 Bingham, *Family Newspapers*, pp. 188–90.
52 Ibid., p. 169.
53 Weeks, *Sex, Politics and Society*, p. 243.
54 Bingham, *Family Newspapers*, p. 168.
55 Mark Jarvis, *Conservative Governments: Morality and Social Change in Affluent Britain* (Manchester: Manchester University Press, 2005), p. 101.

Chapter 6: A Permissive Society? 1964–1970
1 Ina Zweiniger-Bargielowska, 'Explaining the gender gap', in Martin Francis and Ina Zweiniger-Bargielowska (eds), *Conservatives and British Society, 1880–1990* (Cardiff: University of Wales Press, 1996), pp. 192–224.
2 OPCS, *Marriage and Divorce Statistics: Historical Series, 1837–1983*. FM2 No 16 (London: HMSO, 1995); Lewis, *The End of Marriage?*, p. 30.
3 Coleman, 'Population and family', p. 62.
4 Claire Langhamer, *The English in Love: the Intimate Story of an Emotional Revolution* (Oxford: Oxford University Press, 2013).

5 Brian Abel-Smith and Peter Townsend, *The Poor and the Poorest* (London: Bell and Co., 1965).
6 Ibid., pp. 33, 48.
7 Pat Thane and Ruth Davidson, *The Child Poverty Action Group, 1965–2015* (London: Child Poverty Action Group, 2016).
8 David Butler and Gareth Butler, *Twentieth-Century British Political Facts* (New York: St. Martin's Press, 2000), p. 350.
9 Kiernan et al., *Lone Motherhood*, p. 42.
10 Cook, *The Long Sexual Revolution*.
11 A.H. Halsey and Jean Floud, *Social Class and Educational Opportunity* (London: Heinemann, 1956).
12 Howard Glennerster, *British Social Policy Since 1945* (Oxford: Blackwell, 1995), pp. 139–40.
13 Halsey, 'Further and higher education', in Halsey and Webb (eds), *Twentieth-Century British Social Trends*, pp. 228–9.
14 Ibid., pp. 224–32.
15 Phoebe Hall, 'Creating the Open University', in Phobe Hall, Hilary Land, Roy Parker and Adrian Webb, *Change, Choice and Conflict in Social Policy* (London: Heinemann, 1975), pp. 155–276.
16 Department of Education and Science, *The Plowden Report: Children and Their Primary Schools* (London, HMSO, 1967), https://education-uk.org/documents/plowden/plowden1967-1.html.
17 Royal Commission on Trade Unions and Employers' Associations, 1965–1968, *Report* (London: HMSO, 1968), pp. 90–3.
18 N. Seear, *The Position of Women in Industry*, Research Paper for the Royal Commission on Trade Unions and Employers Associations (London: HMSO, 1968).
19 McCarthy, *Double Lives*, pp. 269–71.
20 Ibid., p. 274.
21 E. Younghusband, *Report on Social Workers in Local Authority Health and Welfare Services* (London: HMSO, 1959).
22 McCarthy, *Double Lives*, p. 275.
23 Ibid., pp. 281–4.
24 Bingham, *Family Newspapers*, p. 87.
25 Andrew Holden, *Makers and Manners: Politics and Morality in Post-war Britain* (London: Politico's, 2004), p. 131.
26 Ibid., pp. 133–4.
27 Ibid., pp. 140–1.
28 Hall, *Sex, Gender and Social Change*, p. 179.
29 Coleman, 'Population and family', p. 50.
30 Cook, *Long Sexual Revolution*, pp. 268–74.
31 Caroline Rusterholz, *Responsible Pleasures: The Brook Advisory Centres and Youth Sexuality in Postwar Britain* (Oxford: Oxford University Press, 2024).
32 Ibid., pp. 296–317; Hall, *Sex, Gender and Social Change*, pp. 176–7.
33 Hall, p. 171.
34 Ibid., p. 168. Rebecca Jennings, *Lesbian Intimacies and Family Life: Desire, Domesticity and Kinship in Britain and Australia, 1945–2000* (London: Bloomsbury Academic, 2024).

35 Hall, *Sex, Gender and Social Change*, pp. 164–8.
36 R.H.S. Crossman, *Diaries of a Cabinet Minister, 1966–68*, Vol. 2 (London: Hamish Hamilton, 1976), p. 407, 3 July 1967.
37 David Butler, 'Electors and elected', in A.H. Halsey (ed.), *Trends in British Society Since 1900* (London: Macmillan, 1972), p. 318.
38 Holden, *Makers and Manners*, p. 128.
39 Ibid., p. 129.
40 Peter Tatchell, 'Fifty years of gay liberation? In Britain it's barely four', *Guardian*, 23 May 2017, p. 31.
41 K.O. Morgan, *Callaghan: A Life* (Oxford: Oxford University Press, 1998), pp. 297, 320.
42 Cretney, *Family Law*, pp. 318–91.
43 Ibid., pp. 134–6, 420–1.
44 Ibid., p. 379, n. 392.
45 Elizabeth Meehan, *Women's Rights at Work: Campaigns and Policy in Britain and the US* (New York: St Martin's Press, 1985), pp. 43–56.
46 Barbara Castle, *Fighting All the Way* (London: Pan, 1993), pp. 408–9.
47 Ibid., p. 412.
48 Ibid., p. 427.
49 Ibid.
50 Holger Nehring, 'The growth of social movements', in Paul Addison and Harriet Jones, *A Companion to Contemporary Britain, 1939–2000* (Oxford: Blackwell, 2005), pp. 389–406.
51 Peter Hitchens, *The Abolition of Britain: from Lady Chatterley to Tony Blair* (London: Continuum, 1999; 2nd edn, Bloomsbury, 2008).

Chapter 7: The Seventies, 1970–1979
1 A. Atkinson, *Incomes and the Welfare State: Essays on Britain and Europe* (Cambridge: Cambridge University Press, 1996), p. 17.
2 Ina Zweiniger-Bargielowska, 'Housewifery', in Zweininger-Bargielowska (ed.), *Women in Britain*, p. 160.
3 Robert J. Wybrow, *Britain Speaks Out, 1937–78: A Social History as Seen Through the Gallup Poll Data* (London: Macmillan, 1989), p. 102.
4 Coleman, 'Population and family', p. 62.
5 Lewis, *The End of Marriage?*, p. 34; Langhamer, *The English in Love*.
6 Lewis, *The End of Marriage?*, p. 30.
7 Coleman, 'Population and family', p. 34.
8 Lewis, *The End of Marriage?*, p. 35.
9 DHSS, *Report of the Committee on One-Parent Families*, Cmnd 5629 (1974), Vol. 1, pp. 490–1.
10 Ibid., p. 261.
11 Ibid., p. 260.
12 Ibid., p. 425.
13 Ibid., p. 510.
14 Ibid., p. 516.
15 Ibid., pp. 513–14.
16 Castle, *Fighting*, pp. 469–70.

17 For a detailed account of the work of the Finer Committee and responses to it, see Thane and Evans, *Sinners?*, pp. 140–68.
18 Ibid., p. 166.
19 Including *Hidden from History: 300 Years of Women's Oppression and the Fight Against It* (London: Pluto, 1974); *Women, Resistance and Revolution: A History of Women and Revolution in the Modern World* (London: Random House, 1973). See her account of the women's movement in *Threads Through Time: Writings on History and Autobiography* (London: Penguin, 1999), pp. 13–83.
20 Brixton Black Women's Group, 'Black women organizing', *Feminist Review*, 17 (1984), pp. 84–8; Natalie Thomlinson, *Race, Ethnicity and the Women's Movement in England, 1968–93* (London: Palgrave, 2016).
21 Lori Williamson, *Power and Protest: Frances Power Cobbe and Victorian Society* (London: Rivers Oram, 2005), pp. 80–4.
22 Erin Pizzey, *This Way to the Revolution: A Memoir* (London: Peter Owen, 2013).
23 Cretney, *Family Law*, pp. 753–5.
24 Amnesty International UK, *Violence against Women* (London: Amnesty International UK, 2025), www.amnesty.org.uk/violence-against-women#.VMTOG1.
25 Jackson, *Women Police*, pp. 185–93.
26 Bingham, *Family Newspapers*, pp. 155–6.
27 Thomlinson, *Race, Ethnicity and the Women's Movement*; George Stevenson, *The Women's Liberation Movement and the Politics of Class in Britain* (London: Bloomsbury, 2019).
28 Women and Equality Unit, *Key Indicators of Women's Position in Britain* (London: UK Government, Department of Trade and Industry, 2001), p. 83.
29 Meehan, *Women's Rights at Work*, pp. 72–96; Antonio Zabalza and Zafiris Tzannatos, *Women and Equal Pay: The Effects of Legislation on Women's Employment and Wages in Britain* (Cambridge: Cambridge University Press, 1985).
30 Reid, *United We Stand*, pp. 354–5.
31 Roger King and Neill Nugent (eds), *Respectable Rebels: Middle Class Campaigns in Britain in the 1970s* (London: Hodder and Stoughton, 1979).
32 https://womenshistorynetwork.org/the-first-40-years-the-working-womens-charter/.
33 Reid, *United We Stand*, p. 387.
34 Ann Oakley, *Housewife* (London: Allen Lane, 1974).
35 Louise Toupin, *Wages for Housework: A History of an International Feminist Movement, 1972–77* (London: Pluto Press, 2020); Emily Callaci, *Wages for Housework: The Story of a Movement, an Idea, a Promise* (London: Allen Lane, 2025).
36 Dyhouse, *Students*, p. 99.
37 Butler and Butler, *Twentieth-Century British Political Facts*, p. 366.
38 Zweiniger-Bargielowska, 'Housewifery', p. 158.
39 McCarthy, *Double Lives*, pp. 325–30.
40 Ibid., p. 348.
41 Ibid., p. 349.
42 Ibid., pp. 332–3.
43 Ibid., pp. 335–6.
44 *Services for Young Children with Working Mothers: Report by the Central Policy Review Staff* (London: HMSO, 1978).
45 McCarthy, *Double Lives*, p. 338.

46 Jennings, *Lesbian Intimacies*, pp. 101–26.
47 Nehring, 'Growth of social movements', pp. 393–5.
48 For a discussion of local differences in LGBTQ experiences in England since the 1960s, see Matt Cook and Alison Oram, *Queer beyond London* (Manchester: Manchester University Press, 2022).
49 Ibid., p. 1.
50 Ibid., p. 3.
51 Hall, *Sex, Gender and Social Change*, p. 181.
52 Jan Morris, *Conundrum* (London: Faber and Faber, 1974).

Chapter 8: The Lady's Not for Equality, 1979–1997
1 Thames TV, 13 December 1982. Thatcher Foundation Website: https://ww.margaret thatcher.org.
2 Richard Vinen, *Thatcher's Britain: The Politics and Social Upheaval of the 1980s* (London: Simon and Schuster, 2009), p. 25.
3 Sarah Childs, Joni Lovenduski and Rosie Campbell, *Women at the Top 2005: Changing Numbers, Changing Politics* (London: Hansard Society, 2005), 'International comparisons', pp. 75–93.
4 Emma Nicholson, *Secret Society: Inside – and Outside – the Conservative Party* (London: Indigo, 1996), pp. 85–105.
5 Hansard Society, *The Report of the Hansard Society Commission on Women at the Top* (London: Hansard Society, 1990).
6 Vinen, *Thatcher's Britain*, p. 25.
7 The MPs were Bernie Grant, Diane Abbott, Paul Boateng and Keith Vaz.
8 Jeffrey Weeks, Brian Heaphy and Catherine Donovan, 'Families of choice: autonomy and mutuality in non-heterosexual relationships', in S. McRae (ed.), *Changing Britain: Families and Households in the 1990s* (Oxford: Oxford University Press, 1999), pp. 297–316.
9 Kiernan et al., *Lone Motherhood*, p. 56.
10 Office of National Statistics (ONS hereafter), 'Fastest increase in the oldest old', 1 April 2011, www.ons.gov.uk/ons/index.html.
11 ONS, *Statistical Bulletin: Older Peoples' Day*, 30 September 2010, p. 3, www.ons.gov.uk/ons/rel/mortality-ageing/focus-on-older-people/older-people-s-day-2011/index.html.
12 Women's Royal Voluntary Service, 'Gold age pensioners contribution outweighs cost by £40 billion', 2011, www.goldagepensioners.com.
13 Holden, *Makers and Manners*, p. 227.
14 Ibid.
15 Margaret Thatcher, *The Downing Street Years* (London: HarperCollins, 1993), pp. 630–1.
16 Ibid., p. 628.
17 Holden, *Makers and Manners*, p. 264.
18 *British Social Attitudes. Cumulative Sourcebook: The First Six Surveys*, compiled by Social and Community Planning Research (Aldershot: Gower, 1992), tables N1-16-25, N2-2.
19 Quoted in Hilary Macaskill, *From the Workhouse to the Workplace: 75 Years of One-Parent Family Life, 1918–1939* (London: National Council for One Parent Families, 1993), p. 45.
20 Thane and Evans, *Sinners?*, p. 172.

21 Ibid., p. 173.
22 Thatcher, *Downing Street Years*, p. 630.
23 Mavis MacLean with Jacek Kurzewski, *Making Family Law: A Socio-legal Account of Legislative Process in England and Wales* (Oxford: Hart, 2011).
24 Cretney, *Family Law*, pp. 563–5.
25 E. Breitenbach and F. Mackay, 'Feminist politics in Scotland from the 1970s–2000s: engaging with the changing state', in Breitenbach and Thane (eds), *Women and Citizenship*, pp. 157–9.
26 P. Chaney, 'Devolution, citizenship and women's political representation in Wales', in Breitenbach and Thane (eds), *Women and Citizenship*, pp. 189–208.
27 J.W.B. Douglas, J.M. Ross and H.R. Simpson, *All Our Future: A Longitudinal Study of Secondary Education* (London: Panther, 1971), pp. 42–7; Michele Cohen, 'Knowledge and the gendered curriculum: the problematisation of girls achievement' (2004), www.historyandpolicy.org/policy-papers/category/michele-cohen.
28 B. Parekh, *The Future of Multi-ethnic Britain* (London: Runnymede Trust, 2000).
29 Howard Glennerster, 'Education', in Howard Glennerster and John Hills (eds), *The State of Welfare: The Economics of Social Spending*, 2nd edn (Oxford: Oxford University Press, 1998), pp. 57–63.
30 Ibid., pp. 65–6.
31 Halsey, 'Further and higher education', p. 239.
32 McCarthy, *Double Lives*, pp. 358–9.
33 https://www.hansardsociety.org.uk.
34 McCarthy, *Double Lives*, pp. 359–60.
35 Ibid., p. 360.
36 Susan McRae, *Women at the Top: Progress after Five Years. A Follow-Up Report to the Hansard Society Commission on Women at the Top* (London: Hansard Society King-Hall Paper, 1996).
37 McCarthy, *Double Lives*, p. 361.
38 Ibid., p. 362.
39 Ibid., pp. 364–5.
40 Ibid., pp.368–9.
41 Timothy J. Hatton, 'Population, migration and labour supply: Great Britain, 1871–2011', in Roderick Floud, Jane Humphries and Paul Johnson (eds), *The Cambridge Economic History of Modern Britain*, Vol. 2, *1870 to the Present* (Cambridge: Cambridge University Press, 2014), p. 108.
42 Maria Evandrou and Jane Falkingham, 'Personal Social Services', in Glennerster and Hills (eds), *The State of Welfare*, p. 217.
43 Ruth Lister, 'The family and women', in Dennis Kavanagh and Anthony Seldon (eds), *The Major Effect: An Overview of John Major's Premiership* (London: Macmillan, 1994), pp. 357–9.
44 Kathleen Sherit, *Women on the Front Line: British Servicewomen's Path to Combat* (Stroud: Amberley, 2020).
45 Polly Toynbee, *Hard Work: Life in Low-Pay Britain* (London: Bloomsbury, 2003).
46 McCarthy, *Double Lives*, p. 170.
47 Ibid., p. 271.

48 Ibid., pp. 375–6; House of Commons, *Third Special Report from the Employment Committee (Session 1981–2), Homeworking* (31 March 1982).
49 Vinen, *Thatcher's Britain*, p. 183; David Kynaston, *The City of London*, Vol. 4, *A Club No More, 1945–2000* (London: Chatto and Windus, 2002), p. 713.
50 Thane and Evans, *Sinners?*, pp. 184–6.
51 Ibid., pp. 187–8.
52 *Daily Mail*, 5 July 1993.
53 Thane and Evans, *Sinners?*, pp. 189–93.
54 Mortimore and Blick (eds), *Butler's British Political Facts*, p. 621.
55 Jonathan Cribb, Robert Joyce and David Phillips, *Living Standards, Poverty and Inequality in the UK* (London: Institute for Fiscal Studies, 2012).
56 Mel Porter, 'Gender identity and sexual orientation', in Pat Thane (ed.), *Unequal Britain: Equalities in Britain Since 1945* (London: Continuum, 2010), pp. 159–61.
57 'Life blood or death', *The Times*, 21 November 1984, quoted in ibid., p. 151.
58 Cook and Oram, *Queer Beyond London*, p. 1.
59 Holden, *Makers and Manners*, p. 248.
60 Ibid., p. 298.
61 Ibid., p. 300.
62 Ibid., pp. 300–1.

Chapter 9: Things Can Only Get Better? New Labour, 1997–2010

1 Helen McCarthy, 'Gender Equality', in Thane (ed.), *Unequal Britain*, pp. 120–2.
2 https://www.equalityhumanrights.com.
3 Childs et al., *Women at the Top 2005*, pp. 80–2.
4 Fiona Mackay and Meryl Kenny, 'Women and political representation in post-devolution Scotland: high time or high tide?', pp. 171–3; Paul Chaney 'Devolution, citizenship and women's political representation in Wales', pp. 190–2, both in Breitenbach and Thane (eds), *Women and Citizenship*.
5 Esther Breitenbach and Fiona Mackay, 'Feminist politics in Scotland from the 1970s to 2000s: engaging with the changing state', in Breitenbach and Thane (eds), *Women and Citizenship*, p. 164.
6 Laura Shepherd-Robinson and Joni Lovenduski, *Women and Candidate Selection in British Political Parties* (London: Fawcett Society, 2001).
7 Robert Taylor, 'New Labour, new capitalism', in Anthony Seldon (ed.), *Blair's Britain, 1997–2007* (Cambridge: Cambridge University Press, 2007), pp. 232–3.
8 Polly Toynbee and David Walker, *The Verdict: Did Labour Change Britain?* (London: Granta, 2010), p. 203.
9 McCarthy, 'Gender and equality', p. 116.
10 ONS, 'Fertility. UK fertility remains high', 24 June 2011, https://www.ons.gov.uk/index.html.
11 Mortimore and Blick (eds), *Butler's British Political Facts*, p. 274.
12 George Smith, 'Schools', pp. 210–12; Halsey, 'Further and higher education', pp. 226, 234; McCarthy, 'Gender equality', pp. 117–18.
13 Equal Opportunities Commission, *Women and Men in Britain: Professional Occupations* (London: EOC, 2001); Michael Beloff, 'Law and the judiciary', in Seldon (ed.), *Blair's Britain*, pp. 297–311.

14 EOC, *Women and Men in Britain*, pp. 5–6.
15 Ibid., p. 6.
16 Ibid., pp. 6–7.
17 Ibid., pp. 3–4.
18 EOC, *Women and Men in Britain: Management* (London: EOC, 2002).
19 Cabinet Office Briefing, *Women's Incomes Over the Lifetime: The Mother Gap* (London: The Women's Unit, Cabinet Office, 2000).
20 T. Anderson, J. Forth, H. Metcalf and S. Kirby, *The Gender Pay Gap: Final Report to the Women and Equality Unit* (London: Cabinet Office, Women and Equality Unit, July 2001).
21 Karen Escott and Dexter Whitfield, *Promoting Gender Equality in the Public Sector* (London: EOC, Working Paper No. 2, 2002).
22 https://www.fawcettsociety.org.uk.
23 Karen Ross, 'No more funny handshakes', *Times Higher Education Supplement*, 15 December 2000.
24 Karen Ross, *Women at the Top 2000: Cracking the Public Sector Glass Ceiling* (London: The Hansard Society and Fawcett Society, 2000).
25 Robert Taylor, *Diversity in Britain's Labour Market* (Swindon: ESRC Future of Work Programme Series, 2001).
26 Toynbee, *Hard Work*, p. 99.
27 Ibid.; McCarthy, *Double Lives*, pp. 377–80.
28 Fawcett Society, Commission on Women and the Criminal Justice System, *Interim Report on Victims and Witnesses* (London: Fawcett Society, 2003).
29 Tony Blair, 'Beveridge revisited: a welfare state for the 21st century', in Robert Walker (ed.), *Ending Child Poverty: Popular Welfare for the 21st Century* (Bristol: Policy Press, 1999), p. 7; Kitty Stewart, 'Equality and social justice', in Seldon (ed.), *Blair's Britain*, p. 441.
30 John Hills, *Good Times, Bad Times: The Welfare Myth of Them and Us* (Bristol: Policy Press, 2015), p. 132; Stewart 'Equality and social justice', pp. 434–5.
31 Thane and Evans, *Sinners?*, p. 196.
32 Stewart 'Equality and social justice', pp. 425–6.
33 Ibid., pp. 419–21.
34 Michael Marmot, *Fair Society, Healthy Lives: Strategic Review of Health Inequalities in England* (2010), www.marmotreview.org.
35 David Willetts, *The Pinch: How the Baby Boomers Took Their Children's Future – and Why They Should Give It Back* (London: Atlantic Books, 2010); E. Howker and S. Malik, *Jilted Generation: How Britain Has Bankrupted Its Youth* (London: Icon Books, 2010).
36 Pat Thane, 'Demographic futures', in Peter Taylor-Gooby (ed.), *New Paradigms in Public Policy* (Oxford: Oxford University Press/British Academy, 2013), pp. 139–66; Emily Grundy, 'Reciprocity in relationships: socio-economic and health influences on intergenerational exchanges between third age parents and their children in Great Britain', *British Journal of Sociology*, 56:2 (2005), 233–55.
37 https://www.agediscrimination.info/case-reports/2011/1/10/oreilly-v-bbc.
38 Home Office Citizenship Surveys 2001/11: www.ukdataservice.ac.uk.
39 Porter, 'Gender identity', pp. 156–9; Holden, *Makers and Manners*, pp. 336–43.

40 Holden, *Makers and Manners*, pp. 380–1.
41 Ibid., pp. 346–8.
42 Porter, 'Gender identity', p. 158.
43 Ibid., p. 128.
44 Holden, *Makers and Manners*, pp. 356–7.
45 Porter, 'Gender identity', p. 158.
46 Cook and Oram, *Queer Outside London*, pp. 5–6.
47 Porter, 'Gender identity', pp. 159–61; Cook and Oram, *Queer Outside London*, p. 219.
48 Ibid., pp. 311–12, 315–18, 336–58.
49 International Lesbian, Gay, Bisexual, Trans and Intersex Association, *State-Sponsored Homophobia: A World Survey of Sexual Orientation, Criminalization, Protection and Recognition*, 11th edn (Brussels, 2016), www.ilga.org/worldwide-legislation.
50 Tessa Jowell, 'We are the most feminist government in history', *Guardian*, 15 April 2002.
51 McCarthy, *Double Lives*, pp. 381–3.

Chapter 10: Austerity, 2010–2024

1 Joseph Rowntree Foundation, *UK Poverty 2023. The Essential Guide to Understanding Poverty in the UK* (York: Joseph Rowntree Foundation, 2023), p. 91. See also www.resolutionfoundation.org/publications/the-living-standards-audit-2018/.
2 Child Poverty Action Group website: https://www.cpag.org.uk.
3 Jonathan Cribb, Agnes Norris Keiller and Tom Waters, *Living Standards, Poverty and Inequality in the UK, 2018* (London: Institute for Fiscal Studies, 2018).
4 Joseph Rowntree Foundation, *UK Poverty 2024. The Essential Guide to Understanding Poverty in the UK* (York: Joseph Rowntree Foundation, 2024), https://www.jrf.org.uk/uk-poverty-2024-the-essential-guide-to-understanding-poverty-in-the-uk.
5 Ruth Patrick, Kate Andersen, Mary Reeder, Aaron Reeves and Kitty Stewart, *Needs and Entitlements: Welfare Reform in Larger Families* (London, 2023), https://largerfamilies.study/publications/needs-and-entitlements/.
6 'Regional employment and wage gaps have narrowed but inequality proves deeply entrenched as child poverty gaps widen further' (London: Resolution Foundation, 6 August 2024), https://www.resolutionfoundation.org/press-releases/regional-gaps-have-narrowed.
7 'Two-child cap is cementing inequalities, Starmer told', *Guardian*, 6 August 2024.
8 *State of Ageing, 2023* (London: Centre for Ageing Better, November 2023); see also the National Life Tables published annually by ONS, https://www.ons.gov.uk/peoplepopulationandcommunities/birthsdeathsandmarriages/lifeexpectancies/bulletins/nationallifetablesunitedkingdom.
9 'Obesity blamed as rising life expectancy stalls', *Guardian*, 19 February 2025.
10 Women Against State Pension Inequality website: https://www.waspi.co.uk.
11 Ibid.
12 For further detail, see DWP, *The Gender Pensions Gap in Private Pensions*, Department of Work and Pensions, June 2022, https://www.gov.uk/government/statistics/gender-pensions-gap-in-private-pensions/the-gender-pensions-gap-in-private-pensions.
13 'Nearly 1m over-66s are living in deprivation, figures show', *Guardian*, 17 April 2024.

14 Denise Wilkins, 'Unpaid carers like me prop up a failing system', *Guardian*, 3 June 2023; *Key Facts and Figures about Caring* (London: Carers UK, 2023), https://www.carersuk.org/policy-and-research/key-facts-and-figures/.
15 ONS, *Census 2021*, www.ons.gov.uk/census.
16 Elizabeth Parkin and Bukky Balogun, *Quality and Safety of Maternal Care*, House of Commons Library Research Briefing, 14 May 2024.
17 Fawcett Society, 'The gender health gap', 20 February 2024, https://www.fawcettsociety.org.uk/the-gender-health-gap-our-stories.
18 Fawcett Society, 'The impact of the menopause on the progression of women into senior leadership roles', 2022, https://www.fawcettsociety.org.uk/the-impact-of-the-menopause-on-the-progression-of-vwomen-into-senior-leadership-roles.
19 Department of Work and Pensions, Policy Paper, 'Menopause and Workplace: How to Enable Fulfilling Working Lives: Government Response', July 2022, https://www.gov.uk/government/publications/menopause-and-the-workplace-how-to-enable-fulfilling-working-lives-government-response.
20 *Equality and Human Rights Monitor* (Equality and Human Rights Commission, November 2023), pp. 237–8.
21 Government Equalities Office, *Gender Equality at Every Stage: A Roadmap for Change*, 3 July 2019, https://www.gov.uk/government/publications/gender-equality-at-every-stage-a-roadmap-for-change.
22 Fawcett Society, *Equal Pay Day, 2023. Unlocking Flexible Work*, 22 November 2023, https://www.fawcettsociety.org.uk/news/equal-pay-day-2023-is-november-22.
23 Lizzie Ville, *The Gender Pay Gap in the UK Explained* (London: Fawcett Society, 2023).
24 Alison Andrew, Oriana Bandiera, Monica Costas Dias and Camille Landais, *Women and Men at Work* (London: Institute for Fiscal Studies, 2021).
25 'The second shift for women is still unfair, unpaid and unvalued', *Guardian*, 3 February 2025.
26 Ville, *Gender Pay Gap*, pp. 11–12.
27 Ibid., p. 9.
28 Fawcett Society, *Diversifying the Tech Sector, Addressing the Gender Gap in Tech* (London: Fawcett Society, 2023), https://www.fawcettsociety.org.uk/diversifying-the-tech-sector.
29 Ibid.
30 Catherine Marren and Andrew Bailey, *Sex and Power* (London: Fawcett Society, 2022), pp. 13–16, https://iknowpolitics.org/sites/default/files/thefawcettsociety-sexpower2022.pdf.
31 FTSE *Women Leaders*, Annual Report 2023, https://ftsewomenleaders.com.
32 UK Government Cabinet Office, *Report. High Growth Woman-led Taskforce*, March 2024, https://www.gov.uk/government/groups/woman-led-high-growth-enterprise-task force.
33 'Reversal of diversity drive risks undoing decades of progress', *Guardian*, 15 February 2025.
34 Ibid.
35 Marren and Bailey, *Sex and Power*, p. 5.
36 Scottish Government, *A Fairer Scotland for Women: Gender Pay Gap Action Plan* (Edinburgh, 8 March 2019), https://www.gov.scot/publications/fairer-scotland-women-gender-pay-gap-action-plan/.

37 *Equality and Human Rights Monitor* (London: Equality and Human Rights Commission, 2022), p. 257.
38 Z. Azad, A. De-Freitas and Lizzie Ville, *Transforming Early Childhood Education and Care: Sharing International Learning*. Part 1 (London: Fawcett Society, 2023), https://www.fawcettsociety.org.uk/transforming-early-childhood-education-and-care-sharing-international-learning.
39 Department for Education, *Budget 2023: Everything You Need to Know About Childcare Support*, Blog, The Education Hub, 16 March 2023, https://educationhub.blog.gov.uk/2023/03/budget-2023-everything-you-need-to-know-about-childcare-support/.
40 Quoted by Z. Azad et al., *Transforming Early Childhood*, p. 5.
41 Pregnant then Screwed, 'A third of parents eligible for new childcare funding considering leaving job or reducing work hours due to recent hike in childcare costs', press release, 22 February 2024, https://pregnantthenscrewed.com/childcare-fee-hikes.
42 Women's Budget Group, 'Early Education and Childcare', https://www.wbg.org.uk/research-analysis/topics/early-education-and-childcare/.
43 Azad et al., *Transforming Early Childhood*, p. 7.
44 Ibid.
45 Coram, *Families facing growing childcare shortages while costs rise by 7%* (London: Coram, 2024), https://www.coram.org.uk/news/families-facing-growing-childcare-shortages-while-costs-rise-by-7/.
46 Azad et al., *Transforming Early Childhood*, p. 7.
47 Ibid.
48 Fawcett Society, *Closing the Gender Play Gap*, March 2023, https://fawcettsociety.org/closing-the-gender-play-gap.
49 All Party Parliamentary Group on Women in Parliament, *Open House: Where Next for Gender Equality in Parliament?* (London: Fawcett Society, September 2023), https://www.fawcettsociety.org.uk/appg-on-women-in-parliament.
50 Ibid., pp. 5–6.
51 Ibid., p. 7.
52 Ibid., p. 10.
53 Ibid., p. 19.
54 Ibid., p. 20.
55 Fawcett Society, *StopGap 2024*, 'Campaigning for change, centring all women's voices' (London: Fawcett Society, Autumn 2024).
56 Ibid.
57 The Trussell Trust, *State of Hunger*. Year 2, main report. May 2021, https://www.trusselltrust.org.
58 Fawcett Society, 'The impacts of coronavirus on women', https://www.fawcettsociety.org.uk/the-impacts-of-coronavirus-on-women.
59 *Parenting in Lockdown: Coronavirus and the Effects on Work–Life Balance* (Office of National Statistics, 20 July 2020).
60 Fawcett Society, 'Coronavirus: impact on parents', evidence, August 2020. https://www.fawcettsociety.org.uk/parenting-and-covid-19.
61 *Equality and Human Rights Monitor 2023* (London: EHRC, 2023), p. 232.
62 Ibid., pp. 253–4.
63 'Watchdog: women face an epidemic of violence', *Guardian*, 31 January 2025.

64 *Equality and Human Rights Monitor 2023*, p. 233.
65 'Labour pledge: the action needed to halve violence against women', *Guardian*, 14 October 2024.
66 'London mayor urges primary schools to tackle misogyny', *Guardian*, 19 October 2024.
67 'Nicola Sturgeon confirms trans rapist moved to male prison', *Herald*, 26 January 2023.
68 'Report has potential for positive change', *Guardian*, 13 April 2024.
69 Hilary Cass, *The Cass Review. Independent Review of Gender Identity Services for Children and Young People: Final Report. April 2024*, https://cass.independent-review.uk/home/publications/.
70 'Drawing a line: hopes Cass report will end "culture of fear" in gender research', *Guardian*, 13 April 2024.
71 *Guardian*, 13 April 2024.
72 'Tories allow ban on trans women in single-sex spaces', *Guardian*, 3 June 2024.
73 *Stop Gap*, 2024, p. 3.
74 Fawcett Society, 'Labour's first 100 days: a new era for women?, https://www.fawcettsociety.org.uk/blog/labour-first-100-days-a-new-era-for-women.
75 'Reversal of diversity drive risks undoing decades of progress', *Guardian*, 15 February 2025.

Conclusion
1 Fawcett Society, 'Fawcett celebrates publication of Equal Rights Bill', 11 October 2024, https://www.fawcettsociety.org.uk/blog/fawcett-celebrates-draft-employmen-rights-bill.
2 Fawcett Society, 'Equal Pay Day 2024', https://www.fawcettsociety.org.uk/news/equal-pay-day.

Index

Tables are denoted by the use of **bold**.

A Taste of Honey (play/film), 93
Abbott, Diane, 140, 164
Abel-Smith, Brian, 99
abortion, 11, 43–4, 106–8
Abortion Act (1967), 106–7
Abortion Law Reform Association (ALRA), 43, 106
Abse, Leo, 110, 111
Action for Lesbian Parents, 136
Admiral Duncan pub bombing (1999), 185
adoption, 36–7, 61, 182, 185, 203
Advisory, Conciliation and Arbitration Service (ACAS), 131
ageing society, 42–3, 141, 182–4
AIDS/HIV, 160–1
Albany Trust, 96
All-Party Parliamentary Groups (APPGs), 208
all-women shortlists (AWS), 164–5
Amos, Valerie, 145, 165
Anderson, Dr Louisa Garrett, 19
Anglican Church, 29, 44, 185
Anglican Mothers Union, 29
Anglo-Boer war (1899–1902), 10
'Angry Young People', 93–4
ante-natal care, 40, 41, 51
apprenticeships, 85, 102
Archbishop of Canterbury, Michael Ramsey, 112
armed services, 154, 162
Arran, Lord, 110–11
Astor, Lord, 77
Astor, Nancy, 27, 32, 39
Attlee, Clement, 49, 58
Audit Commission, 173
austerity, 189–224
    Coronavirus pandemic, 210–12
    election (2024), 220–3
    health inequalities, 194–6
    inequalities at work, 196–208
    poverty and inequality, 190–4
    transgender inequalities, 215–20
    unequal representation in parliament, 208–10
    violence against women and girls, 213–15
Australia, 8, 13, 36, 77
Auxiliary Territorial Service (ATS), 46

'baby-boomers', 59, 68, 74, 183–4
Badenoch, Kemi, 220
Baldwin, Stanley, 33, 38, 39–40, 56
banking profession, 31, 52, 88–9, 149, 155–6, 172
Bastardy Act (1923), 36
Batley, Yorkshire, 11
Batt, Anne, 106
BBC, 31–2, 58, 103, 151, 184
beauty contests, 124
Beauvoir, Simone de, 81
Berkeley, Humphrey, 110
Bermondsey, South London, 87–8
Bevan, Aneurin, 64
Beveridge, William, 56–8, 64, 75
Bevin, Ernest, 46
biological differences, 16
birth certificates, 35, 59, 137, 186
birth control, 11, 42, 100, 108–9
birth rates, 10, 11, 21, 43, 59, 119, 134, 150, 152, 169–70
Black, Asian and Minority Ethnic groups (BAME)
    Amos and, 145
    childcare and, 205
    criminal justice system and, 178
    education and, 147, 148, 170
    gender pay gap, 203
    income inequalities, 180
    in lockdown, 210–11, 212
    in lower-skilled occupations, 155
    Malhotra on, 222
    maternity services, 194
    'motherhood penalty', 198
    as MPs, 140, 164
    in public life, 165
    racism at work, 200
    single-parent households, 169
    unions and, 130
Black Women for Wages for Housework, 131
Blair, Cherie, 170
Blair, Richard, 62
Blairism, 164–88
Blasphemy Act (1697), 136
blood transfusion services, 51
Boateng, Paul, 165
Bogarde, Dirk, 110

INDEX

Bondfield, Margaret, 55
Boothroyd, Betty, 150
Bottomley, Virginia, 148
Bourne case (1938), 43–4
Bowlby, John, 66, 80
Bradshaw, Ben, 184
Brexit, 193, 228
Brighton, 136
British Employers Confederation, 71
British Federation of Business and Professional Women (BFBPW), 85, 89
British Federation of University Women (BFUW), 85
British Institute of Public Opinion (BIPO) polls, 54–5
British Medical Association (BMA), 50
British Nationality Act (1948), 73
British Restaurants, 49
British Social Attitudes Survey, 143, 198
British Society for the Study of Sex Psychology, 35
Brook Advisory Centres, 108
Brooks, Edwin, 109
Brown, Ernest, 50
Brown, Gordon, 169, 180, 182
Burgess, Guy, 95
businesswomen, 25
Butler, R.A., 56, 96, 97

Cabinet Family Policy Group (1982), 141–2
Callaghan, James, 113, 123, 134
Cameron, David, 117, 189, 192
campaign, 214
Campaign for Homosexual Equality (CHE), 112, 136
Campaign for Nuclear Disarmament (CND), 116
campaigns for gender equality, 145–6
Canada, 36, 206
career ambitions, 5
carers, 58, 75, 131, 141, 152, 193–4
Carers Allowance, 193
Carpenter, Edward, 35
Cass, Hilary, 217–19
Castle, Barbara, 98, 114, 115, 123
Catholic Church, 36, 42, 44–5, 106, 109, 113, 185
Cazalet Keir, Thelma, 56
Centre for Economic Performance (CEP), LSE, 199
Chamberlain, Neville, 36, 38, 46
charitable work, 8, 10, 13, 28
Charter for Working Women (TUC), 130
Chesser, Eustace, 78
Child Benefit, 122, 123, 142, 181, 191, 212
child mortality, 49, 51
Child Poverty Action Group (CPAG), 99, 123, 190–1
Child Support Acts (1990/91/95), 144, 156
Child Support Agency (CSA), 156

Child Tax Credit (CTC), 181, 191
child welfare, 40
childbirth, 10
childcare, 52–3, 66–7, 134–5, 141–2
  by grandparents, 169, 183, 184, 211
  high cost, 198, 203, 205
  lack of, 134, 169, 176, 204
  lack of affordable, 57, 79, 89, 105, 143, 189
  in lockdown, 210, 211–12
  'New Deal' and, 169
  profit-making providers, 205–6
  publicly funded, 52, 67, 182, 184, 203–6
  qualified staff in, 204–5
  workplace creches, 78, 134
  see also day-care; nurseries
childminders, 69, 122, 134, 182, 205
children
  Coronavirus pandemic, 210–11
  custody of, 7–8, 36, 136, 144
  as evacuees, 47–8, 52, 53
  gender stereotypes, 206–8
  malnutrition, 210
  vaccination, 49
  vulnerable, 80, 206
Children's Commissioners, 191–2
Church of England
  abortion, 106
  divorce, 112, 113
  homosexuality, 95, 110
  ordination of women, 29, 150
Churchill, Winston, 49, 51, 56, 58
Civil Partnership Act (2004), 186
civil partnerships, gay, 186
civil service
  equal pay, 79
  marriage bar, 30, 68, 78
  senior ranks, 89, 133, 150–1, 174
  unequal pay, 33, 70–1
  unions and, 44
  in wartime, 52
class division, 75–6, 148
class inequality, 5–6
Cobbe, Frances Power, 125
Code of Conduct, Parliamentary, 209
cohabitation, 16, 18, 22, 100, 113–14, 140
Colleges of Advanced Technology, 101
Colquhoun, Maureen, 184
Committee on One-Parent Families, 100, 119
comprehensive schools, 100, 103, 147
Confederation of British Industries (CBI), 104–5, 114, 129, 151
conscription, 22–3, 47, 48, 52
consent, age of, 36
constitutional reform, 166–8
contraception, 11, 42, 100, 108–9
Cook, Robin, 166
Cooper, Yvette, 215
Coram Children's Charity, 205

253

INDEX

Corbett, Robin, 127
Coronavirus pandemic, 197, 210–12
council housing, 64, 79, 143, 158
Council of Europe, 214, 216
Council of Women Civil Servants, 29, 71
councils, local, 7
Craigie, Jill, 78
Crime and Disorder Bill (1998), 185
criminal justice, 178–9, 213–14
Criminal Justice Bill (1994), 162
Criminal Law Amendment Act (1922), 36
Crosland, Anthony, 100–1
Crossman, Richard, 109, 111
Crowther Report (1959), 85
Culture, Media and Sport, Department of, 187, 190, 208
Currie, Edwina, 162

Davison, Emily Wilding, 9, 10
day-care, 67, 87, 122
death rates 14, 15, 51
Delaney, Sheila, *A Taste of Honey*, 93
Design of Dwellings Committee (1942), 55–6
diplomatic service, 68
disability, 58, 75, 107, 141, 180, 182, 189, 193, 195, 203
Disability Rights Commission, 166
diversity and inclusion, racial inequality, 222
divorce, 15–16, 44–5, 91–2, 112–14
  British nationality and, 6
  court, 113–14
  difficulties obtaining, 5, 7, 36, 74
  insurance benefits, 58
  legal aid and, 158
  pensions and, 159
  rates, 92, 99, 119, 140
  stigma of, 80
Divorce Law Reform Union (DLRU), 113
Divorce Reform Act (1969), 113, 119
Dodds, Anneliese, 221–2
Domestic Abuse Act (2021), 213
Domestic Abuse Commissioner, 213
domestic help, 57, 89, 105
domestic service, 5, 17, 31, 32
domestic violence, 3, 15–16, 125–8, 144, 178–9, 211
Domestic Violence and Matrimonial Proceedings Act (1976), 126
(Donovan) Royal Commission on Trade Unions and Employers' Associations (1968), 102–3
Duncan, Alan, 187
Duncan Smith, Iain, 187
Dunn, Nell, 93–4

Eagle, Angela, 184
early childhood education and care (ECEC), 198, 203–6
Early Years Alliance, 212

East London, 17–18
Economic and Social Research Council (ESRC), 175
education
  11+ exam, 65, 100
  comprehensive schools, 100, 103, 147
  free period products, 195–6
  GCSEs, 148
  gender inequality in, 85, 102, 147–8
  girls outperforming boys, 147, 170, 196, 225
  leaving with no qualifications, 132, **147**, 172
  in lockdown, 210, 211, 212
  misogyny, 215
  school meals, 142
  wartime, 56
  see also types of education
Education Act (1944), 56, 65
Education, Department of, 208
Educational Maintenance Allowances (EMAs), 180, 189
elections, general, 26, 27–8
  1900s–1940s, 9, 12, 38, 40, 64
  1950s, 76, 79, 139
  1960s, 97, 98, 105, 106, 110–11, 114
  1970s–1980s, 101, 115, 117, 138, 161
  1990s, 148, 153, 164, 184
  2000s–2010s, 165, 188, 190
  2020s, 189, 197, 205, 209, 214–15, 220–3
Emergency Medical Service (EMS), 50
employers' associations
  Donovan Commission, 102–3
employment *see* work, women and
Employment, Department of, 129, 148
Employment Equality (Sexual Orientation) Regulations (2003), 185
Employment Protection Act (1975), 130–1
Employment Relations (Flexible Working) Act (2023), 201
employment rights, 122, 131, 153, 186
Employment Rights Bill (2024), 201, 223, 229
Engineering Employers' Federation, 129
Equal Franchise Bills, 38, 39, 40
equal opportunities at work, 86–7, 168–78, 226
Equal Opportunities Commission (EOC), 129–30, 145, 149, 153, 166, 170–4, 177
equal pay, 54–5, 56, 70–3, 78, 79, 114–16
Equal Pay Act (1970), 114, 122, 130, 145
Equal Pay Campaign Committee (EPCC), 54, 70, 78, 79
Equal Pay Day, 197, 229
Equalities Office, Government, 208
Equality Acts (2006/10), 186, 215–16
Equality and Human Rights Commission (EHRC), 166, 177, 199, 202
Equality (Race and Disability) Bill (2024 ongoing), 222
Equality Units, 165, 167

254

INDEX

ethnic minority groups *see* Black, Asian and Minority Ethnic groups (BAME)
European Commission on Human Rights, 185
European Community (EC), 114, 131, 144, 145, 146, 148, 228
European Convention on Human Rights (ECHR), 166, 185, 186, 214
European Court of Human Rights (ECtHR), 112, 145, 146, 159, 162, 185, 186, 216
European Court of Justice (ECJ), 159, 162, 186
European Union (EU), 152, 153–4, 168, 193, 228
evacuation (WW2), 47–8, 52, 53

Fabian Society, 13, 193
Fabian Women's Group, 12–13, 72
Fair Pay Agreements, 223
family allowances, 33, 58, 64, 74
Family Law Reform Act, (1987), 144
family life
    1979–97, 140–4
    families at war, 17–19
    gender, sexuality, marriage and the family, 34–8
    marriage, sex and family, 58–62
    permissive society, 99–100
    post-Second World War, 74–6
    during Second World War, 58–62
    The Seventies, 118–23
Family Planning Act (1967/1972), 108, 109
Family Planning Association (FPA), 42, 109
Fawcett Commission, 178–9
Fawcett, Millicent Garrett, 5, 8, 17, 23, 26, 39
Fawcett Society, 194–5, 197–201, 205–7
    briefings by, 211, 212
    campaign against misogyny, 214
    on the Employment Rights Bill, 229
    equal pay and, 72
    'Labour's First 100 Days' blog, 222
    Parliament and, 208, 209–10
    surveys, 167, 174
Female to Male support group, 159
feminists/feminism, 41, 43, 57, 81, 124, 131–2, 146
    see also individual movements
Ferguson, Sheila, 60–1
Finch, Peter, 110
Finer Joint Action Committee (FJAC), 123, 135
Finer, Sir Morris, 119, 123, 131
Finland, 8
First Aid Nursing Yeomanry (FANY), 19
First World War (1914–18), 16–24
Fitzgerald, Hilde, 60–1
flexible working hours, 168, 197, 203, 205
food banks, 210
food rationing, 49
Ford sewing machinists strike, Dagenham (1968), 114–15
France, 148

franchise
    extension to skilled working men, 7
    extension to all men 23, 25
Friendly Societies, 40–1
FTSE Women Leaders Annual Review, 201–2
Fulham, Bishop of, 21
furlough scheme, 210

Gardiner, Gerald, 112
gas and electricity corporations, 79
Gavron, Hannah, 90
gay couples, 119, 140, 185
Gay Liberation Front (GLF), 112, 116, 118, 127
Gay Pride marches, 135
gay rights, 160–2, 166, 184–7, 228–9
gay support groups, 136
gender dysphoria, 186–7, 216
'Gender Equality at Every Stage, a Roadmap for Change' (2019), 196–7
'gender inequality' (definition), 1
gender pay gap, 171–2, 173, 196–9, 202–3, 222, 229
gender reassignment, 159, 186, 216–20
Gender Recognition Act (2004), 186–7, 216, 217
Gender Recognition Certificate (GRC), 216
Gender Recognition Reform (Scotland) Act (2022), 216
Gender Representation on Public Boards (Scotland) Act (2018), 202
Germany, 148
Gielgud, John, 95
Glasgow, 18–19
'glass ceiling', 171, 174, 176
Good Law Project, 219
Gordon Walker, Patrick, 105
graduates, university, 25, 47, 82–3, 86–7, 89, 176
'Great War' *see* First World War (1914–18)
Greater London Authority (GLA), 168, 173
Greater London Council (GLC), 154, 160
Greenham Common peace camp, Berkshire, 146
Grunwick strike, Willesden (1976–78), 130
Guaranteed Maintenance Allowance (GMA), 121, 122, 123
Gunter, Ray, 114

Haire, Norman, 95
Hall, Radclyffe, 35
Hansard Society for Parliamentary Democracy, 149–50, 174
Hart, Judith, 98
Health and Social Security, Department of (DHSS), 120, 121, 126
health, birth and death, 40–4
health services, 3, 22, 50–1, 194
    see also National Health Service
health visitors, 21–2, 40–1, 207
Heath, Edward, 118, 128, 135, 138
Herbert, A.P., 44
History Workshop movement, 124

INDEX

Hitchens, Peter, 117
Hollis, Patricia, 158–9
home schooling, 210, 211, 212
homelessness, 75, 190
homophobia, 3, 136, 160–1, 184, 186
Homosexual Law Reform Society (HLRS), 96, 110, 135
homosexuality, 6, 15, 94–7, 185
   rights, 109–12, 135–7, 160–2, 227, 228
Hormone Replacement Therapy (HRT), 195
Horsbrugh, Florence, 77
hostels, 37, 75, 169
housewives, 18, 33, 52, 90, 131–2
housework, 33, 79, 81–2, 88, 118, 131–2, 152, 198
housing, affordable, 64, 88, 121–2, 159, 169, 191
Housing Benefit, 159, 191
housing costs, 58, 126, 169, 172, 179, 183, 191
Housing (Homeless Persons) Act (1977), 123, 127, 143
housing, improving, 55–6, 64
Howe, Elspeth, 149
Howe, Geoffrey, 149
Hubback, Judith, 86
Human Rights Act (HRA) (1998), 166, 185
Human Rights Commission, 166
Hunt, Audrey, 82, 84

ill-health, 10–14, 20, 41, 88
'illegitimate' births, 22, 36–7, 59–62, 74, 100, 140, 144, 158, 170
income inequality and poverty, 179–82
Income Support (IS), 140, 156
Independent Complaints and Grievance Scheme, Parliamentary, 209
industrial work, 32, 52, 67, 82–3, 87, 142
   engineering, 54–5, 71, 85, 115, 129, 171
infant care, 21–2
infant mortality, 11, 14, 21, 43, 51, 74, 194
inflation, 123, 132, 159, 169, 172
Inner London Education Authority (ILEA), 160
Institute for Fiscal Studies (IFS), 191, 197–9, 204
Institute of Directors, 151
Institute of Personnel Management, 129
International Council of Women (ICW), 13
International Lesbian, Gay, Bisexual, Trans and Intersex Association, 187
International Women's Day, 125
Ireland, 36, 70, 77, 108
Isle of Man, 8, 112

Jeger, Lena, 115
Jenkins, Roy, 106, 110, 111, 113
Jephcott, Pearl, 87–8
Jersey, 112
Joseph Rowntree Foundation (JRF), 190
Jowell, Tessa, 187
jury service, 30
justice system, 3, 92–3

Kean, Ann, 185
Khan, Sadiq, 215
Kilmuir, Lord, 110
King, Oona, 164
Kinsey, Alfred, 95
Klein, Melanie, 66
Klein, Viola, 80–1, 82, 90–1

labour market deregulation, 148
Labour Party Women's Section, 28
labour shortages
   post-war, 67, 69, 70, 82, 86–7
   wartime, 17, , 46, 53
Lambeth, South London, 13
Law Commission, 214
Lawson, Nigel, 143
League of the Church Militant, 29
Leeds, 136
legal profession, 30, 93, 151, 170, 175
lesbianism, 6, 35, 109–12, 125, 136–7, 162, 178, 227
   rights, 109–12
life expectancy, 12, 14, 42, 74, 141, 192
Lilley, Peter, 156–7, 158
literacy, 47
Livingstone, Ken, 154, 168
local government, 7, 27–8, 40, 71, 79, 146, 189
Local Government Act (1987)
   Section 28 and, 161, 184, 185
Local Housing Allowance, 212
lockdowns, Covid-19, 210–12
London and National Society for Women's Service, 72
London County Council (LCC), 69, 79, 103
London Gay Switchboard, 136
London School of Economics (LSE), 83–4, 87
lone-parent families, 135, 140, 142, 143–4, 156–8, 169, 179, 190, 192
Lords, House of, 77, 110
Low Pay Unit, 133

MacDonald, Ramsey, 38
Maclean, Donald, 95
Macmillan, Harold, 88
maintenance, 7, 36, 73, 120, 144, 156
Major, John, 138, 139, 145, 146, 148, 150–63
Malhotra, Seema, 222
Manchester City Council, 160–1
Markham, Violet, 62
Markiewicz, Countess Constance, 27
marriage
   ages, 15, 74, 78, 99, 119
   fall in, 119
   gender, sexuality, marriage and the family, 34–8
   inequalities in, 5–6, 14–16, 57, 91–2
   in lockdown, 211
   rise of, 99
   same sex, 189

INDEX

and separation, 7, 15–16, 36, 58, 73, 74, 80
  sex and family, 58–62
  'shot-gun', 74
marriage bar, 30, 31, 52, 56, 57, 68
'married couple's allowance', 145–6
Married Women's Association (MWA), 73, 91, 98, 145
Married Women's Property Act (1964), 98
Mass Observation surveys, 51, 95
'maternal deprivation' theories, 66, 81
maternal/maternity
  benefit, 75, 152
  mortality, 11, 22, 43, 51, 194
  pay, 75, 152, 181
  services, 194
  welfare, 21–2, 40
maternity leave, 130–1
  extended, 80, 153, 168
  introduction of, 69, 78
  paid, 70
  returning to work after, 132, 149
Matrimonial Causes Acts (1923/37), 36, 44
Matrimonial Proceedings and Property Act (1970), 113
May, Theresa, 187, 189, 190
McKinsey, 201
McRae, Susan, 150–2
means-tested benefits, 58, 99, 140–1, 181, 182–3, 191, 204
medical profession, 19–20, 70, 88, 103–4, 106, 130, 133, 170–1
Medical Women's Federation, 88
menopause, 72, 194–5
Menopause Employment Champion, 195
mental health, 11, 66, 193, 206, 211, 218
Methodist Church, 113
#MeToo movement, 200–1
middle-class women
  campaigning by, 9
  education, 65–6
  employment, 32, 45, 68, 195
  marital status, 34, 73, 90
  as volunteers, 13, 52
  voters, 75–6
  younger, 128
  see also 'white blouse' occupations
milk provision, 22, 40, 49
Mill, John Stuart, 7
Miller, Maria, 190
minimum wage, 87, 130, 168, 177, 181, 198, 204, 223
Ministry of Defence (MoD), 162
Minorities Research Group, 109–10
misogyny, 3, 214–15, 222, 227–8, 229
Modernization of the House of Commons, 166
Montagu, Lord, 95
Moral Welfare Council (CofE), 95
Morgan, Nicky, 190

Morris, Jan, 137
mother and baby homes/hostels, 75
'motherhood penalty', 172–3, 198
mothers at home, 89–91
MPs, female, 27–30, 139–40, 164–5, 208–10, 220–2
  Cabinet ministers/senior posts, 148, 150, 187, 190
  increasing numbers of, 64, 98, 167, 225
  MSPs, 167
  see also individual MPs
multi-generational households, 134
murders, by men, 136, 161, 209, 213, 214–15
Murray, Dr Flora, 19
Myrdal, Alva, 80–1

Nabarro, Gerald, 111
National Assistance Act (1948), 75
National Assistance Board (NAB), 58, 65, 75
National Association of Women Civil Servants (NAWCS), 69, 78
National Audit Office (NAO), 205, 214, 215
National Childbirth Trust, 89
National Childcare Strategy, 180
National Conference of Women, 54
National Council for the Unmarried Mother and her Child (NCUMC), 36, 37, 61, 75, 123
National Council of Women (NCW), 13, 29, 30, 32, 33, 91, 92–3
National Dock Labour Board, 87
National Health Insurance (NHI) system, 11, 12, 34, 38, 40
National Health Service (NHS)
  employees, 70, 82
  equal pay, 79
  gender reassignment, 159, 186, 218–19
  increased funding, 183
  introduction of, 64
  maternity services, 194
  unmarried mothers and, 75
National Housewives Register, 90
national identity, 6
National Insurance (NI), 57–8, 75
national opinion polls (NOP), 106, 110, 185
National Police Chiefs Council, 214–15
National Spinsters' Pensions Association (NPSA), 34
National Union of Seamen, 111
National Union of Societies for Equal Citizenship (NUSEC), 26, 28, 36, 38
National Union of Women Teachers (NUWT), 29, 69, 70, 78
National Union of Women Workers (NUWW), 13, 14, 17
National Union of Women's Suffrage Societies (NUWSS), 8–10, 23
National Victims Advisory Panel, 178

257

INDEX

national vote protests, 2, 8
'New Deal' (1998), 169, 181
New English Law of Property (1926), 37
New Labour (1997–2010), 164–88
   the ageing society, 182–4
   constitutional reform, 164–8
   criminal justice, 178–9
   equal opportunities at work, 168–78
   gay and transgender rights, 184–7
   income inequality and poverty, 179–82
New Opportunities for Women (NOW), 133
New Zealand, 8, 13, 77
NHS England, 217, 218
   see also National Health Service
Nicholson, Emma, 139
night-working, 168–9
'non-binary' people, 215
Northern Ireland, 44–5, 58–9, 191–2
   abortion, 108
   adoption, 185
   birth control, 109
   childcare, 203
   divorce, 36, 113
   gender equality, 173
   homosexuality, 112
   human rights, 166
   same sex marriage, 189
   transgender rights, 187
Norwich, Bishop of, 59
nurseries, 52–3, 79, 87, 134, 152, 153

Oakley, Ann, 131
Obscene Publications Acts, 35
OECD countries, 199, 205
Office for National Statistics (ONS), 198, 211
office work, 20, 32
'oil shock' (1974), 122–3, 132
older people, 34, 50, 75, 125, 141, 166, 180, 182–3, 193
Olympic Games (2024), 217
One Parent Benefit, 158
online abuse, 209, 214
Open University, 101
Opportunity 2000, 151
O'Reilly, Miriam, 184
Organization of Women of Asian and African Descent (OWAAD), 125
Orwell, George (Eric Blair), 61–2
Osborne, George, 189, 191

paid leave, 168
Paisley, Ian, 112, 113
Pankhurst, Adela, 9
Pankhurst, Christabel, 9, 14, 16
Pankhurst, Emmeline, 8–9, 16, 17, 39
Pankhurst, Sylvia, 9, 17–18, 23, 26
parental leave, 198, 207, 212
Parliamentary Reform Act (1867), 7

part-time work, 69, 78, 86, 131–3, 152–3, 168, 203, 205
paternity leave, 152, 153, 168, 182, 198, 207
Patten, John, 153
Patterson, Mrs Marie, 129
pay gap, 20–1, 31–4, 52, 54–5, 70–3, 78–85
penal reform organizations, 30
Pension Credit (PC), 182–3
pensions, 182–3
   benefits, 180
   Beveridge and, 57
   divorce and, 159
   gender pay gap, 172–3, 193, 199
   improving, 64
   introduction of, 12
   low, 78, 99
   pension age, 34, 58, 146, 192
   single mothers and, 38, 53
   transsexuals and, 160
permissive society (1964–1970), 98–117
   family life, 99–100
   towards the 'permissive society', 106–16
      abortion, 106–8
      birth control, 108–9
      divorce, 112–14
      equal pay, 114–16
      homosexual and lesbian rights, 109–12
   work, 102–5
Personal Injuries Act 1(939), 54
Phillipson, Bridget, 221, 222
Pizzey, Erin, 125–6
Plath, Sylvia, 94
Plowden Report (1967), 101
policewomen, 13–14, 16–17, 32, 36, 171
policing, 96, 121, 157, 171, 179, 213, 223
Political and Economic Planning (PEP) think tank, 129
political parties, membership of, 8
polytechnics, 101
Poor Law Boards, 7
Poor Law Guardians, 28
Portillo, Michael, 153
poverty, 3–4, 49, 142–4, 159, 179–82
   during austerity, 190–4
   child poverty rates, 180–2, **181**
   pensioner, 182–3, 193
   poverty, ill-health and gender inequality, 10–14
   single mothers, 15, 99, 142, 157, 169, 179, 190, 228
Pre-School Playgroup Association, 90, 134–5
pregnancy, 41–2
   teenage, 122, 143, 158
   vulnerable, 43, 61
   work and, 69, 78
   see also 'illegitimate' births
Pregnant Then Screwed, 204
prejudices, workplace, 27, 29–30, 51–2, 83–4
premarital sex, 22, 35, 59–60, 74

INDEX

Press for Change, 159, 217
Prices and Incomes Bill (1970), 115
Pride events, 135, 186
prison population, female, 178
privatization, 148, 154–5
professional occupations, 70, 88–9, 133–4, 149, 151–3, 170–2
  senior posts, 103–4, 149–51, 154, 174, 177, **177**, 190, 201–2
  see also individual professions
property rights, 5, 7, 24, 25, 30, 73, 98, 113
proportional representation (PR), 139, 167–8
prostitution, 13, 73, 94–5, 96–7
Protestant Church, 36, 45, 108, 109
public services
  cuts to, 147, 176
  decline in, 141, 180, 193
  increased funding, 130, 173
  privatized, 155, 206
  see also individual services

Queer as Folk (Ch4), 185

Race Relations Act (1965), 105
racial diversity/equality, 70, 173
Racial Equality, Commission for (CRE), 166
racism, 70, 105, 143, 194, 200
rape, 3, 14, 44, 127–8, 154, 162, 178–9, 213–14, 217
rape crisis centres, 127
Rathbone, Eleanor, 18, 26, 28–9, 33, 39, 57, 64–5, 91, 131
rationing, 49, 53
Rayner, Angela, 220–1
Reading, Lady Stella, 47
'Reclaim the Night' marches, 127
redundancy, protection against, 201
Redwood, John, 157, 158
Rees, Merlyn, 134
Reeves, Ellie, 221
Reeves, Maud Pember, 13
Reeves, Rachel, 221, 222
religion, women and, 29
rent strikes, 18–19
Representation of the People Act (1918), 23
Resolution Foundation, 192, 211
retail sector, 20, 207, 211
retirement, 4, 183–4
Rhondda, Lady, 39, 77
Richardson, Jo, 126
Robinson, Kenneth, 109
Rodgers, Adrian, 184
Ross, Karen, 174–5
Rothermere, Lord, 39
Rowbotham, Sheila, 124
Royal Commission on Divorce (1956), 92
Royal Commission on Equal Pay (1944/46), 54, 56, 70–3

Royal Commission on Population (1944/49), 59, 74
Royal Commission on Trade Unions and Employers' Associations (1968), 102–3
Ruddock, Joan, 165
Rue, Rosemary, 104
Russia, 51

same sex marriage, 189
Scarman, Lord Justice, 130
school medical services, 40
schoolchildren, 12, 42, 49, 53
science and technology graduates, 83
Science, Technology, Engineering, and Mathematics (STEM), 82–3, 83, 85, 132, 170, 171, 199–200, 225
Scotland, 58–9, 166–7, 216–17
  abortion, 108
  child poverty, 191, 192
  childcare, 203, 204
  divorce, 5, 15, 44, 92, 113, 119
  domestic violence, 213
  education, 100
  employment policies, 202
  Equality Network, 184
  female MSPs, 167
  free period products, 196
  gender equality, 146, 173
  homosexuality, 112
  infant mortality, 43
  professional occupations, 171
  same sex marriage, 189
  Section 28, 185
  transgender rights, 187
Scott, Joan, 1
Scottish Homosexual Reform Group (SHRG), 112
Second World War (1939–45), 46–63
  equal pay, 54–5
  evacuation, 47–8
  marriage, sex and family, 58–62
  social conditions, 48–51
  social reform, 55–8
  women's work, 51–4
secondary education, 56, 65, 85, 100–1
Security, Department of (DSS), 144, 157, 158, 159
Seear, Nancy, 83–4, 87, 102, 128–9
Select Committee on Violence in Marriage, 126
separation, marriage and, 7, 15–16, 36, 58, 73, 74, 80
service families, 34, 49, 53
services sector, 132, 210
Seventies, The (1970–79), 118–37
  changing families, 119
  gay liberation, 136–7
  inequality at work, 128–35
  single-parent families, 120–3
  Women's Liberation Movement, 123–8

259

INDEX

Sex Discrimination Acts (1975/86), 104, 129, 133, 145
Sex Discrimination (Gender Reassignment) Regulations (1999), 159, 186
Sex Disqualification (Removal) Act (1919), 29–30
sex education, 35, 108
Sex Education Society, 95
sex/sexual relationships, 16, 22, 34–8, 58–62
sex work, 155
sexual assault, 9, 30, 60, 178
Sexual Discrimination (Election Candidates) Act (2002), 165
sexual harassment, 3, 44, 60, 154, 201, 215, 223
Sexual Offences Acts (1967, 2003, 2004), 110–12, 162, 178, 185–6
Sexual Offences (Amendment) Act (1976/98), 127, 185
sexual violence *see* violence, physical and sexual
Shelter, 123
Shepherd, Gillian, 148, 150
shop assistants, 32, 34
Simms, Madeleine, 106
single mothers, 79–80, 143–4, 156–8
    affordable childcare, 135
    in lockdown, 211
    pensions and, 38, 53
    poverty and, 15, 99, 142, 157, 169, 179, 190, 228
    Rayner as, 221
    support for, 75, 140
single-parent families, 99, 140, 143–4, 169
Smith, Chris, 184
Smith, John, 164, 165, 166, 173
Soames, Nicholas, 162
social conditions (WW2), 48–51
social media, 209, 214, 227–8
social reform, 55–8
social science studies, 80–1
social security benefits, 64
Social Security, Department of (DSS), 165, 180
social services, 7, 28, 33, 60–1, 74, 133
social work profession, 75, 104, 122, 157
Society for the Protection of Unborn Children (SPUC), 106–7
soldiers, Black US, 59, 61
soldiers' separation allowances, 18
Soviet Union, 35
Special Educational Needs and Disabilities (SEND), 182, 196, 205, 206
St Joan's Social and Political Union, 29
Starmer, Sir Keir, 220, 221
State Pension Act (1995), 146
Status of Women Committee of Women MPs, 69
Steel, David, 106
Stonewall, 161, 186
Stonewall riots (1970), 135
Stopes, Marie, *Married Love*, 34, 35, 42
Street Offences Act (1959), 96–7

strikes, 18–19, 54, 114, 130
suffrage, equal, 38–40
suffrage movement, 2, 5–10, 22–4
suicide, 90, 94, 95, 110, 207, 211
Summerskill, Edith, 54, 98, 129
Sunak, Rishi, 220
Supplementary Benefit, 121, 141
Supplementary Benefits Commission (SBC), 120–1, 122
Sure Start centres, 180, 182, 189, 203
'sweated' trades, 12–13
Sweden, 207, 212
Swinney, John, 216

Tatchell, Peter, 161, 184
Tate, Mavis, 54
Tavistock Centre, London, 218
tax allowances, 70, 73, 78, 105, 145
Taylor, Ann, 166
Taylor, Robert, 175, 176
teaching profession
    equal pay, 56, 79
    gender pay gap, 31, 71
    maternity leave, 69
    needs of lone-parent families, 122
    re-entering, 88
    science and technology graduates, 84
    shortages, 68, 86–7, 103
    teaching unions, 44, 69
    women in, 134, 171
Technical Education White Paper (1956), 85
teenage mothers, 122, 143, 158, 169
Tender, 215
Terence Higgins Trust, 160
textile industries, 32, 71
Thatcher, Margaret, 118, 148, 149, 154–7, 160–2, 228
Thatcherism, 138–47
    campaigns for gender equality, 145–6
    families, 140–4
    Thatcher in power, 139–40
Timber Corps, 47
#TImesUp, 201
To Be a Woman (1951 film), 78–9
Townsend, Peter, 99
Toynbee, Polly, 176
Trade Boards, 155
Trade Boards Act (1909), 12
trade unions, 12–13, 102, 114–15, 129–31
    Blair and, 168–9
    Donovan Commission, 102–3
    EOC and, 145, 172
    expansion of, 44
    membership of, 118, 155
    under Thatcher, 148
    TUC and, 72
    wartime, 21
    see also individual unions

INDEX

Trades Union Congress (TUC), 72, 104–5, 114, 115, 129, 130–1, 133, 135
Trans-Actual, 219
transgenderism
  campaigns, 137, 166
  inequalities, 215–20
  rights, 186–7, 227
  'Rolling Back the State', 154–9
  transition, gender, 215–20
Transport Act (1985), 154–5
Transport and General Workers' Union (TGWU), 129
transsexuals and, 227
Trident nuclear missiles, 146
Truss, Liz, 189
Trussell Trust, 210
Turing, Alan, 95

unemployment, 17, 32–4, 43, 132–3, 141–2, 155, 169, 210–11
Unemployment Insurance scheme, 12
unfair dismissal, 122, 131, 133, 168, 223
Union of Jewish Women, 29
United States (US) 14, 36, 61, 77, 146, 154
United Suffragists, 23
Universal Credit (UC), 191, 192, 212
universities, 101, 130, 132, 148, 150, 151, 170, 171, 211
unmarried mothers, 22, 36–8, 59–62, 75, 119, 121
unmarried partnerships, 15, 18, 22, 49, 186, 211
  see also cohabitation; 'illegitimate' births
unmarried women, 27, 31, 34, 58
unpaid leave, 168
upper-class women 9, 13
Up the Junction (Dunn), 93–4
upskirting, 213

Vaughan, Janet, 51
venereal disease (VD), 13, 14, 22
Vietnam Solidarity Campaign, 116
violence, physical and sexual
  domestic violence, 3, 15–16, 125–8, 144, 178–9, 211
  reporting, 14
  against women and girls, 60, 213–15, 227, 229
voice, fighting for a political, 5–24
  families at war, 17–19
  'Flapper Vote', 39
  The 'Great War', 16–17
  inequalities in marriage, 14–16
  infant and maternal care, 21–2
  poverty, ill-health and gender inequality, 10–14
  The vote, 22–4
  votes for women, 6–10
  work for women, 19–21
voluntary action, 184
Voluntary Aid Detachments (VADs), 19

voting equality
  fighting for a political voice, 5–10
  votes for men and women, 22–4
  what difference did the vote make?, 25–45
    equal suffrage, 38–40
    gender, sexuality, marriage and the family, 34–8
    health, birth and death, 40–4
    inequalities at work, 31–4
    the struggle continues, 44–5
    women in parliament, 3, 27–30
  WSPU and, 16
Voyeurism (Offences) Act (2019), 213

'Wages for Housework' campaign, 33, 131
Wages for Lesbians, 131
Wales
  childcare, 204
  Children's Commissioner, 191–2
  devolution, 166–7
  employment policies, 202
  female MPs, 167
  feminist activists, 146
  gender equality, 173
  'Period Proud Wales Action Plan', 196
  professional occupations, 171
  Redwood on single mothers, 157
  same sex marriage, 189
  transgender rights, 187
War Cabinet Committee on Women in Industry, 21
Ward, Irene, 54
Ward, Mrs Humphrey, 7
Waterhouse, Keith, 157–8
Webb, Beatrice, 7
welfare services, 61, 99, 144
  centres 11
  'rolling back the state', 154–9
'welfare state' (1945–51), 64–76
  family life, 74–6
  other gender inequalities, 73
  Royal Commission on Equal Pay, 70–3
  work, 66–70
'white blouse' occupations, 20, 31, 71
White, Florence, 34
'white slavery', 13
Whitehead, Phillip, 109
Whitehouse, Mary, 136
Whiteley, William, 39
Whittle, Prof Stephen, 159, 217, 219
Wider Opportunities for Women (WOW), 133
widows, 6, 15, 38, 53, 80, 120, 140
Wildeblood, Peter, 95
Wilkinson, Ellen, 27, 39, 64
Wilson, Harold, 98, 111, 123
Winnicott, Donald, 66
winter fuel payments, 182
Wintringham, Margaret, 27, 32

INDEX

Wolfenden Report on Homosexual Offences and Prostitution (1957), 96–7, 110, 111
Woman-led High Growth Enterprise Taskforce, 201
woman-only environments, 217, 220
Woman Power Committee MPs, 54
Women Against State Pension Inequality (WASPI), 192–3
Women and Equalities, Minister for, 190
Women and Equalities Select Committee, 195, 208–9
Women and Equality Unit, Cabinet Office, 165, 172–3
Women and Equality Unit (DSS), 165, 173
Women in Parliament (APPG), 208–9
Women into Science and Engineering (WISE), 171
Women's Advisory Housing Council, 55–6
Women's Aid Federation (WAF), 126
Women's Army Auxiliary Corps (WAAC), 19, 62
Women's Auxiliary Air Force (WAAF), 46
Women's Budget Group, 204, 211
Women's Caucus, Parliamentary, 209–10
Women's Citizens Association (WCA), 28
Women's Co-operative Guild (WCG), 9, 11, 12–13, 29, 55
Women's Engineering Society, 85
Women's Freedom League (WFL), 14, 23
Women's Group on Public Welfare, 55
Women's Health Enquiry Committee, 41
Women's Hospital Corps, 19
Women's Housing and Planning conference (1942), 55
Women's Institutes (WIs), 28–9, 33, 55
Women's Labour League (WLL), 11
Women's Land Army, 19, 47
Women's Liberation Movement (WLM), 116, 118, 123–8, 134, 145
Women's Liberation Workshop, 116
Women's Local Government Society (WLGS), 7
Women's Police Service, 16–17
Women's Royal Air Force (WRAF), 19, 47
Women's Royal Naval Service (WRNS), 19, 46–7
Women's Sick and Wounded Convoy Corps, 19

Women's Social and Political Union (WSPU), 8–10, 16–17, 23
Women's Taxation Action Group (WOTAG), 105
Women's Voluntary Service (WVS), 47, 51, 55
Woolf, Virginia, 35
Work and Pensions, Department of (DWP), 191, 195
'work-life balance', 152
work, women and, 29–30, 31–4, 132–4, 226
  1979–97, 148–54
  1997–2010, 168–78
  during austerity, 196–208
  exploitation of, 133
  permissive society, 102–5
  post-war, 66–70, 94
  The Seventies, 128–35
  wartime, 19–21, 51–4
Workers Protection Act (2024), 215
working-class women, 87–8
  access to health care, 40–1, 43
  campaigning by, 9, 128
  divorce and, 15
  employment, 31, 32–3
  experiences in work, 87–8
  at home, 68, 90
  living standards, 17, 28, 65, 66
  married, 18–19
  menopause and, 195
  as mothers, 11
  in Parliament, 222
  portrayals of, 93–4
  voters, 10, 76, 111
working conditions, 13
Working Families Tax Credit (WFTC), 181
working from home, 149
Working Tax Credit (WTC), 181
World Health Organization (WHO), 194
Wynn, Margaret, 79–80

YouGov, 216
Young, Janet, 139
Younghusband, Eileen, 104

Zweig, Ferdynand, 80, 81